"A must-read for fans of true crime and Hollywood history, *A Murder in Hollywood* never disappoints! Casey Sherman deftly serves just the right mix of glamour, glitz, and grit to keep the reader turning pages. It's a stunner from start to finish."

—Kristin Dilley, cohost of the *Mind over Murder* podcast

"In his stunning new book, *A Murder in Hollywood*, Casey Sherman takes us behind the glitz and glamour of 1950s Technicolor to a front row seat at a real-life film noir, the story of Lana Turner and her terrifying love affair with LA gangster Johnny Stompanato. It's a violent and harrowing tale of female empowerment, a page-turner more gripping than any film in which she ever starred."

—Terence Winter, executive producer of *The Sopranos* and creator of *Boardwalk Empire*

"Casey Sherman's *A Murder in Hollywood* is a riveting page-turner. This book shines a much-needed light on sexism and overt violence against women in Hollywood during the twentieth century. Bravo to Sherman for exposing a toxic Hollywood culture against the backdrop of one of Tinseltown's most famous crimes."

—Tamara Leitner, bestselling author of *Don't Say a Thing*

PRAISE FOR HELLTOWN

"With *Helltown*, Casey Sherman delivers the kind of true crime that keeps eyes glued to the pages—smart, impeccably researched, and utterly absorbing. Destined to be on all the year-end best nonfiction lists, this is an unqualified triumph by a writer at the top of his game!"

—Gregg Olsen, #1 *New York Times* bestselling author of *If You Tell*

"Searing and important, *Helltown* is an immaculately researched and rivetingly propulsive chronicle illustrating a pivotal part of our history. Brilliantly weaving together true crime, a grotesque criminal, the political landscape, and the brilliant minds who wrote about it, Casey Sherman is a master at bringing history alive. Compelling, complex, and revealing—do not miss this!"

—Hank Phillippi Ryan, *USA Today* bestselling author of *Her Perfect Life*

"Master storyteller Casey Sherman takes us back in time to the 1960s and into the dark mind of a charismatic killer. Set against the idyllic backdrop of Cape Cod, *Helltown* is a riveting, often spine-tingling true crime story."

—Terence Winter, executive producer of *The Sopranos*, creator of *Boardwalk Empire*

"*Helltown* is an immersive and captivating journey into the mind of a serial killer."

—*Associated Press*

"*Helltown* will render even the calmest reader unsettled when the book has been concluded. Author Casey Sherman continues his excellent work in the true crime realm with his latest effort. The narrative relayed by Sherman is engrossing and never wavers in its intensity."

—*Seattle Book Review*

PRAISE FOR
THE LAST DAYS OF JOHN LENNON

"Incredibly tense and thriller-like… I totally recommend it."

—Lee Child, #1 bestselling author of the Jack Reacher series

"A must read for music fans, true crime aficionados, or anyone looking for a deep, insightful dive into a dark chapter of American history."

—*Town & Country*

"A first-rate book…a winner."

—*Baltimore Post Examiner*

PRAISE FOR HUNTING WHITEY

———

"A page-turning saga of a real-life killer."

—*Boston Herald*

"*Hunting Whitey* feels like pulling up to the bar to hear the story of a lifetime. With extraordinary access to firsthand witnesses, Casey Sherman and Dave Wedge report the incredible real story of how America's most wanted criminal met his final judgment."

—Joseph Finder, *New York Times* bestselling author of *House on Fire*

"*Hunting Whitey* actually breaks new ground many times with its revelations about Bulger's post-crime life put in print for the first time."

—*Houston Press*

"Sherman and Wedge have crafted a thorough, detailed, and gripping story of a larger-than-life crime boss who met a disturbing end. Compelling read for true crime buffs."

—*Library Journal*

ALSO BY CASEY SHERMAN

A Rose for Mary: The Hunt for the Real Boston Strangler

Search for the Strangler: My Hunt for Boston's Most Notorious Killer

Black Irish

Black Dragon

*The Finest Hours: The True Story of the U.S.
Coast Guard's Most Daring Rescue*

Bad Blood: Freedom & Death in the White Mountains

Animal: The Rise and Fall of the Mob's Most Feared Assassin

Boston Strong: A City's Triumph over Tragedy

The Ice Bucket Challenge: Pete Frates and the Fight Against ALS

*Above & Beyond: John F. Kennedy and America's
Most Dangerous Cold War Spy Mission*

12: The Inside Story of Tom Brady's Fight for Redemption

*Hunting Whitey: The Inside Story of the Capture and
Killing of America's Most Wanted Mob Boss*

The Last Days of John Lennon with James Patterson

Helltown: The Untold Story of a Serial Killer on Cape Cod

A MURDER
IN
HOLLYWOOD

THE

UNTOLD STORY

OF

TINSELTOWN'S

MOST SHOCKING

CRIME

CASEY SHERMAN

This publication is designed to provide accurate and authoritative information in regard
to the subject matter covered. It is sold with the understanding that the publisher is not
engaged in rendering legal, accounting, or other professional service. If legal advice
or other expert assistance is required, the services of a competent professional person
should be sought. —*From a Declaration of Principles Jointly Adopted by a Committee
of the American Bar Association and a Committee of Publishers and Associations*

Published by Sourcebooks
P.O. Box 4410, Naperville, Illinois 60567-4410
(630) 961-3900
sourcebooks.com

Cataloging-in-Publication Data is on file with the Library of Congress.

Printed and bound in the United States of America.
MA 10 9 8 7 6 5 4 3 2 1

For my beloved brother Todd Forrest Sherman—
artist, poet, author, and bringer of joy.
1965–2022

PROLOGUE

Lana Turner paced the pink carpeted floor with a cigarette gripped tightly between her fingers. She took a deep drag into her lungs and blew out a cloud of smoke toward the ceiling of her spacious bedroom. Her fourteen-year-old daughter, Cheryl, was in her own bedroom, sobbing hysterically. Lana sucked on her cigarette once more, smoking it down to the nub, and looked down at the man lying on her carpet.

Lana Turner and Johnny Stompanato are greeted by Cheryl Crane upon their return from Acapulco, Mexico, in 1958 (Courtesy: Associated Press)

Months of vicious beatings and emotional torment now seemed to be over. Her movie career would be dead too, she thought. As dead as the man lying on her rug.

Mildred Turner, Lana's mother, was on her knees over the man's body with her ear pressed against his chest.

The doorbell rang, and Lana ran downstairs to answer it. Standing before her was her longtime physician and Beverly Hills neighbor, Dr. John McDonald. Lana led him back upstairs to her master bedroom in the rented house that she had moved into only a few days before. Mildred Turner was giving the man mouth-to-mouth resuscitation when Dr. McDonald entered the room. She stood up and stepped away while the doctor took off his jacket and opened his medical bag. He reached in the bag for a stethoscope, inserted the ear tips, and ran the stem down to the body so that he could listen to the man's heart with the chest piece. Not getting any sign of life, the physician grabbed hold of the man's wrist to check for a pulse.

Lana looked on with Mildred.

Dr. McDonald removed his stethoscope and looked up at Lana.

He was speechless. Instead of saying a word, he simply shook his head—*No.*

The doctor then reached back into his bag and retrieved a syringe. He inserted a dose of adrenaline into the tube and plunged the needle into the man's heart. Dr. McDonald picked up the stethoscope once more and listened to the man's heart. He shook his head again.

"Call Jerry Giesler," he ordered Lana.

Lana reached for the telephone and asked the operator for the famed defense lawyer's number.

She wrote down the information and dialed Giesler's office.

"John Stompanato is dead," she told him.

"Where's the body?" Giesler asked her.

"He's here. He's right here."

"I'll be right there," he told her. "Give me your address."

Giesler summoned his driver and told him the address. "Take me to 730 North Bedford Drive!"

The roads were slick, but Giesler ordered his driver to be hasty. He had to get there before someone called the police. As they raced toward Lana Turner's house, Giesler stared out the car window and watched the rain fall, his genius brain absorbing what he had just learned, calculating what needed to be done, and predicting what could happen next.

The gangster Johnny Stompanato was officially dead, and his boss, the powerful Los Angeles crime lord Mickey Cohen, would be hell-bent on revenge and out for Lana's blood.

CHAPTER ONE

A MURDER BY THE BAY

It was mid-December, and the temperature in the city by the bay hovered around forty degrees. The sky was moist but there was not a drop of rain in sight, which was unusual for this time of year. What was usual was the heavy fog floating like an elevated carpet outside the small window to Virgil Turner's cramped hotel room, which was located at the corner of Fourth and Mission Streets, a short distance from the newly opened and far more glamorous Pickwick Hotel.

Turner, a handsome and athletic-looking thirty-four-year-old Alabama native and decorated veteran of the Great War, had recently checked into the hotel, which was popular with transients, under the name Ernie Johnson. While most other hotel guests were catching up on their sleep, Turner was moving about his hotel room searching for his clothes. His wristwatch told him that it was just before 2 a.m. At that hour, all was eerily quiet. The rattle of the cable cars had ceased at midnight and would not begin again for a couple of hours. Restaurants and diners were shuttered for the evening, and there was even a lull in the labyrinthian opium and gambling dens that spread across Chinatown.

Turner quickly put on his pants and shirt, ran a comb through his thick, wavy blond hair, and reached for his overcoat. It had been more than a decade since Virgil Turner had returned home from World War I, but he remained as fit as he had been while serving as an infantry platoon sergeant in the mud-caked, blood-filled trenches of Europe. With broad shoulders and narrow hips, Turner turned heads wherever he went. He had worked as a miner and a stevedore, opened and failed a dry-cleaning business, and operated a distillery brewing corn liquor in his basement before cops came in and busted it up. Most recently, Turner had been making a living with his body. He had moved into a home in San Francisco's fashionable Nob Hill neighborhood with an elderly and wealthy insurance executive, leaving his wife, Mildred, and their young daughter behind. Turner had promised that the move was only temporary and that the money he would earn as a personal assistant, as much as fifty dollars per week, was too good to pass up.

Mildred suspected the duties performed by her husband in his new job went far beyond dictating and managing the executive's busy schedule. When they had arrived on the West Coast three years before, Mildred recalled a steady stream of older men arriving by car at their tiny flat in Stockton and whisking her husband away by car for hours at a time. Turner brushed off her inquiries by telling her the men were merely business partners working with him on a number of lucrative deals, opportunities that never came to fruition. Often, when he would return from these outings, the normally virile husband paid little attention to his young, attractive wife.

Inside the hotel room at the corner of Fourth and Mission Streets, Turner added a diamond stickpin to the lapel of his jacket and stuffed a thick wallet filled with cash in the pocket of his overcoat. The stickpin had been a parting gift from his former employer and lover from Nob Hill.

He left the hotel with a quick nod to the overnight bellman, climbed into his beat-up jalopy, and drove off through the steep, winding streets of the city. Turner was seeking action. He needed to make some quick cash, and he needed to keep a promise for once in his life. As he drove in the darkness, he thought of his young daughter and what a mess he had made of her childhood thus far. Turner knew his marriage to Mildred was over, but his nine-year-old child was the relationship that he cared for most.

The girl was now living with strangers in Modesto, California, while he and his estranged wife worked to cobble together enough money to care for and raise their child. She had been sent to live in Modesto when Mildred was fired from her job as a hairdresser after the salon owner accused her of stealing money from the cash register. Turner had recently paid a visit to the foster home, where his daughter complained that she was being treated like a scullery maid and forced to clean the house for her guardians, the Hislops, and wash and iron their clothes. In an effort to bring a little cheer to her sad face, Turner asked her what she wanted him to bring her on his next visit.

"I want a bike, Daddy!" she squealed. "Pretty please?"

"Okay, I'll get you one. I'll get you a nice shiny red one!"

Turner knew a glistening red bicycle would be hard to come by, especially at the beginning of the Great Depression, when families did not have enough money to eat or put a roof over their heads, let alone afford an extravagant gift like a new bike. But it was the one promise to her that he had sworn he would not break.

At roughly 2:30 a.m. on December 14, 1930, Turner pulled his old Star Car into the dirt parking lot of a darkened warehouse at the corner of Mariposa and Minnesota Streets in the slaughterhouse district known as Butchertown, which was built on stinking marshland just south of the city. He met up with some local gamblers and bought his way into a game of craps under his alias, Ernie "Tex" Johnson. Turner had a small cash reserve and probably figured that he could put up the diamond stickpin as collateral if he hit a losing streak. But instead, Turner won big.

After several lucky rolls in the smoky, dimly lit confines of the warehouse, he gathered his winnings and headed for the door. It was now early Sunday morning. Turner would have to find a safe place to keep his gambling winnings back at the hotel until he could visit a department store to purchase the gift for his daughter the following day.

The war veteran apparently did not see the deadly blow coming.

Turner was struck once over his left eye by a heavy object, probably a blackjack. The force of the assault was so strong that the single blow triggered a cerebral hemorrhage, knocking him to the ground. There, his killer or killers quickly rifled through his pockets, stealing the cash winnings from Turner's wallet and swiping the diamond stickpin from his lapel.

Just after 7:00 a.m., as the first light of dawn stretched over the city, a wild-eyed railroad conductor on his way to work burst through the front doors of the nearby Potrero police station. "There's a body lying on the sidewalk on Minnesota Street," the conductor shouted.

He led two uniformed police officers to the scene where Virgil Turner's body was in a sitting position, propped against the side of the warehouse. His coat was pulled partly over his head, and his hat and left shoe were found at the left side of his body. His left sock was missing. According to his wife, Turner made a habit of stashing extra cash in his left sock. The cops checked his vital signs. Turner was not breathing. To the officers, it appeared that his body had been left in a sitting position by his killers, possibly to give the illusion that Turner wasn't really dead, just dead drunk and sleeping it off.

His body was removed at 7:20 a.m. and taken to a nearby morgue where an autopsy was performed later that morning. The medical examiner noticed a discoloration of Turner's eye, just below the spot where he was struck by a blunt object. There were no other injuries or the appearance that the decorated soldier put up any defensive struggle. Turner's killers had taken him by surprise. In cop speak, it meant that he had been taken "for a ride," which was how investigators described it to local reporters. The next day's headline of the *Oakland Tribune* read, "Murdered Man Believed to Be Robber Victim: Veteran Found Lying Near Warehouse, with Money and Diamonds Gone." The article went on to describe the items stolen from

Turner and the single blow that caused his death. The news reporter added that his body was identified at the morgue by his wife, Mildred, who said she was a nightclub entertainer and told investigators that she had spoken to her husband just hours before by telephone.

In the last paragraph of the *Oakland Tribune* report, there is mention that Virgil and Mildred Turner were married for eleven years and had a daughter named Julia Jean Turner. The young girl, who was called "Judy" and "JuJean" by her parents, did not read the newspaper article and was totally confused when her foster mother, Julia Hislop, a stern woman who was prone to fits of rage, marched into her bedroom and said, "Put on your nice dress. We're going to San Francisco."

"Why?" the daughter asked.

Hislop did not answer. She simply said, "Never mind."

The foster mother, who had once beaten the girl with a stick of kindling wood that left her covered with dark bruises, did not lash out violently against her this time. She merely pointed to the girl's dress and left the room.

But Judy quickly realized the trip was important. At first, she beamed with excitement during the long train ride from Modesto to San Francisco.

Is my mother having a baby? Judy asked herself.

She was an only child. Mildred had suffered a miscarriage a few years prior and had sworn off sex. Another reason for her abstinence was her husband's brute aggression in bed. There was no lovemaking between Virgil and Mildred Turner. She was merely a receptacle for his manly urges. Naively, Judy thought that having another sibling might reunite her parents. Mildred and Virgil had been happy once. Judy remembered watching and laughing as her parents danced the foxtrot across the kitchen floor to the song "You're the Cream in My Coffee," played on a wind-up Victrola. The pair had met in Picher, Oklahoma, when Mildred was just fifteen years old. She had been escorted to a local dance by her father at a rooftop beer garden, where she spotted Turner hoofing away in tap shoes on a small stage. They locked eyes and both were swept off their feet. A brief courtship led to an elopement. There would be no big church wedding, as Mildred's father adamantly disapproved of their union and the nine-year age difference between them. Although Mildred respected her husband, always calling him "Mr. Turner" and never by his first name, she soon wanted to break free from the drudgery of marriage. Whenever Mildred earned a little money, she'd buy dresses for their young daughter and herself and catch a train out of town without a destination in mind. She would only telegraph or call Mr. Turner when she ran out of money someplace miles away from their home.

Little Judy found herself on a train once again with Mrs. Hislop by her side. The foster mother had told her to keep her mouth shut about the beatings and the hours of housework she was forced to provide for the family. Instead, Judy kept her mind on what would hopefully be a joyous reunion with her mother at the train station, but Mildred was in no mood to celebrate when they met up later that day in San Francisco. Her mother barely said a word a short time later when the two had dinner at a Chinese restaurant. The silence did not faze Judy, as she had become used to Mildred's erratic behavior. Once, Mildred had Judy wave to a woman in a passing train and told the girl that the stranger was her real mother, just to make her cry. During dinner, Judy peppered Mildred with questions, which her mother ignored between mouthfuls of chop suey and sips of hot tea.

Back at the hotel that evening, Judy believed she had seen a vision, which she later described as a "huge medallion of shining gold, and on it was embossed the face of God, a shimmering countenance…and benign." The apparition told her that her father, Virgil Turner, was dead, which surprisingly comforted her.

Consolation turned to sheer terror the next morning when she saw Turner's lifeless body stuffed in a casket at the funeral home. Lying before her was her father, the only man who had ever cared for her, the only man she had ever loved.

"Do you want to kiss your father goodbye?" Mildred asked.

Instead, the daughter reached out and touched her deceased father's folded hands. The hands were cold. They were the same hands that had hugged her and danced with her, but they were alien to her now. She recoiled quickly and hid behind Mildred's mourning dress. Judy flinched once more a few hours later at Virgil's burial at the National Cemetery at the Presidio surrounded by Monterey cypress and overlooking San Francisco Bay, where a line of American soldiers in full military dress fired three rifle volleys over the flag-draped coffin of the U.S. Army sergeant, first class.

The murder of Virgil Turner would never be solved.

Two decades later in 1951, when the daughter took time to reflect on her father's death, she wrote, "The shock I suffered then may be a valid excuse for me now. It explains things I do not myself understand. I know that my father's sweetness and gaiety, his warmth and his tragedy have never been that far from me—that, and a sense of loss and of growing up too fast."

Julia Jean "Judy" Turner penned the article in the pages of *Woman's Home Companion*. By this time, she was called by a new name, Lana Turner, and she was the biggest star in Hollywood.

CHAPTER TWO

FROM BROOKLYN TO BOYLE HEIGHTS

Long before Lana Turner would stake her claim as queen of Hollywood, its underground king, Meyer Harris "Mickey" Cohen, arrived in Los Angeles when he was just three years old with his older sister, Lillie, and their mother, Fanny, an immigrant from Kiev, Ukraine, who did not speak English.

They had migrated west from the Brownsville neighborhood of Brooklyn, New York. Fanny was a young widow. Max Cohen, her fishmonger husband and Mickey's father, died in 1913 when the boy was less than two months old. At the time, Brownsville was described as New York's "rawest, remotest, cheapest ghetto," populated by Jews fresh off the boat from eastern Europe. But the close-knit Jewish enclave could not support single mother Fanny and her six children, so she left four of them behind with relatives when she hopped on a train to the West Coast with Lillie and little Mickey in tow. They settled in another Jewish ghetto, Boyle Heights, located on a set of bluffs just east of the Los Angeles River, better known as East LA today. Its namesake, an Irish developer named Andrew Boyle, had survived being stood up in front of a firing squad during the Mexican-American War. Years later, he plonked down $4,000 for twenty-two acres of land in the area then known as Paredón Blanco, or White Bluffs, where immigrants from the French Basque region herded their sheep on Mount Pleasant.

When Fanny Cohen got off the train in Los Angeles, there were about ten thousand Jews living in the city. Many flocked to the Boyle Heights neighborhood called Russian Town, where fig, lemon, and peach trees grew among the small row houses. Nearby Brooklyn Avenue was the center of activity for Jewish residents, filled with the aroma of smoked meat, bagels, and knishes from the old country wafting out of butcher shops, bakeries, and delicatessens. The ghetto was also home to hundreds of Italian, Japanese, and Mexican immigrants, adding more exotic smells and impossible-to-read signage atop small storefronts, creating a micro League of Nations next to the river.

Once settled, Fanny called for the rest of her children to join them in Los Angeles. Mickey Cohen's earliest memories centered on his job as a paperboy for the *Los Angeles Record* when he was six years old. The diminutive tyke stood on a high box and waved copies of the daily newspaper to all who passed by. Young Cohen was also industrious. He would sleep in the men's room at the newspaper on big news days, such as a presidential election or a Jack Dempsey fight, waiting for the sheets to roll off the presses just so he would be the first one to sell those extra editions, which could earn him up to a dollar a newspaper.

Occasionally, he was forced to fight with other paperboys in an effort to keep his coveted spot at the corner of Soto and Brooklyn Streets. Cohen was smaller than the other boys, but what he lacked in stature, he more than made up for with an insatiable hunger to survive. He often walked away victorious from these childhood scrapes. He was tough and knew how to earn money and keep it.

"I was really looking to make a buck at a very young age," he would later recall to a biographer.

Mickey Cohen's official FBI file, which is more than four hundred pages long, shows that he entered grammar school but dropped out before reaching junior high school. Fanny Cohen opened a small grocery store and pharmacy in the Russian Orthodox section of Boyle Heights, and young Mickey entered the family business. When he wasn't rinsing produce and bagging avocados and lemons for customers from the old country, he helped run Fanny's thriving bootlegging business, which operated out of the back of the store.

Cohen's first arrest came when he was nine years old after he tangled with local cops who came to inspect Fanny's store and bust up her illicit liquor business.

"I was making gin the way I was taught to make it, when the Prohibition coppers caught me," he remembered years later. "It was the first time I ever got in a beef with the coppers, so when one of them reached for the still, I kind of got peeved and I hit him with a plate of hot food." The officer wiped the food off his face, slapped a pair of handcuffs on Cohen's tiny wrists, and brought him downtown in the police wagon. The youngster was charged with bootlegging, but the case was thrown out of court.

The arrest gave Cohen his first taste of criminal activity, which he relished. He quickly set his sights on a bigger score: targeting the burgeoning movie business. Cohen watched theatergoers hand over their meager earnings to the box office manager at the nearby Columbia Theater, which ran silent movies like *Sacred and Profane Love* starring Conrad Nagel and *The Idol of the North* with Dorothy Dalton. One day, he picked up a thick piece of wood and wielded it as a weapon, threatening to cudgel the ticket taker if he did not hand over a bag of coins. Staring down at the tiny tyrant, the box office manager refused Cohen's demand and flagged down a local beat cop, who arrested him on the spot. Instead of getting a slap on the wrist this time, Cohen was sent to a juvenile detention center at Fort Hill in Los Angeles. The reform school guardians spent little time attempting to reform and educate the juvenile delinquents. Instead, they were unforgiving and sadistic, handing out daily beatings to Cohen and other children using a bicycle tire as a makeshift whip.

If Cohen had any ideas about turning his young life around, they were quashed by the constant abuse inflicted by his adult tormentors. The soft boy grew hard at Fort Hill. When he was released after serving a seven-month term, he was ordered to attend public school, but he barely ever found his way to class. Instead, Cohen got his education inside smoke-filled pool halls where he learned to hustle men twice his age. He was so talented with a pool cue that he began earning more money than his mother, Fanny, did owning her own grocery store and unlawful booze business.

"I got a kick out of having a big bankroll in my pocket," he would later write in his memoir. "Even if I only made a couple hundred dollars, I'd always keep it in fives and tens so that it would look big. I had to hide it from my mother, because she'd get excited when she'd see a roll of money like that. One time when I was twelve, I left my pants hanging over a chair with three-four hundred dollars in my pocket… So when my mother went to hang them up, this roll fell out and spread out all over the floor. She called in my older brother Sam, and they must have thought I'd robbed a bank, because he kicked the shit out of me."

During his probation from reform school, Cohen was ordered by the court to meet weekly with a counselor or "big brother" named Abe Roth, a popular boxing referee in LA. Roth had built a reputation as a tough guy in and out of the ring. During one bout, he refused to allow a beaten boxer's cornermen to throw in the towel. To Roth, that wasn't manly enough. He ordered the battered pugilist to come out for the next round, only to see him get pummeled some more before stopping the fight. In Cohen, Roth saw a younger, smaller version of himself. But he would not tutor Cohen on the finer points of working as a referee. Instead, he groomed the twelve-year-old to become a boxer.

Roth booked the boy to fight in several bootleg joints around the city. Cohen had to lie to his mother, Fanny, who despite her own criminal activity abhorred violence. He would tell her that he was going to the beach, when in reality he was fighting in the back of clubs in East Los Angeles, Compton, and Watts, wearing oversize boxing trunks and a pair of boxing gloves that went up to his sharp elbows. Standing just over five feet tall and weighing only 115 pounds, Cohen terrorized the flyweight boxing circuit, winning more than a dozen matches with his wild, windmill punching style and capturing the newsboy flyweight championship. He earned one dollar for each round and more if he won. Cohen liked boxing as it sharpened his fighting skills and made him a sought-after bodyguard for teenage news hawkers looking to protect their own coveted street corners from violent rivals. Always looking for new ways to earn cash, Cohen quickly muscled out most of the paperboys and took their street corners for himself.

Unlike kids in the neighborhood where Cohen had been born back in Brooklyn, kids living in Boyle Heights did not stick to their own. "It seems all us Mexicans, Jews, and Italians got along very well," Cohen later recalled. "If anyone called someone a kike, spic, or wop in our neighborhood, we would all gang up and beat his head in."

Fanny Cohen feared that her youngest son would end up dead in some alleyway and demanded that he give up boxing and go back to school, where his older brothers were thriving and preparing to enter college. Cohen scoffed at the idea. Unlike for his siblings, school was not for him. He decided to take his boxing career to the next level and turn pro. He hopped a train to the Midwest, where he would meet his destiny through a charismatic, murderous father figure named Al "Scarface" Capone.

CHAPTER THREE

THE SODA FOUNTAIN

Judy Turner and her mother, Mildred, made the move from Northern California to Los Angeles in 1936 after Mildred was stricken with San Joaquin Valley fever, also known as desert rheumatism. After living in San Fransisco and then Sacramento, Mildred was told by her doctor that she move to a drier climate in an attempt to cure her wretched cough. With her now-teenage daughter in tow, Mildred Turner gathered their belongings and hitched a ride south with two other women in a borrowed car. When they reached Paso Robles, about two hundred miles north of LA, their car flipped over in a rainstorm and landed in a ditch. Mildred suffered broken ribs, and Judy received a nasty bump on her head along with several scrapes and bruises while climbing out of the wreck. Surprisingly, the dented car was still roadworthy. After getting the vehicle upright and pushed out of the mud, the travelers got Mildred patched up at a nearby hospital, found a motel, and continued on with their journey the following day.

"We rattled our way into Los Angeles," Lana Turner wrote in her memoir. It was "the biggest city I'd ever seen, its wide streets lined with ornate stone buildings, with bright imposing signs."

The brightest sign of all read *Hollywoodland*. Standing forty-three feet tall and stretching thirty feet wide, the sign straddled the rocky hillside over the city. Its thirteen giant letters were supported by a frame of scaffolding, pipes, wires, and telephone poles that were hauled to the site by pack mules up steep, winding dirt roads. The sign had been erected more than a decade earlier by Harry Chandler, publisher of the *Los Angeles Times*, to promote his posh new real-estate development in the Hollywood Hills, at the end of Beachwood Canyon, where lots were selling for $150 to $400. Chandler paid $21,000 to have the sign built, and it was supposed to be taken down after eighteen months. The sign, adorned with thirty-seven hundred light bulbs, flashed *Holly* then *Wood* and then *Land*. Coinciding with the giant sign was an early advertisement that read "Where will you live when the second million has come? Will your family enjoy a delightful home in the clean, pure mountain air of Hollywoodland, with its wonderful climate, broad open spaces and plenty of 'elbow' room—or—will you live in a 'dwelling' in the flat, uninteresting houses-in-a-row sections of the City, your family's freedom hampered by this maelstrom of human existence?"

Long after the last lots were sold off, the sign remained on its lofty perch, now a symbol of the city and its most profitable industry: movie making.

When mother and daughter were unceremoniously dropped off at the corner of Sunset Boulevard and Highland Avenue, they never gave a second thought to what their lives might be like "when the second million has come." Judy and Mildred stared down at their two suitcases, which were caked with crusted dirt, and wondered where their next meal would come from. From time to time, when money was tight and Virgil Turner was still alive but nowhere to be found, mother and daughter had survived on a diet of crackers and milk. But Mildred had not make the long trek from San Francisco to Los Angeles without a plan, at least in the short term. She had contacted a friend named Gladys Taylor, who offered not only to pick them up when they reached LA but to give them a place to stay while Mildred looked for a job. Gladys Taylor, or "Gladdy" as she was known, had a small Spanish Colonial-style, two-bedroom house on Glencoe Way in the

Hollywood Hills. There was also a tiny utility room with a cot where Judy could sleep. When Gladys pulled up in her car at the corner of Sunset and Highland, mother and daughter looked like a pair of refugees with their suitcases and a few beat-up boxes and crumbled bags.

After loading Gladys's car, Judy climbed into the back seat and enjoyed the ride through town. "All I noticed were those glorious art deco buildings… with their gleaming fluted stone and chrome—so modern, so sophisticated."

She also got a closer look at the Hollywoodland sign, where the broken body of a young, aspiring actress had been found by a hiker four years earlier. Her name was Peg Entwistle, and she had jumped from high atop the sign's giant letter *H*. Entwistle's purse contained just one item—a handwritten suicide note that read "I'm afraid I'm a coward. I am sorry for everything. If I had done this a long time ago, it would have saved me a lot of pain." Entwistle had recently been released from her contract with RKO Pictures following

The famed Hollywood sign as it looks today (photo by Casey Sherman)

her cameo in the film *Thirteen Women*. The deadly plunge by a relatively unknown actress off the Hollywoodland sign became one of the biggest scandals and mysteries to hit the town in years, discussed with the same macabre glee as the rape and manslaughter trials involving silent film star Roscoe "Fatty" Arbuckle.

Mildred Turner quickly found a job at a Hollywood beauty salon, whose beauticians proudly claimed they could transform the average

Hollywood housewife into the second coming of Joan Crawford or Bette Davis. In September, Judy enrolled at Hollywood High School, where actors such as Carole Lombard, Lon Chaney Jr., Joel McCrea, and Fay Wray, the recent star of RKO's *King Kong*, had once roamed the halls. While her Hollywood High classmates Judy Garland and Mickey Rooney dreamed of following in the footsteps of those famed alums, Judy Turner yearned for a career off camera, possibly as a fashion designer. She had always marveled at how well put together Mildred was despite having little money for clothes. Mother and daughter bonded over old copies of *Vogue* magazine and read aloud to each other passages from Emily Post's book *Etiquette in Society, in Business, in Politics, and at Home.* Judy's mother, however, saw her fifteen-year-old daughter best suited for a future in the secretarial pool and urged her to take typing classes. Judy listened to Mildred and enrolled in typing class at Hollywood High.

But one day in October 1936, Judy made a decision that would change her life forever. Feeling bored and thirsty, she cut class and ran across Highland Avenue to get a soda. She strolled into Currie's Ice Cream Parlor, adorned by a giant sign featuring two vanilla ice cream cones at 6775 Sunset Boulevard, and took a stool along the wooden counter opposite the soda fountain. She craved a tall glass of chocolate malted or a strawberry soda, but she only had a nickel in her pocket, which was just enough for a glass of Coca-Cola. Judy offered the soda jerk her coin, and he filled up a tall glass of ice-cold Coke, sank a straw in the middle, and slid it over to the young brunette, who was blessed with a soft, spotless complexion.

"As I sipped the Coke, a man at the fountain kept staring at me. He was well dressed and in his midforties, with sharp features, a mustache, and dark hair," she later recalled.

Judy heard the strange man whispering to the soda jerk.

"Who is that girl?"

"That's Judy, Mr. Wilkerson."

The man desperately wanted to meet the teenager, who he thought was "breathtakingly beautiful."

"I'll ask," the soda jerk promised.

The counterman walked toward Judy and leaned over.

"There's a gentleman who wants to meet you."

Judy was wearing a tightly fitted white sweater, and she could feel the strange man undressing her with his eyes, focusing his attention mainly on her youthful but well-formed breasts. The soda jerk could sense that she was feeling uncomfortable.

"He's all right. He works down the street and eats here all the time," he said, trying to put her at ease. "Do you mind if he speaks to you?"

She was nervous but nodded her consent to the counterman. "Well, if you say so. But stay close."

The mustachioed man was direct in his approach.

"Hello, young lady. I'm Billy Wilkerson, the publisher of the *Hollywood Reporter*. Would you like to be in movies?"

"I don't know," she replied, stumbling over her words. "I'll have to ask my mother."

Wilkerson flipped out a business card that read *W. R. Wilkerson—The Hollywood Reporter* and placed it on her palm. "Yes, ask your mother about it and have her call me."

Judy stuffed the business card into her notebook and headed back to Hollywood High just in time for her next class.

That night, when Mildred arrived home from the beauty parlor, her daughter handed her Wilkerson's card. Mildred was tired from a long day at the salon and did not appear interested in Judy's random meeting with a stranger. But Gladys recognized the name immediately.

"He publishes the *Hollywood Reporter*," Gladys told Mildred. "It's a respectable paper and he seems legitimate. You should find out what he wants."

Mildred was new to town and did not know any Hollywood types. She asked Gladys if she would follow up with Wilkerson. Gladys placed the call to Wilkerson's office as Judy huddled next to the telephone, and an appointment was set up for the following day.

Billy Wilkerson had made his way to Hollywood in 1930 with his wife, Edith, their dog, and $2,000 in his pocket. He had come from New York with an idea to publish a newspaper that cranked out stories about film productions and the daily happenings of the movie industry. He had been told by friends that the idea was insane. "Save your money," they all urged Wilkerson. "The picture business has too many papers now, and a Hollywood paper will never pay!"

A gambler like his father had been, Wilkerson blocked his ears and plowed ahead with his plan. He rented a small office, filled it with secondhand furniture and a couple of old typewriters, and went to work. The first edition of the *Hollywood Reporter* was published on September 3, 1930, and six years later, it was considered by many industry insiders as the most important newspaper covering the motion picture industry in the world. President Franklin Delano Roosevelt even had his own subscription to the *Reporter*, which was delivered by airmail to the Oval Office every day. Wilkerson enjoyed rubbing elbows with both celebrities and politicians. Within the pages of the *Hollywood Reporter*, he printed a column known as "Billy's List" in which he listed the names of suspected Communist sympathizers. The list later evolved into the infamous Hollywood blacklist that ruined many careers in the entertainment industry. But somehow, the publisher managed to survive the scandal unscathed. In fact, he prospered.

When Judy walked into Wilkerson's office with Gladys Taylor by her side, she did not see any secondhand furniture or ratty typewriters. The spacious office had ornate furnishings with rococo designs. The publisher had come a long way in a relatively short period of time. Not only was Wilkerson the publisher of the town's hottest newspaper, but he also owned Hollywood's glitziest new nightclub, the Café Trocadero. The place was glamorous, decorated with striped silk chairs, gold-spackled walls, and shimmering chandeliers. It was also filled every night with many of Hollywood's biggest stars, including Clark Gable, Bing Crosby, and Fred Astaire.

Billy Wilkerson believed the girl he had just discovered at the malt shop could become a movie star on par with those Hollywood legends. But Wilkerson did not just happen to be at the ice cream parlor that day. It was part of his daily routine. He had a fascination with young girls. The powerful trade publisher would disappear from the office for half an hour each day to ogle pretty teenagers from Hollywood High at Currie's Ice Cream Parlor and the nearby Top Hat Café, both of which were popular with high school students. Gawking at underage girls was one thing; approaching one was another. There is little doubt that Wilkerson, middle-aged and married, fantasized about Judy Turner, whose measurements were 35–24½–34½, but instead of cultivating his own version of Lolita in this case, Wilkerson kept their relationship on a professional level.

"You're a very pretty girl," he beamed as she sat in a chair across from his desk.

The compliment caused Judy to blush and giggle. She was still a child, and all the attention was new to her.

Wilkerson continued to praise her looks and told her that she needed a talent agent. He then scribbled a note on a piece of paper, folded it, and stuck it in an envelope.

"This should get you into Zeppo's office."

The agent Wilkerson was referring to was Zeppo Marx, who had retired from his family's famed comedy act, which starred his older brothers Groucho, Harpo, and Chico. Zeppo Marx now managed the careers of Clark Gable, Barbara Stanwyck, and other famous actors.

Wilkerson's note opened the door for the teenager, who met with Zeppo Marx a few days later. Just as Wilkerson had done at the soda fountain, Marx gazed longingly at Judy before engaging her in conversation.

"Tell me, Judy, how old are you?" he asked.

"Fifteen, Mr. Marx."

Marx could hardly believe it. "Oh, no you're not."

"Yes, I really am," she replied. "Honest."

Marx gave her a stern look.

"Don't ever say that again," he scolded her. "As far as this industry goes, you're eighteen!"

With that one sentence, Zeppo Marx had stolen what remained of Judy Turner's childhood. At that moment, the teenager had no idea why concealing her age would be so important. Marx then introduced her to Henry Willson, one of his top talent scouts. The jowly agent quickly schooled the Hollywood High School student about the seedy underbelly of the Hollywood dream factory.

"Men go home to fuck their wives out of duty," Willson told Judy. "But what the bastards really want is to bed a gal who looks like you."

Willson was also surprised that Wilkerson had not made a pass at the teenager.

"I don't know how you escaped. When [Wilkerson's] not losing money gambling, he sleeps with every gal not named Mrs. Billy Wilkerson."

Willson recognized a predator when he saw one. He would eventually launch the careers of Hollywood stars like Rock Hudson and Tab Hunter, often trading movie auditions for sexual favors. Willson also was known to serve up young women to *Gone with the Wind* producer David O. Selznick and his infamous casting couch.

Willson took Judy to every studio in town, where she was turned down flatly time and again. After each rejection, she would go back to class at Hollywood High or to her job at a lingerie shop on Hollywood Boulevard, where she earned just over twelve dollars each week.

It was David O. Selznick who gave Judy her unofficial start in films. With Willson's urging, the producer cast the teenager as an extra in a crowd scene in the first adaptation of *A Star Is Born* with Fredric March and Janet Gaynor in the lead roles. But the brief screen appearance did nothing to advance her career. A photographer then offered to pay her money to pose for nude photos, which she declined. Gaining little traction with his teenage client, Henry Willson gave up on her and turned his attention to an emerging stable of beefcake actors, who were all looking for their lucky break in Tinseltown.

Next, Zeppo Marx passed Judy on to a young talent scout named Solly Biano at Warner Brothers. Biano had heard that acclaimed film director Mervyn LeRoy was looking for a girl to fill out the cast of his upcoming movie. LeRoy was a surefire hitmaker of Hollywood crime films, most notably *Little Caesar*, starring Edward G. Robinson in the role of an up-and-coming gangster hell-bent on taking over the Chicago rackets. The film was an obvious nod to real-life organized crime kingpin Al Capone.

LeRoy's new project was an adaptation of a book written by Atlanta-based novelist Ward Greene titled *Death in the Deep South*, about the lynching of a northerner in a stereotypical southern town following the murder of a local girl. Before meeting with LeRoy, Judy was paraded in front of the casting director. It was part of the job and something she was now getting used to, but there was a different, darker tone in this meeting.

"Lift your skirt," he barked at her. "Walk and turn around."

Judy felt uncomfortable and bit down hard on her lip, trying not to cry. No one had ever asked her to do anything like this before. The teenager felt like cattle being led to slaughter. She showed her thighs to the casting director and waited nervously for another demand. Judy stared at the couch in the casting director's office and feared the worst. But instead of pouncing on her, the director dismissed Judy with a wave of his hand.

The teenager breathed a sigh of relief and fled the room.

Later, when LeRoy got a look at her inside his office bungalow, he recognized her beauty right away. She wore very little makeup, and her youthful complexion was radiant.

"Well, you're very pretty," he said while chomping on a cigar. "Tell me what you've done."

"Nothing," she replied honestly.

LeRoy asked her if she had performed in any stage productions at Hollywood High. Judy smiled nervously and shook her head no.

"No elocution class? No acting classes?"

"No, sir."

LeRoy noticed that her hands were shaking.

She can't even look me in the eye, the director thought to himself. *But there's something endearing about her. She has tremendous appeal, which I know the audience will feel.*

"Please wait outside," LeRoy told her.

Judy left the bungalow and stepped back out into the bright Southern California sunshine. If it didn't go well here, she would go back to school and learn how to make dresses for those talented and experienced actresses who would make it on the silver screen.

Solly Biano joined her out on the Warner Brothers lot a few minutes later after speaking one on one with the director.

"You're in the picture," he said with enthusiasm. "It's a small part, but a good one. And we're getting you fifty a week!"

Fifty dollars per week was more than twice as much money as Mildred earned working at the beauty parlor. Judy Turner signed her first movie contract on February 12, 1937, just a few weeks after she turned sixteen. With her first fifty-dollar check in her pocket, she told Mildred to sit down and close her eyes before placing it in her hands.

"Now you'll never have to work again," Judy promised.

In an unusual move, LeRoy signed her to a personal services contract, not a contract with the studio. This would allow the director to haul the teenager around like a piece of luggage from back lot to back lot, depending on which studio he was working for at the time.

He also had another big decision to make regarding the teenage actress. She needed a new name. LeRoy felt that Judy Turner was too plain. The director figured there was probably a Judy Turner in just about every town in America, but Hollywood was not "every town." The place was special, and it served as an escape for ordinary folks struggling through their ordinary, mundane lives. The teenager suggested her birth name, Julia Jean. The director scoffed at the idea.

"Nope, that's almost as bad," he told her. "Turner sounds nice and American, but we need a new first name."

LeRoy pulled out a book of baby names, one he kept for moments such as this, and began searching for names that started with the letter L.

"What about Lurlene?" he asked her. "Or Leonore?"

She turned her delicate nose up at both suggestions.

Suddenly, a name popped into her head. "What about Lana?"

LeRoy asked her to spell it. She did and then she repeated the name, this time stretching the vowels—*Lah-nah*.

The director let the name swim around in his head for a few moments.

"Lana Turner," he said aloud. "Lah-nah Turner. It sounds right. That's it. You're Lana Turner!"

Cameras rolled on her first film, titled *They Won't Forget*, in early March 1937. She found herself sitting on a stool at a soda fountain, just as she had done in real life at Currie's Ice Cream Parlor a few months before. But this time, everyone around her called her Lana, and she was playing the role of Mary Clay, an attractive college student who is about to be murdered.

LeRoy did not have his young actress sitting for long. He sent Lana to wardrobe to be fitted in a tam hat, a skirt that showed off her calves, and a tight blue sweater. When she returned to the set, he gave her a simple instruction.

"Just walk," he told her. "Just walk from *here* to *there*."

Lana took the direction and walked in front of a building facade during a seventy-five-foot tracking shot while a brass band played "Dixie" in the background. The sixteen-year-old didn't have to really act or speak; her lithe body did all the acting and talking for her. Lana bounced down the street with a style that made her appear much older than her sixteen innocent years. But LeRoy was not looking for innocence in the character. Cameraman Arthur Edeson sexualized her with his lens. Up to this point in her life, Lana had barely even kissed a boy. Now she was being put on display for the erotic enjoyment of grown men.

"Lana's debut didn't require great screen acting," LeRoy recalled. "All she had to do was walk, and boy, did she know how to do that. I had the music scored to match the up and down movements of her tits and ass."

She was immediately dubbed Hollywood's "Sweater Girl." Law enforcement had long considered the "sweater girl" phenomenon a plague on America's youth and the root cause for the rise in sex crimes around the country. "Women walk the street, their curves accentuated by their dresses," Pittsburgh police superintendent Harvey J. Scott told a United Press reporter. "But our real problem is with bobby-soxers. They are the sweater girls—just kids showing off their curves and apparently liking it. What kind of wives and mothers are they going to be?"

The fear now was that Lana Turner would take the phenomenon to a dangerous new level.

Lana's star-maker Billy Wilkerson penned one of the first reviews of the film in the *Hollywood Reporter*. "Short on playing time is the role of the murdered schoolgirl," he wrote. "But as played by Lana Turner it is worthy of more than a passing note. This young lady has vivid beauty, personality, and charm." Wilkerson made no mention of discovering the teenager at Currie's Ice Cream Parlor, but word of the encounter soon made its way around Hollywood and beyond. Suddenly, pretty girls from all over the

United States cobbled together what little money they had and purchased bus and train tickets to Hollywood, where they would park themselves on soda fountain stools at Currie's Ice Cream Parlor, the Top Hat Café, and Schwab's Pharmacy on nearby Sunset Boulevard, hoping to be discovered by a talent agent. Lana Turner's Hollywood story had eclipsed the tragedy that had befallen failed actress Peg Entwistle just a few years before.

Chapter Four

CHICAGO AND AL CAPONE

Mickey Cohen had an important job. He was ordered to keep a close watch on an illegal card game that operated in the back of a Jewish restaurant near the Edgewater Beach Hotel on Chicago's North Side. The game was run by a gangster named Joe Barron, who had taken a liking to the young tough kid from Los Angeles. Barron put Cohen on his payroll to make sure that the money was counted properly each night and that no disgruntled gambler tried to get their losses back with a knife or a gun. Cohen stood guard over the game like an angry pit bull, watching and sometimes snarling at the poor suckers who reluctantly handed over their wages to the casino's boss. Piles of cash poured in and needed to be protected.

"Never leave the joint unless you're with me or it is a must," Barron told him.

Cohen followed Barron's orders explicitly. His allegiance to the mob up to this point was one of the main reasons that gangsters had sent him to Cleveland, then on to New York City before ultimately placing him in Chicago, the world capital of organized crime. Originally, Cohen had been a stickup guy for the Cleveland syndicate while taking prize fights on the side. The Italians called him "that Jew kid," and they admired the gumption he showed in knocking over card games and getting away with as much as $5,000 in a single score. He continued to hone his skills later in New York, where he connected himself with his first criminal mentor—the Irish gangster Owney Madden.

Madden was a boxing promoter and owner of the Cotton Club, Harlem's historic jazz club, where Black entertainers like Louis Armstrong and Cab Calloway played trumpet, danced, and sang in front of a "Whites Only" crowd. Madden was known as "the Duke of the West Side" for his flashy appearance and tailor-made suits. This royal title did little to mask Madden's ferocity. Actress Mae West called him "sweet, but oh so vicious." Owney Madden's other nickname was more fitting—"the Killer." As a former leader of the notorious New York City gang the Gophers, Madden had learned how to maim and kill with an assortment of weapons, including stilettos, lead pipes, slingshots, and knuckle dusters. But nothing compared to his favorite murder tool, a Smith & Wesson that he used to shoot and kill at close range.

Mickey Cohen studied Madden closely and began to copy the way he dressed and mimic his mannerisms. Cohen was a self-professed "punk kid" who matured quickly under Madden's tutelage. "Owney was really a guy to respect and admire—quite a guy," Cohen gushed years later. He was "a man of his word all the way through. His faithfulness to his own kind is the strongest thing a man can have, and if Owney felt that you were an all right person, there wasn't nothing that he wouldn't do for you."

Madden's influence on Cohen would manifest itself for many years in the way Cohen treated those he deemed loyal. But young Cohen had a habit for coloring outside the lines. He may have sworn his allegiance to the Syndicate, but he also put together his own criminal crews in Cleveland and in New York City.

"We were stepping on the toes of the outfit," he recalled. "But we just figured, the hell with it, we had ourselves to worry about."

There were many times when Cohen came within a hair of getting his "lights put out" for screwing with the wrong people—gangsters with better connections in the racket world than he had.

One time, Cohen was ordered to shoot a rival for the mob, but he put a bullet in an innocent man instead after a lookout identified the wrong guy. In return, Cohen pistol-whipped the mob spotter for the mistake and was called before a Mafia roundtable to explain his actions.

"Look, when I learned for sure that this was the wrong guy, I says, what the fuck. I ain't that rotten. I'm lucky I didn't kill this son of a bitch," he said, sharing his frustrations with members of the roundtable. Cohen could have signed his own death warrant for beating up the mob lookout, whose older brother held a position of power in the rackets. But gangsters like Owney Madden and others saw through Cohen's impetuous personality and recognized his potential. That is how he ended up in the Windy City, the ultimate finishing school for organized crime.

In Chicago, Cohen resorted to violence only when necessary and with great efficiency. One day, three gangsters turned up at Joe Barron's restaurant looking for the casino boss. Cohen had locked the front door, so the mobsters opened fire through a large glass window. Cohen ducked for cover and then shot back, hitting two of the gunmen and killing them on the sidewalk. He was arrested for double homicide. Cohen was handcuffed and taken to the nearest Chicago police precinct where he sat in a jail cell, wondering whether he would face the gallows for what he had done.

But Cohen would never face trial or even be forced to make a plea. His boss, Joe Barron, had the local cops on his payroll and convinced them it was an act of self-defense, which truly it was.

News of Cohen's dead aim with a pistol reached the Lexington Hotel where Al "Scarface" Capone had taken a ten-room suite on the top floor, which he had converted into his office and residence. Capone's office had a sweeping view of his criminal kingdom, Chicago's South Side, where nearly every storekeeper and business owner paid some amount of tribute to Big Al and his army of thieves, thugs, and trained killers. Capone had gained control over the city's rackets on February 14, 1929, St. Valentine's Day, when his men, dressed as police officers, entered a garage at 2122 North Clark Street, which served as headquarters for George "Bugs" Moran, Capone's archrival in the multimillion-dollar bootlegging business. Moran's crew figured it was nothing more than a police shakedown and lined up facing the garage wall. Instead of pulling out handcuffs, the fake cops whipped out tommy guns and fired seventy rounds, killing seven members of the gang. Capone was never charged in connection with the dramatic slaying because he was conveniently visiting his home in Florida at the time, but everyone in the city knew the St. Valentine's Day Massacre was his dirty work.

"Only Capone kills like that," a defeated Moran told reporters.

Capone was impressed by Cohen and probably saw a little of himself in the brash Jewish gangster from Los Angeles. Capone called for Cohen and invited him into his inner sanctum.

"I walked into his office kinda awed," Cohen remembered. "Al Capone was like the king of Chicago. If you were disfavored by him, your life wasn't worth a damn. But if you did something good, then he would show you his appreciation… It built you up in the eyes of other people."

Seated in a leather chair with an armor-plated back and under large, framed portraits of George Washington and Abraham Lincoln, the boss of bosses told the young gangster "what a nice piece of work it was." Capone did not make any direct reference to the double shooting at Joe Barron's place, but the compliment was implied. The five-foot-ten-inch Capone stood up and wiggled his large girth out from behind his bulletproof chair. He strode over to the diminutive Cohen, grabbed him by the head, and kissed him on both cheeks. Cohen's life changed in an instant. The meeting and the gesture had opened up a whole new world for the young gangster from Los Angeles.

"People who never *knew* me *knew* me now," Cohen recalled years later.

"I wasn't just a punk kid anymore. I was someone who had done something to justify the favor of Al Capone."

Soon after, Cohen began working with Capone's younger brother Mattie as the pair operated a poker game in the Chicago Loop. Cohen was even invited to the Capone household for Sunday dinner.

"How are ya fixed for money?" Capone would ask Cohen before patting the young man's pockets. If Cohen was light on dough, Capone would stuff a couple hundred dollars into his jacket pocket. Cohen looked up to Capone like a god.

"I respected his ways," Cohen later wrote. "Like a kid [who] has an admiration for a great boxer or some idol that you want to kind of follow in his footsteps, or mold your life in his way."

Although Cohen greatly admired Capone, he still chewed at his own leash from time to time. Without authority from Big Al, Cohen and Mattie Capone decided to add craps to their poker game setup. But Cohen's craps game was biting into the profits of other Capone enterprises, and the boss had no tolerance for anyone who took money off his plate.

"What the fuck is the goof up in the crap game in the Loop?" Capone asked angrily of a key lieutenant, who then caught up with Cohen and launched into a tirade.

"Are you crazy?" Capone's lieutenant asked. "We gave you an okay for poker. We don't have any craps in the Loop, and you come around and open a fucking crap game? Are you out of your mind?"

Cohen stood his ground. "I couldn't make any money with poker," he replied. "I got guys that gotta eat."

Cohen finally agreed to close down the craps game. But the decision only lasted a short while. He reopened the game in another location, infuriating Capone. Five days later, a black car rolled up on Cohen as he stood in the snow outside a place called Chew Tobacco Ryan's. Guns pointed out the windows, and muzzle flashes lit up the darkened street. Cohen stood still, not moving in his new camel-hair coat. He did not dive into a snowbank and out of the line of fire because he didn't want to get his new coat dirty. Surprisingly, the gunmen missed their open target.

"I got ribbed about this for about a year," Cohen remembered with pride. "They were all talking about that crazy little Jew bastard that wouldn't fall."

Cohen did not fall, but he was forced out of town a while later after a bloody encounter with an enforcer who worked for a local cab company. The thug pulled a gun on Cohen in the street. Cohen jammed his own finger in the trigger, preventing the gun from firing. He convinced the thug to discuss the matter over coffee at a nearby pharmacy. The men walked closely together, with Cohen's finger still jammed in the trigger. Once at the coffee shop, the thug let his guard down for a split second, which was all Cohen needed. He grabbed a sugar bowl and smashed it over the mobster's skull, splitting his head open like a watermelon. Blood spattered across the counter, and the waitress screamed in terror. The sound of the ruckus caught the attention of some nearby police officers who ran into the coffee shop with guns pulled. The cops recognized Cohen and saw the thug slumped over, covered in blood.

"Why did you break his head?" one of the officers asked.

"I didn't break his head," Cohen protested. "He fell off the stool. He's drunk."

Although it had been an attempt on Cohen's life, he stayed true to the code of the streets and told police nothing, even when they asked him about the gun. Cohen was charged with assault with intent to murder. The case was later dismissed when authorities determined on their own that the pistol did not belong to Mickey Cohen. He was released from jail and saw his freedom as a sign to leave Chicago.

After a brief stint in Detroit, Mickey Cohen returned to the place of his youth, Los Angeles, where he would take all the hard lessons he had learned in Cleveland, New York, and Chicago and use them in his bloody bid to seize control over the city.

CHAPTER FIVE

TOO FAST, TOO SOON

Lana gazed up at a small flag as it flapped against the mast of Errol Flynn's yacht, the *Sirocco*. Stitched into the flag's canvas was the image of a crowing rooster. The sixteen-year-old actress steadied herself and then stepped off the dock and onto the long, black-hulled vessel, where she grabbed the older actor's firm hand for balance. Flynn had purchased the boat in 1930 for about $4,000 and then sailed it on a voyage across the Pacific Ocean from Australia to New Guinea. That was more than a decade before he shot to fame as a swashbuckling action star in the Warner Brothers seafaring epic *Captain Blood*. Errol Flynn's amazing physicality in the lead role sent young men and women to movie theaters in droves, earning over $1 million at the box office, a huge number for any film studio at the time. Studio head Jack Warner called him "a dueling Fred Astaire."

Flynn's Tasmanian skin was deeply tanned, and his tightly coiled muscles gave him the appearance that he could slide down a sail on a rapier blade with a pirate's panache. In reality, his liver was deteriorating from heavy drinking, and he was drowning in debt. But he was still considered big box office.

The word circulating through Hollywood was that Warner Brothers was going to tap Flynn to star in its most expensive film to date, a $2 million big-screen version of *The Adventures of Robin Hood*, where Flynn would get the opportunity once again to perform most of his own stunts. This was positive gossip for the actor, different from the salacious rumors that were whispered across studio lots. For years, the twenty-eight-year-old actor had been plagued by scurrilous talk and outright scandal over his reputation as a dangerous predator who targeted teenage girls.

Lana had recently been introduced to Flynn by her friend Olivia de Havilland at the commissary on the Warner Brothers lot. The twenty-two-year-old British actress had shared the screen with Flynn in *Captain Blood* and was now being eyed to act opposite him again in the role of Maid Marian in *The Adventures of Robin Hood*. She was in love with her costar despite his marriage to French actress and ballerina Lili Damita. De Havilland, six years older and wiser than Lana, did not act on her feelings toward Flynn, who was married, but her younger friend was naively smitten with the action hero. Shortly after their introduction, Flynn whisked Lana away to his dressing room, where he kissed and groped the teenager. The actor considered his own behavior to be commonplace in Hollywood. "You saw a young lady you fancied and you'd say, 'Star's perks!'—which meant to back off," Flynn later wrote in his memoir.

But their brief tryst was interrupted by movie director Michael Curtiz, who had some acting notes for his future leading man. The director, who was working on the script for *Robin Hood*, was undoubtedly more familiar with Flynn's sordid past than Lana was, and he came crashing into the dressing room to prevent the actor from getting hauled off to jail and charged with statutory rape.

But Flynn did not let Lana out of his sight. During her next visit to his dressing room, he offered her bourbon. Then he invited her to join him and his friends aboard the *Sirocco* for a cruise to the Catalina Islands. Despite their twelve-year-age difference, Flynn and Lana shared similarities. Both were insecure in the fact that neither one could act, dance, or sing. They were impostors in the land of make-believe. Regarding his acting ability, Flynn often said, "I just happened to look well in a doublet and hose."

But the sweater girl and the swashbuckler smoldered on-screen. Flynn was ready to assume Douglas Fairbanks's mantle as the number one action hero in Hollywood, while young Lana was preparing to compete against the town's top actresses, including Joan Crawford, the queen of Metro-Goldwyn-Mayer (MGM). Aboard the *Sirocco*, Lana shared a cabin with several other young women; all had been assigned bunk beds. Each night, Lana's bunk stayed empty while Flynn molested the teenager in his cabin, demanding that he be allowed to perform oral sex on her until she finally gave in. Her young life was now moving at the speed of a freight train. It seemed to her that one moment, she was sipping Coke at a soda fountain just like any other teenager, and the next, she was below deck getting mauled by Captain Blood.

After the encounter, Lana never stepped aboard the *Sirocco* again. But one thing became clear to her: her childhood—for what it was—was now over.

The publicity department at Warner Brothers then began using the teenager as arm candy for the studio's rising male stars. Lana was ordered to escort a twenty-six-year-old former lifeguard from Illinois named Ronald Reagan to the world premiere of *Jezebel*, starring Henry Fonda and Bette Davis. Reagan had just signed a seven-year contract at Warner Brothers, earning him $200 a week. He had his own new movie coming out in a few weeks, his first starring role as an insurance investigator in a film called *Accidents Will Happen*. To help drum up publicity for that movie, Warner Brothers wanted Reagan to be seen everywhere, especially at nightclubs and red carpet premieres. The handsome, rugged-looking actor had only been on the Warner lot for a short while, but he had already earned a dubious reputation as a "greater swordsman" than the lecherous Errol Flynn.

For the *Jezebel* premiere, Lana borrowed a white gown from the Warner

Brothers wardrobe department. Reagan picked her up in a taxi, too ashamed to pull up in front of the theater in his battered old car.

"He said that I was the most beautiful girl he'd ever seen," she told historian Darwin Porter years later. "But he was not the best-looking man I'd ever seen. I mean, he was handsome, but not a beauty contest winner. I found him very appealing with the most wonderful manners, and he knew how to treat a lady. He made me feel grown up even though I was still a teenager."

After the movie, Reagan treated Lana to a dinner of hot dogs and ribs and then took her back to his apartment. The next day, he boasted about the evening to fellow actor Dick Powell during a round of golf.

"Lana is just as oversexed as I am," Reagan said. "I spent the night with her and I'm hoping it will be the beginning of many more nights to come. Lana was one of my greatest conquests, a flamboyant feather in my cap."

She admitted as much to the historian Porter. "He taught me how to ride a horse before getting into the saddle himself. Did I say that diplomatically?"

Reagan, known as "Dutch" to his friends, went on to pose for publicity photos with young Lana and did not hide the fact that he was a grown man dating a teenager.

"Dutch was not yet a one-girl guy. He was seen squiring dishy Lana Turner around town, and joked that he 'wasn't acting' in her company," wrote Edmund Morris, Reagan's official biographer. "He also dated Margaret Lindsay, Mary Jane Crane, and the exquisite Anita Louise. How much sex he was getting was a matter of speculation."

Lana's affair with the much older Ronald Reagan did not last long, especially after she moved over to the MGM lot in Culver City when Mervyn LeRoy left Warner Brothers. She was no longer attending Hollywood High, as all young contract players were ordered to study at the studio between takes. MGM had built a white plaster building with Mediterranean tiles, which was dubbed the Little Red Schoolhouse. Lana took her math and

English courses while sitting at a desk next to Judy Garland and Andy Rooney, two of MGM's biggest child stars. Between classes, Lana would excuse herself to smoke cigarettes with her teachers in an effort to show off her new maturity. She was now earning $100 a week, which was enough money to move out of Gladys Taylor's place and into a three-bedroom house on Kirkwood Drive in Laurel Canyon.

Lana's new rented home was high up in the hills, and it took seventeen steps to reach the front door. Inside, the furnishings were all painted white with a polar bear rug spread out next to a marble fireplace in the living room. Lana slept on a giant four-poster bed fit for an emerging Hollywood princess. She no longer had to rely on a diet of crackers and milk. Those days were far in the past. She was now a girl who had everything, except a strong male presence in her life. Her father, Virgil Turner, was buried under six feet of moist earth at the Presidio in San Francisco while his teenage daughter was about to take Hollywood by storm.

"We had youth, we had beauty, we had money, we had doors open to us," Lana later recalled. "We were so alive and caught up in the business… Industry talk made us feel so grown up."

She was cast in the movie *Love Finds Andy Hardy* with her Little Red Schoolhouse classmates Mickey Rooney and Judy Garland. Lana played the attractive new girl, one who had her eyes on Andy Hardy in the fictional town of Carvel, which was built on Lot 2 at the MGM studio. Lana begged the producer not to dress her in tight sweaters in an effort to distance herself from the noxious "sweater girl" label. But the producer had not cast her for her acting skills. He needed to take full advantage of her curves, so he dressed her in a bathing suit for a pivotal scene with Rooney.

The executives at MGM demanded physical perfection from their stable of young stars. On the outside, actors like Lana, Rooney, and Garland were presented as wholesome, all-American boy- and girl-next-door types. They were told never to be photographed with a cigarette or a cocktail in their hands. But behind the scenes, they were tortured by their studio handlers and were fed a regimen of black coffee, cigarettes, chicken broth, and diet pills to keep their weight down. This treatment would have a disastrous effect on many, especially Garland, who became addicted to amphetamines and died from a drug overdose at age forty-seven.

"They'd give [me and Mickey Rooney] pills to keep us on our feet long after we were exhausted," Garland admitted years later. "Then they'd take us to the studio hospital and knock us out with sleeping pills...then after four hours, they'd wake us up and give us pep pills again so we could work seventy-two hours in a row. Half the time we were hanging from the ceiling, but it was a way of life for us."

Lana arrived at the studio lot each day at six a.m. so that she could get into her hair and makeup chair an hour later. Rehearsals started at nine a.m., and filming began just after lunch and would continue until two o'clock in the morning.

"I could have slept in my dressing room, as Judy Garland and Mickey Rooney sometimes did—but I always insisted on driving home," Lana recalled. Overtired and blurry eyed, Lana drove herself home from these marathon studio sessions in her new fire-engine-red Chrysler coupe along the steep and winding roads of Laurel Canyon, where one wrong turn could have sent her plunging off the hillside to her death.

Lana and her actor friends rebelled against the studio by acting out with their own scorched-earth policy, blazing a trail through Hollywood's night-club scene—drinking, smoking, and dancing on tables at hotspots like Billy Wilkerson's Café Trocadero and the Coconut Grove. Not one to let a good opportunity go by, Wilkerson and his fellow gossip columnists wrote about Lana and Hollywood's other wild children in the pages of their magazines and newspapers. A stack of newspapers with Lana's picture on the covers landed on the desk of MGM cofounder Louis B. Mayer, and he exploded with anger. He had built a successful formula designed around wholesome family entertainment, and he was not about to let the studio's newest emerging teenage star ruin MGM's image.

He immediately called Lana and her mother, Mildred, to his office. Standing just five foot five and weighing 175 pounds, Louis B. Mayer was the most powerful mogul in the movie business and was described by at least one Los Angeles civic leader as "an all-American, in heart, in spirit and in soul." But the MGM honcho was also called "a monster" by those who felt trapped under his iron thumb. His presence was felt everywhere on MGM property, which covered 167 acres. MGM was not just a movie studio; it was Mayer's personal kingdom, where up to eighteen films were being shot simultaneously with more than ninety actors and directors under contract. MGM also had its own police department with fifty uniformed and undercover officers and detectives.

Mayer ran MGM with the efficiency of General Motors, and no detail escaped his close and discerning eye. If he called you to his third-floor office in the Thalberg Building at MGM, it was almost never to praise you. Mayer had sent his biggest stars, including Mickey Rooney, away in tears after his bombastic teardowns. A meeting with the studio head could go one of two ways: he would either break your spirit or steal your soul. When it came to Judy Garland, Mayer would hold meetings with her seated on his lap with a hand on her breast urging her to "sing from the heart."

Lana had no idea what to expect when she entered Mayer's office, which had white leather walls and a white custom-built wrap-around desk, all designed to feed his god complex. With Mildred Turner in the room, Mayer did not attempt to grope his teenage star. Instead, he went on an emotional rant about protecting Lana's carefully crafted image.

"You're keeping late hours and making the papers," he scolded her. "You're ruining your wonderful future!"

Lana offered no excuse or explanation. Instead, she began to cry.

Mayer jumped out of his chair and stood behind his crescent-shaped desk.

"The only thing you're interested in is [this]!" he shouted, pointing at his crotch.

Mildred Turner gave Mayer a horrified look. "How dare you, Mr. Mayer," she screamed back. "In front of my daughter!" Mildred grabbed Lana by the elbow and marched her out of Mayer's office.

Chapter Six

The Return of the King

Mickey Cohen walked under the drooping fronds of a large palm tree toward the Clover Club at 8477 Sunset Boulevard with a shotgun tucked under his coat. The place was owned by restaurateur Eddie Nealis, and its management catered to film studio executives and Hollywood's top stars. The Clover Club was located along a sparse stretch of the road, just beyond Los Angeles's city limits. From the street, the place looked uninviting and fortress-like. Inside, however, the Clover Club was outfitted with hidden gambling rooms where celebrities could bet against the house. Producers like David O. Selznick lost vast amounts of money on a weekly basis. The club also had one-way mirrors to signal card dealers of impending raids so the gaming tables could be flipped over at a moment's notice.

Cohen led a small group of gangsters through the back door and into a large gambling den where they all showed their weapons and demanded that the patrons put their money and jewelry on the tables. "I had the stick [shotgun] on everybody. Everyone else had pistols," Cohen recalled.

He had targeted the nightclub under orders from Benjamin "Bugsy" Siegel because Nealis had refused to hand over his profits to the Syndicate. During the stickup, Cohen noticed a beautiful young blonde standing nervously next to big-band trumpeter Harry James. Cohen did not see the musician as a threat, so he shifted his steely gaze to the other well-dressed men in the room. The heist was over in a few short minutes, and Cohen then fled with the other members of his gang.

Despite the brazen robbery ordered by Siegel and carried out by Cohen, Nealis refused to give up control of the Clover Club. Cohen was dispatched once again, this time to kill the club's security man, a notorious Irish gangster named Jimmy Fox. Cohen shot him up but failed to kill him. Still, the message had been sent, and Nealis relinquished club control to Siegel and fled to Mexico.

Cohen thought back to the night of the original raid, as he could not get the image of the beautiful blonde who had placed her diamond necklace into his fedora out of his mind.

"Who was that gorgeous woman we just heisted?" Cohen asked.

"That was Betty Grable," one of the henchmen replied.

At twenty-two years old, Grable was pure Hollywood gold. She worked out of the 20th Century Fox lot and would later become known more for her pinup shots than for her screen performances. Cohen did not know it, but Betty Grable could have been his biggest score at the Clover Club, as her legs would soon be insured for $1 million in a publicity stunt orchestrated by 20th Century Fox.

The cross-pollination between Hollywood glamor and gangsterism was becoming more commonplace in Los Angeles. Movies like *Little Caesar* and *The Public Enemy* starring James Cagney put millions of dollars in the studio coffers while also depicting hardened criminals as big-screen antiheroes. Screenwriters lifted their ideas from the gruesome headlines in newspapers from cities like Chicago and New York, but there was very little organization involving the crimes happening on a daily basis in LA. While Mexican youth gangs calling themselves *palomillas*, or flocks of doves, operated with limited success in Boyle Heights, the Italian Mafia had depended on a sleepy-eyed killer from Corleone, Sicily, to seize control of all vice operations being run out of Los Angeles. His name was Jack Ignatius Dragna.

A former soldier in the Italian army, Dragna had taken over the rackets in LA after the previous mob boss, Giuseppe "Joe Iron Man" Ardizzone disappeared and was declared dead. Dragna operated a 538-acre vineyard in the nearby hills and ran a floating casino ship called *Monfalcone*. Born in a Mafia stronghold before the turn of the century, Dragna had Sicilian blood, but he lacked the brains to expand the mob's operations in Los Angeles. His LA outfit was known as "the Mickey Mouse Mob." The Syndicate, which operated mainly out of New York and was made up of notorious mobsters like Al Capone, Charles "Lucky" Luciano, Meyer Lansky, Frank Costello, and others, sent one of their own to the West Coast to get Dragna in line or get rid of him altogether. Bugsy Siegel was their handpicked emissary. Siegel was even more dangerous than Dragna, and his handsome movie star looks made him a natural fit for Hollywood.

Siegel was already an underworld legend by the time he reached Los Angeles. He was born in 1906 in a dreary, overcrowded tenement on Cannon Street in New York's Lower East Side. The boy grew fast and was taller and stronger than most of the other kids in his Jewish neighborhood.

By the time he was twelve years old, Benny, as he was then known, put his muscles to work extorting protection money from pushcart peddlers and threatening to poison carriage horses if their drivers did not pay up. Siegel's fearsome reputation spread quickly through the Lower East Side, where terrified merchants began referring to the preteen in hushed tones as a *vilde chaye*, Yiddish for "wild animal." At sixteen, Siegel partnered with a slightly built Jewish immigrant from Grodno, Russia, named Meyer Lansky. They formed a small gang and fought constantly with their Irish and Italian rivals. Siegel was skilled with his fists and quick to pull a weapon on his foes.

"He was young, but very brave. He liked guns," Lansky recalled years later. "His big problem was that he was always ready to rush in and shoot. No one reacted faster than Benny."

When he would get angry, the handsome Siegel would go "bug-eyed" and unleash a torrent of bullets on his enemies, earning him the nickname

"Bugsy," which no one ever dared to call him to his face. When the FBI began to track him years later, the Bureau called Siegel "insane along certain lines."

Jack Dragna may have been worried about Siegel's arrival in Los Angeles, but Mickey Cohen did not seem to care. Cohen had been ordered to report to Siegel and serve as his number two for the Syndicate's plot to strong-arm Dragna.

"Jack [Dragna] wasn't pulling [in] the counties or [getting] the political picture together," Cohen later explained. "There wasn't even a casino open [on land]. There was no combination, everyone was acting independently. The organization had to pour money on Dragna at all times. So Benny come[s] out here to get things moving good."

But Cohen was in no rush to work for his fellow Jewish mobster from New York.

If I get in touch with Benny too quickly, he'll lock me up in his gang right away, Cohen thought to himself. *I won't be able to plan any scores. I have to get a hold of some money, and I have some things to do.*

Operating independently and with a flair for the dramatic, Cohen targeted an LA gambling joint called the Continental Press, where bets were made on horse races over a wire service that telegraphed and reported race results. The gambling parlor had thirty-five telephones for incoming and outgoing bets. Twenty-five men worked the phones inside, while two armed sheriffs stood guard at the door. Cohen knocked casually on the front door. As it opened, he pushed his way in with a shotgun.

"You cocksucker," he told one of the sheriffs. "You just move and you're gone!"

Next, Cohen eyed a man who claimed that he had only come in to place a bet. The guy was carrying a large satchel. Cohen pointed his shotgun at the bagman.

"You want it in the head, quick? Or slow in the belly?" he asked.

The bagman handed over the satchel, which contained $22,000 in cash.

Cohen had no idea that Siegel, Lansky, and the Syndicate all had a stake in the Continental Press by way of another "made man," a Mafia lieutenant named Johnny Rosselli.

Siegel sent out word that he wanted to meet Cohen the next afternoon. Cohen strolled into the locker room at the Hollywood YMCA, where Siegel was getting ready to work out. Cohen brought a friend as backup. Siegel stared right through Cohen's companion and told him to take a walk. Now, Cohen was all alone with Siegel.

Siegel immediately dropped the menacing posture and began to laugh out loud. "I heard you were a fucking nut, but how crazy can you be?" he asked Cohen. "You were supposed to call me right away, weren't ya?"

"Yeah, I didn't think it was that important. I wanted to see my family. I've been busy."

Siegel shook his head. "Yeah, I know you've been goddamned busy!" He demanded that Cohen kick back the money he had stolen from the mob.

Cohen refused to back down. "Let me tell you something right now. When I go on a score, I put up my life and liberty. I wouldn't kick back to my own mother!" Cohen turned on his heel and walked out of the locker room.

Siegel could have chased after him with his pistol out and bullets flying, but the gangster played it cool. There was a lot to like about Mickey Cohen.

Instead of an armed showdown, Siegel called another meeting, this time at his lawyer's office.

Jerry Giesler was the most powerful defense attorney in Los Angeles and a well-known "fixer" to the stars. Giesler (pronounced geese-ler) had earned another nickname in Hollywood, "the magnificent mouthpiece." But unlike his clients, including Siegel, Giesler was not flashy or charismatic. Born and raised in the small town of Wilton Junction, Iowa, the attorney was balding, weak chinned, and quiet. He spoke in a reedy voice, dressed sedately in conservative gray suits, and wore horn-rimmed glasses. But if a bad-boy actor, corrupt studio head, or conniving actress found themselves in trouble with the law, they would almost immediately call their publicist with the frantic plea "Get me Giesler!"

The lawyer was in high demand. In the past few years, he had been involved in two of Hollywood's biggest criminal cases. In 1929, movie producer and theater operator Alexander Pantages was arrested and charged with raping a seventeen-year-old aspiring actress named Eunice Pringle. Pantages owned nearly one hundred vaudevillian theater palaces across the United States and Canada and was a business rival of future presidential patriarch Joseph P. Kennedy. Pringle claimed that Pantages had attacked her in a side office at one of his theaters in downtown Los Angeles, located at Seventh and Hill Streets. Pringle had gone to the meeting to talk with Pantages about steps to further her career. She ran out of the theater minutes later, half-naked and delirious. Pantages was convicted of the crime, but Giesler got the conviction overturned on appeal. Following that trial, he was hired by Hollywood director and music man Busby Berkeley after he plowed his car into another vehicle while driving drunk along LA's Roosevelt Highway, killing two people. Despite evidence from witnesses who said Berkeley reeked of alcohol at the time of the crash, Giesler won an acquittal after two hung juries.

Giesler loved to defend both the famous and the infamous, and there was no bigger mob star in Hollywood at that moment than Benjamin "Bugsy" Siegel.

At their meeting with Mickey Cohen, Giesler helped to negotiate the return of a stickpin that Cohen had swiped from a thug during the Continental Press heist.

"It's his family heirloom, it's the thing the guy cannot replace," Siegel explained to Cohen. "You're not gonna get nothing for it anyway."

Nodding at both Siegel and Giesler, Cohen gave in. "All right, don't worry. I'll get it back for ya."

Giesler and Cohen formed an unwritten pact at the meeting—one that would not be broken until years later when both men got involved with Lana Turner.

CHAPTER SEVEN

HOLLYWARS

At seventeen, Lana Turner was unfamiliar with famed attorney Jerry Giesler, as her attention was focused on another lawyer, twenty-seven-year-old Greg Bautzer, who was handling business affairs at MGM.

Unlike the nebbish Giesler, the younger Bautzer was fit and tanned, and he smiled for the paparazzi with sparkling white teeth. He was handsome enough to be a leading man, but Bautzer wielded more power behind the scenes. He took Lana dancing at Ciro's and drinking at the Trocadero. Lana had not given up the nightlife despite Louis B. Mayer's warning. Bautzer also made love to her at the home she shared with her mother. This time, there was nothing rough or forced about the sex. Lana was a willing participant, although she didn't know what to do.

"The act itself hurt like hell, and I must confess that I didn't enjoy it at all," she wrote in her memoir later. "I didn't even know what an orgasm was, but I loved being next to Greg and holding him."

Lana played the role of an adult in bed with Bautzer, but she was still a minor in the eyes of the law. The attorney, who was a decade older, did not seem to care about the age difference and even paraded his young paramour in front of his more seasoned dating partners, including Joan Crawford. Bautzer once escorted Lana to a party at Crawford's fifteen-room mansion on Bristol

Avenue in the Brentwood section of Los Angeles. Like Mayer's office at MGM, Crawford's living room had all-white decor. After cocktails, guests were herded into a projection room to watch movies, including Crawford's own. Lana found a seat next to Bautzer and snuggled up to his shoulder while Crawford watched them with suppressed scorn from her perch in the corner of the room.

While Crawford had a growing animosity toward the young actress, Lana had great admiration for her. The two screen sirens had found a similar niche in Hollywood: playing the bad girl. With eyes like teacup saucers, thick brows, chiseled cheekbones, and pouty lips, Crawford had melted male moviegoers in the 1920s when she first shot to stardom in the silent film *Our Dancing Daughters*, playing a flirtatious flapper named Dangerous Diana. Her performance even won praise from legendary novelist and author of *The Great Gatsby* F. Scott Fitzgerald, who wrote, "Joan Crawford is doubtless the best example of the flapper. The girl you see in smart night clubs, gowned to the apex of sophistication, toying iced glasses with a remote, faintly bitter expression, dancing deliciously, laughing a great deal, with wide, hurt eyes. Young things with a talent for living."

Joan Crawford was no homespun innocent. "If you want to see the girl next door, go next door," she often told the press. Crawford was the undisputed queen of MGM and would burn to the ground any perceived threat to her status.

After the dinner party, she summoned Lana back to her home alone, without Bautzer. "I'd like to talk to you about something very important," Crawford said over the telephone.

Lana was intimidated, even scared, but still, she drove her red Chrysler out to Brentwood for a meeting with the movie star.

"Now, darling, you know I'm a bit older than you, and so I may know some things you haven't learned yet," Crawford said with a forced smile.

At the time, Crawford was close to forty years old, but she had never given anyone her true birth date, so her true age was left up to speculation.

Lana could see under Crawford's makeup to the lines engraved in her forehead and the crow's-feet digging into the edges of her familiar eyes.

"Like what?" Lana replied innocently.

"Well, dear, when you're young, you see things a certain way, but that's not really how they are. As you get older, you realize that life can be very complex," Crawford explained.

Lana began to squirm in her chair. Crawford was talking around the issue and was not being direct. It was a well-rehearsed interrogation.

"Joan, what are you trying to tell me?"

Crawford leaned forward and her eyes grew wide. She stared at Lana with the same terrifying expression that she would later give her daughter, the one she forced to call her Mommie Dearest.

"Well, darling, it's only right to tell you that Greg doesn't love you anymore," Crawford said. "He hasn't for a long time. It's me that he truly loves, but he hasn't figured out a way to get rid of you."

"Get rid of me? Trash is something you get rid of. I am not something you get rid of!" Lana shouted back.

Crawford reached for a cigarette and lit it. She took a long drag and waited as Lana continued her tirade.

"Don't you dare say that to me. You are lying about Greg. I know it isn't true!"

Crawford smiled through the haze of gray smoke, relishing in the teenager's petulant tirade.

"So, Lana dear, why don't you be a good little girl and tell him you're finished—that you know the truth now and that it's over." Crawford stuck the knife in even deeper. "Make it easier on yourself. He doesn't want to hurt you."

Lana did not know how to respond. She could only mutter a soft "Thank you" to her older adversary. She drove back to her house in Laurel Canyon, wiping away tears from her eyes.

As a young star, Lana may not have realized that Crawford had just taught her a valuable lesson, more important than anything she would learn at the Little Red Schoolhouse on the MGM lot. Joan Crawford, in her trademark nasty, condescending way, educated Lana on the idea that love was transactional in Hollywood and that most romances lasted just long enough for the ink to dry in the gossip rags. The encounter in Brentwood also sparked a fire under Lana, as she would now commit herself to dethroning Crawford as queen of MGM.

She screen-tested for the iconic role of Scarlett O'Hara in *Gone with the Wind* but lost it to Vivien Leigh. Lana had read the Margaret Mitchell bestseller and knew that she did not have the acting chops or a credible southern accent to pull it off. Unfazed, she plowed ahead in a role more suited to her abilities in the film *These Glamour Girls*, where she shared top billing with actor Lew Ayres, who would later come under fire by the media as a conscientious objector during WWII. In the movie, which was promoted as an exposé of college life that "blazes across the screen with all of its flaming truth," Lana leads a team of beautiful young women in a plot to turn the tables on a group of privileged young men wearing pedigree polo shirts. The movie also allowed Lana to flex her muscles with the studio. In a Crawford-like move, she demanded her own dressing room—and got it. MGM publicist Emily Torchia opined, "If there was ever a point at which the studio recognized her as an important star, that might be it."

Soon after, Lana was awarded with her own dish on the studio commissary menu called the Lana Allure Salad.

While Lana was beginning to push her weight around at MGM, Mickey Cohen was rolling up wire services across Southern California for his new boss, Bugsy Siegel.

Just as Al Capone had before him, Siegel recognized Cohen's special qualities, particularly that he was smart and would not take shit from anyone. Street thugs were common in Los Angeles, but Cohen was a rare breed of gangster.

"You're a gutty kid, but you need some finesse and polish," Siegel told him. "Or you're gonna wind up being on the heavy for the rest of your life. You got the ability that if used in a proper way would put you [at] a different scale."

Cohen's lucrative heist of the Continental Press showed Siegel how much money could be made in race wire services. Naturally, Siegel's next move was to muscle in on the racket and force the Continental Press out of business. He ordered Cohen to embark on a pistol-whipping tour of wire joints, where he smacked around and bludgeoned any operator who refused to sign up with Siegel's new Trans America wire service. Cohen's terror campaign turned hundreds of LA bookies into eager subscribers of Siegel's telegraph services.

With streams of cash now flooding the pockets of Siegel, Cohen, and the Syndicate, Siegel left Cohen in charge of the Sunset Strip while he set sail for Italy for a meeting with dictator Benito Mussolini. Europe was now on a war footing, and Siegel was looking for a way to cash in. He traveled to Rome with Dorothy di Frasso, a Hollywood socialite and wife of an Italian count. Together, they got Mussolini to pay $40,000 for the access to and development of a new explosive called atomite, which Siegel promised was a powerful smokeless, flashless, and colorless gunpowder. But atomite proved to be a dud, and Mussolini demanded his money back. Siegel was not going to pay the money back and seemed nonplussed over the idea of having the supreme commander of the Italian army breathing down his neck. He was more concerned by the presence of Hermann Goering and Joseph Goebbels, who showed up as guests at the Italian villa owned by Count Carlo di Frasso. Germany had just invaded Czechoslovakia, and the persecution of Jews, with more than four hundred decrees that restricted all aspects of their lives, had been ongoing inside the Reich since Adolf Hitler's rise to power in 1933. Siegel, a proud Jew, voiced his anger to Countess di Frasso.

"Look, Dottie," he told her. "I saw you talking to that fat bastard Goering. I'm going to kill him, and that dirty Goebbels too. It's an easy setup the way they're walking around here." For Siegel, it was no greater challenge than shooting a man in a bustling New York City restaurant or out on a Los Angeles street, but the countess begged him to reconsider the executions, as she knew they would never escape Italy with their lives. Siegel reached Meyer Lansky back in the States for permission to assassinate the Nazi leaders.

"Permission granted," Lansky told him. "But you'll be operating independently and you cannot contact any local Mafia gangs." Siegel would have to go it alone and contemplated what would likely be a suicide mission.

It was Warner Brothers studio head Jack Warner who finally convinced Siegel to give up the plot. Warner was visiting Italy to promote the studio's newest film, *The Life of Emile Zola.* He echoed Countess di Frasso's fear that everyone connected to Siegel would be arrested and hanged. "I talked him out of it on the grounds [that] we couldn't fix the local harness bulls [Italian police] if we got caught."

Months later, on November 9, 1938, more than one hundred Jews would be killed by Nazi brutes across Germany and Austria during Kristallnacht, the Night of Broken Glass.

But Siegel, Cohen, and Lansky would continue to fight Nazis on the home front. Lansky focused his efforts on disrupting German Bund rallies in New York City. He mobilized a small commando unit of Jewish gangsters to attack several gatherings of American Nazis. "We got there in the evening and found several hundred people dressed in their brown shirts," Lansky remembered years later. "The stage was decorated with a swastika and pictures of Hitler. The speakers started ranting and there were only fifteen of us, but we went into action." Lansky's crew grabbed, punched, and kicked every brown shirt they could, tossing some of them out the window to the pavement below. Those Nazis who fled the rally were met outside by members of Lansky's welcoming committee, wielding baseball bats and pool cues. "We chased them and beat them up and some of them were out of action for months," he recalled proudly. "We wanted to show them that Jews would not always sit back and accept insults."

Cohen confronted a popular Nazi Bundist named Robert Noble while both were spending the night in jail on separate charges. Cohen recognized Noble immediately. He had been forced to listen to and read about Noble's "anti-Jew, rabble rousing sentiment" on the radio and in newspapers. Cohen paid off a guard, who allowed him to share a cell with the American Nazi. Noble had been arrested with another Bundist, but that did not seem to concern Cohen, who stepped into their cell. After the jail guard locked the door behind him, Cohen pounced on the Nazis immediately. "I started bouncing their heads together," he remembered. "With the two of them, you'd think they'd put up a fight, but they didn't do nothing."

Cohen fought with everything he had learned inside the boxing ring and out on the streets. Battered and dazed, the two Nazis climbed up the iron bars of the cell and screamed for the guards. Finally, the warden made his way to the jail cell and found the Nazis in a bloodied heap while Cohen sat on his bunk, calmly reading the evening newspaper.

"Them two guys got in a fight with each other," he tried to convince the warden.

"I don't know what happened."

The warden gazed over at the bloodied Nazis and he knew that Cohen was lying.

"Why did you throw us in with an animal, a crazy man?" Noble asked the warden.

Chapter Eight

THE NEEDLE

Lana woke up lying in a strange bed, being called by a different name.

"Where am I?" she asked groggily.

"You're in the hospital," the nurse replied. "But you're doing well, Mrs. Johnson."

Was she dreaming? Was she on some MGM movie set? Lana opened her eyes wider as her blurred vision came into focus. She tried lifting her arm, but the pain was too great. Something had penetrated the skin of her shoulder—a needle perhaps?

More questions.

Again, the nurse called her by that name—*Mrs. Johnson*.

"Who?"

"Mrs. Mildred Johnson, that's who you are."

Lana looked down at the hospital bracelet wrapped loosely around her delicate wrist.

It read *M. Johnson*.

She asked the nurse to bring her a telephone and then dialed a number from memory.

Slurring her words, Lana tried to explain to her mother what was happening.

"Oh, my God!" Mildred Turner shouted into the phone. "My baby! How are you?"

Lana tried to answer but she was choking on tears.

"Where's Artie?" Mildred asked angrily.

Lana had the same burning question: *Where is Artie?*

Artie Shaw was Lana's new husband, and he was the reason she had been sedated and strapped to a hospital bed in Los Angeles.

Lana had met Shaw on the set of her film *Dancing Co-Ed*. It was her first starring role, playing a professional dancer who enters a rigged dancing contest. The movie was based on a script that was typical of the rom-coms being churned out by the studios at the time, heavy on hijinks and music.

Artie Shaw was a famous clarinetist and swing bandleader who had recently scored a massive hit with a recording of Cole Porter's "Begin the Beguine." Shaw was hired to play himself in the movie. Lana shared a kiss with him during rehearsal, but there did not appear to be any sparks. The teenage Lana was immediately turned off by the twenty-eight-year-old bandleader's arrogance.

"He never missed a chance to complain that it was beneath him to appear in a Hollywood movie," she would later write in her memoir. "The crew plotted to drop an arc light on his head. I hated him too, and I even told the press that he was the most egotistical person I'd ever met."

Shaw lacked the rugged good looks of Lana's previous beau, Greg Bautzer. Shaw was erudite and introverted. When he talked, he discussed his affinity for Nietzsche and his desire to leave swing music and Hollywood behind to become a writer. Lana felt no attraction for him, but she agreed to a date in a last-ditch effort to make Bautzer jealous.

Lana had spent most of her nights agonizing about Bautzer's whereabouts. *Is he with Joan Crawford?* she often asked herself. But by that time, the handsome attorney had moved on from Crawford and from Lana to other screen stars like Ginger Rogers, Ingrid Bergman, and Wendy Barrie.

Barrie was a British actress who had appeared in films opposite Jimmy Stewart and Spencer Tracy. She was also dating Bugsy Siegel at the time. When Lana found out that Bautzer and Barrie were seeing each other "under the radar," she trailed Siegel to one of his clubs on the Sunset Strip. Lana was tempted to go after Siegel and seduce the gangster herself. But she listened to the advice their mutual friend, actor George Raft, had given her and others.

"If you go around with Ben Siegel, you'll get hurt," Raft warned. "And I mean hurt. Suddenly, no one will want you in pictures."

It was now time for Lana to move on as well. She had just turned nineteen, and the idea that Shaw, America's most famous bandleader, wanted her appealed to Lana's young ego.

"I'm determined to fuck that little hottie," Shaw boasted to his friend comedian Phil Silvers.

But Shaw did not press Lana for sex during one of their first dates, a drive along the Pacific Ocean. They held hands and talked about the possibility of leading normal lives, where Shaw could retreat from the stage and Lana could be a wife and mother and be called Judy once again.

Both were caught up in the moment, and the next thing Lana realized, she was flying in a charter plane from Burbank, California, to Las Vegas, Nevada, to get married.

"How my life is going to change!" Lana said to herself while staring down at the twinkling lights of Los Angeles as they faded in the distance. "But it seems so right, and it will be. It was destined to happen like this."

After the charter plane touched down in Las Vegas, a hired driver scrambled to find a justice of the peace, who married Lana and Shaw while dressed in his bathrobe and pajamas. Shaw pulled off his own blue star sapphire ring and slipped it on Lana's finger. The driver then brought the newlyweds to the telegraph office, where the bride sent a message to her mother.

Got Married in Las Vegas. Call you later. Love, Lana.

Mildred Turner had no idea that her daughter had married Artie Shaw because Lana had not mentioned him by name in the telegram.

"I've lost her," Mildred muttered while reading the note.

When Lana and Shaw returned to Los Angeles, they were met by a swarm of reporters. The bandleader screamed obscenities as he pushed his way through the growing number of paparazzi. Instead of smiling, kissing, and waving to the media, Lana began to cry.

"I'm sorry, I'm sorry," she told reporters. "I can't talk now. I'm sorry."

Once inside Shaw's home on Summit Ridge Drive, they double locked the front doors. Lana then heard the breaking of glass as photographers began smashing windows, trying to get a photo of the terrified couple. Lana and Shaw waited until midnight before they slipped out of the house and took a spare room at a friend's house. Lana had been wearing the same navy-blue dress for more than twenty-four hours. She felt exhausted and frumpy. She wanted to go to sleep, but it was still her wedding night. They both climbed into the guest bed, and Shaw became aroused. Lana protested softly as he climbed on top of her.

"He was clumsy and fumbling and I didn't help at all," she would write in her memoir. "And when he finally got into position, well, it was horrible. Meaningless and over in a minute. He just went limp and was so quiet about it. As for me—I experienced nothing but a question. What am I doing underneath this man? I don't even know him."

Lana also did not know that Shaw had proposed to Betty Grable just three days before he married Lana in Las Vegas. "That son of a bitch!" Grable told Phil Silvers. "Who does he think he is?"

The next morning, Lana telephoned the studio. Louis B. Mayer had been storming around his plush, white office after hearing the news. "Well, you've really done it this time!" he yelled at her. The story of Lana's elopement with Artie Shaw made headlines around the world.

Judy Garland, fresh off her starring turn in *The Wizard of Oz*, went into a rage when she heard the news. The sixteen-year-old had a big crush on the much older Shaw. When her mother handed her a newspaper with a photo of Shaw and Lana on the cover, Garland ran into her bedroom and repeatedly slammed her head into the wall. "But Artie's in love with me!" she cried. "He told me that he loved me and only me!"

Lana had more pressing matters to worry about than Garland's crush. After marrying Shaw, she quickly came to realize that she was not in Kansas anymore. They moved into a big Spanish-style house on Beverly Glen Boulevard. When Lana returned to Laurel Canyon to pick up her clothes, Mildred had just one question for her daughter.

"Why did you do it?"

"Because I think I'm going to be happy," Lana replied.

But her optimism was just an act. Inside, she also questioned whether she had done the right thing.

Shaw demanded that his young wife not wear lipstick and ordered her to read books to improve her mind.

"I admired Artie's talents as a musician, but it seemed impossible for me to cope with the temperament of a genius," Lana wrote later. "Although I came from a broken home, my parents had only separated, never divorced. I'd still like to think that if my father hadn't been killed, they might have gotten back together. Marriage meant permanence to me. But with Artie, I began to realize, it was no marriage. It was hell."

One evening, Lana returned home late from MGM to find Shaw and two of his buddies hanging around the house waiting for dinner. Lana had admitted early in their whirlwind courtship that she did not know her way around the kitchen. Still, she tried to be a good wife and whipped up a big bowl of spaghetti for her husband and his friends. Lana obediently served the pasta on plates and passed one to Shaw, who was not impressed.

"What is this crap?" he demanded.

Before she could answer, he picked up the bowl and tossed it on the floor of their dining room.

"Clean up that mess!" he shouted.

Lana did not move. Instead, she convulsed. The nineteen-year-old started to shake and cry.

Instead of comforting his young wife, Shaw called a doctor friend, who showed up with a bag of sedatives. He took out a needle and plunged it into Lana's arm. She fell unconscious immediately, and an ambulance was soon called. Lana opened her eyes briefly as she was lifted onto a stretcher. The last thing she remembered was her husband putting a towel over her face so that she would not be recognized.

"Check her in as Mildred Johnson," he ordered the doctor.

Lana woke up the next day feeling groggy, abused, and ultimately betrayed. She returned to the home she shared with Shaw. He never mentioned drugging her and sending her to the hospital alone. But the abuse continued. Shaw even kicked in a door during an argument with her.

A few days later, she called Greg Bautzer. Lana did not want to rekindle an old flame. She just wanted out of her marriage.

"Get your things," he told her. "I'll have you out of there today."

When Shaw returned home from the recording studio, Lana was gone. He had forgotten his house key, so he broke a window to get inside. Once there, he marched from room to room looking for his young wife. There was no trace of Lana, and her closets were empty. Bautzer filed for divorce on her behalf while Lana fled to Hawaii to heal from the ordeal. While on vacation, she missed her period and found a doctor who would give her a pregnancy test. The test came back positive, and Lana called her estranged husband back in Hollywood.

"Well, I just found out that I'm pregnant," she told him.

"So what?" he replied coldly.

Shaw then questioned whether the baby was even his.

"What the hell do you mean by that crack?" she screamed into the telephone. "You know I've never played around. This is your baby!"

Shaw wanted nothing more to do with Lana or their child. She flew back to Los Angeles and discussed the matter with her mother and her new manager, Johnny Hyde, who ran the William Morris Agency. Hyde specialized in beautiful, blonde starlets and would later guide Marilyn Monroe's career. Hyde told Lana that if she wanted the baby, her only choice was to return to her twisted and violent husband.

"MGM has strict taboos," he told her. "One of them being, no children outside marriage. Do you want to continue your career?"

Lana wanted her career and she wanted her baby. But she knew she could not have both, especially if she went back to the explosive Shaw. She vowed that their marriage was over and that meant terminating her pregnancy, which was illegal and dangerous.

"I went by myself," she recalled. "I didn't want anyone with me. The abortion took place in a dirty, dingy private house downtown. It was a terrible place." The abortionist injected her with a fluid and promised her that she would "pass" the fetus later that day. Lana went home in a fog. She experienced minor cramps for several hours before dropping to her knees in agony.

"I'm going to die," she screamed. "Something is wrong and I'm going to die."

Mildred Turner called the abortionist, who did not show up at their house in Laurel Canyon until the next day. He completed the procedure with a sharp loop-shaped tool. Lana bit down on a washcloth to stifle her screams. Mildred had placed towels under her legs on the bed, which was now drenched in Lana's blood. Once finished, the abortionist charged her $500 and demanded that she keep the procedure a secret and not consult her own doctor regardless of any more pain or bleeding she experienced.

"You've threatened the life of my daughter," Mildred shouted at him. "I should have you arrested. You're a bastard!"

Again, Lana felt betrayed by the men in her life. Although she was slow to recover, she could take no time off. Lana had just been cast in a new film, *Ziegfeld Girl* starring Jimmy Stewart and Judy Garland, and production was to begin in a week.

CHAPTER NINE

LANA MEETS BUGSY

Lana's director was yelling at her—again. Victor Fleming stomped around the set of MGM's *Dr. Jekyll and Mr. Hyde* in his customary gray suit, stammering and pointing his finger in Lana's direction. Fleming had helmed forty-one films including *Gone with the Wind* and *The Wizard of Oz*, and now he was growing physically sick because one of his lead actresses could not cry on demand. Lana was cast in the role of Beatrix Emery, the love interest of Dr. Jekyll, played by Spencer Tracy.

After the success of *Ziegfeld Girl*, Lana was offered a role in the big-budget adaptation of the Robert Louis Stevenson Gothic novella playing a barmaid and eventual rape victim named Ivy Peterson. "If you want me for Ivy, I don't think I can do it," Lana admitted to Louis B. Mayer. "I'm afraid. That role is so deep, I don't know if I could trust a director enough to let me try to reach those emotions."

Mayer agreed and gave the role to Ingrid Bergman, who at that time was trying desperately to avoid getting typecast as "the good girl" in her films. While Bergman lost herself in the role, Lana had difficulty finding her character, Beatrix Emery. She was called on by Fleming to break down and cry during a pivotal scene with Tracy near the end of the film. But Lana could not force the tears in her eyes. After numerous takes, a frustrated

Fleming called for "the crystals." They were camphor crystals, used to stimu-late nerves and irritate the eyes. Fleming had the crystals placed inside a thin tube that would be blown into Lana's eyes through a cheesecloth to make her cry. She had heard stories about actresses who had to be rushed to the hospital after "the crystals" treatment.

"Please don't blow anything into my eyes," Lana pleaded.

"Well, you're going to cry and we can't keep doing this all day!"

Fleming's boorish behavior caused Spencer Tracy to walk off the set. It was a noble gesture, but now Lana was virtually alone. She tried once more, this time visualizing that her new puppy had been run over by a car. Still no tears.

The director, who stood six foot three, grabbed Lana's arm and yanked it behind her back violently. Fleming pressed his hulking body against hers with enough pressure that she thought her arm would snap.

"Stop it! You're hurting me."

As the pain increased, the tears began to flow, and Fleming finally released his mighty grip.

Shaken and sobbing, Lana was forced to get in front of the camera and finish the scene. But her eyes were red and swollen now, so Fleming ordered her to recite her lines off camera.

At the end of the day, she contemplated telling Greg Bautzer about the assault, but the Hollywood attorney was neck deep in his own trouble. He had offended Mickey Cohen and feared getting beaten up, stabbed, or shot by the gangster. Bautzer had recently visited the Rhum Boogie jazz club and restaurant on North Highland Avenue. Cohen owned the joint and had an office off the second-story balcony. Bautzer had brought with him singer Martha Raye and a young comedian named Jackie Gleason. Together they ordered mountains of food and several bottles of booze. At the end of the night, Gleason signed the check while Bautzer and Raye grabbed their coats. The club manager brought the check to Cohen's office and waved it in front of his boss.

"I never heard of signing a check in my life," Cohen later wrote of the incident. "It's like walking into a joint and stiffing them."

Cohen bolted from his office and flew down the stairs and grabbed Gleason as the hefty entertainer was about to leave.

"Hey, look-it. What is this bullshit? You come in here and eat and drink and you sign? Who the hell signs a check?"

"Don't you know who I am?" Gleason asked smugly.

"I don't give a fuck who you are," Cohen countered. "You're gonna pay that goddamn check or I'm gonna knock your goddamn head in!" Cohen then rattled off the number of employees that he was responsible for and who he would have to pay cash to at closing time. He grabbed Gleason and whispered in his ear. "Get the fucking money up for this check, or you're not gonna walk outta here."

Martha Raye, who had earned the nickname "the Big Mouth" for her singing and comedy routine, jumped into the fray and began calling Cohen "an animal" and "a thug."

Cohen smacked Gleason on the side of the head as the situation continued to escalate.

Greg Bautzer was well aware of Cohen's reputation, and he knew they were all now in grave danger. He stepped in and tried to mediate. "I'm going to give you my personal check and I'll pay for it."

Cohen was still unfamiliar with the habit of check writing and did not know Bautzer from "a coat hanger."

"Who the fuck are you?" Cohen asked.

Bautzer nervously pulled out his business card and handed it over. "My check is as good as gold," he told Cohen. "You come to my office tomorrow, I'll give you the money. I'll give you the cash." Cohen shoved Bautzer and Gleason out of the club and promised to stop by MGM the next day.

Bautzer could handle the temperaments of entertainers like Artie Shaw, but Mickey Cohen presented a different level of danger. The gangster turned up at Bautzer's office as promised the next day. Actors, extras, and even MGM's private police officers gave Cohen a wide berth as he entered the studio lot and demanded to see Bautzer. The attorney's secretary ushered Cohen into Bautzer's office, where he handed him an envelope stuffed with cash.

As Cohen counted the money, he could not help but comment on Martha Raye's name-calling from the night before.

"All of you were stiff, sloppy drunks," he told Bautzer. "But *I'm* the animal?"

With *Dr. Jekyll and Mr. Hyde*, promoters promised moviegoers that their eyes "have never seen entertainment so graphically filmed." The movie was a box office success for MGM and was nominated for three Academy Awards. Lana was now earning $1,500 per week, the equivalent of about $27,000 today. She purchased a new home on a hilltop in West Hollywood and was getting her pick of roles. One project that she had her eyes on was a remake of 1928's *Our Dancing Daughters*, which had starred a young Joan Crawford. When her old nemesis learned that Lana was being considered for the film, Joan called her at home.

"Darling, I just heard that MGM is considering a remake of my 1928 silent…with you in the lead."

Lana feigned ignorance. "That's the first I've heard of it."

Although she was gaining power at the studio, Lana was still fearful of and intimidated by Crawford.

"Dear heart, you're not good enough as an actress to lie to me," Crawford replied coldly. "Of course you know all about it. But I wanted you to know that if you try to replicate my role as Dangerous Diana Medford, you'll be laughed off the screen."

Lana gathered her strength and seized the opportunity to return some venom toward the older actress.

"I never saw your movie," she told Crawford. "And I know nothing about it. I was just a little girl when it was released. Mother did not let me go to filthy pictures." Lana softened her voice and continued. "Miss Crawford, I really must go. Thank you for the career advice. The next time I need such advice, I'll phone you. Heaven knows you've been in the industry long enough to know everything about it."

Crawford did not respond. Instead, she slammed down the telephone and steamed.

Lana was young and vulnerable, but she was also learning to fight for herself in a town that could celebrate you one day and destroy you the next. Plans for a remake of *Our Dancing Daughters* were eventually scrapped by MGM. But with her renegotiated salary of $1,500 per week, it was a clear sign from the studio that Lana had taken the throne of queen of MGM from her older rival Joan Crawford.

Her unofficial coronation occurred on a Saturday evening at the home of Bugsy Siegel.

The gangster was known to throw lavish parties crawling with Hollywood A-listers, and this was the first time that Lana had received an invitation to rub shoulders with film industry elites. She had met Siegel previously at a cast wrap party for the 1941 Gary Cooper film *Ball of Fire* at the Formosa Cafe, an Asian-themed restaurant and bar built inside a retrofitted cable car in the heart of West Hollywood, directly across the street from Sam Goldwyn's film studio where the romantic comedy was filmed. Siegel kept a hidden safe under the floor of the restaurant. An actor in the film, Dana Andrews, modeled his character, a crime boss named Joe Lilac, after the real-life gangster. Andrews introduced Lana to Siegel, whom she found "extraordinarily handsome."

Lana flirted with Siegel at the bar. He had taken another woman to the party, his new mistress, Virginia Hill. She had a small role in *Ball of Fire*. Hill, nicknamed "the Flamingo" because of her long legs, was a voluptuous and feisty former prostitute who had just started dating Siegel. To prevent a fight between Virginia and Lana from happening inside the tight confines of the Formosa, Siegel poured cold water on Lana's advances and instead invited her to a party at his luxurious Holmby Hills home.

Lana arrived alone and fashionably late to the party that evening and moved flawlessly in her tight-fitting silk dress. She passed the sweeping staircase in the foyer and stepped into the sixty-foot-long living room, where the host was surrounded by several fawning guests. In a room filled with famous actors, starlets, and studio heads, it was abundantly clear to Lana who wielded the most power—it was Benjamin "Bugsy" Siegel.

Seeing her across the crowded living room, he abruptly ended his conversation and moved quickly to her side. All eyes were on the crime king and the movie queen as he kissed her on both cheeks. Lana knew that Siegel was a cold-blooded killer, but she was immediately drawn to his charisma and rugged beauty. He was the best-dressed man in the room. He wore a red silk shirt with a matching tie under a finely tailored suit. He also wore alligator shoes. She had never seen anyone as expensively dressed as the dashing gangster.

Siegel stayed by her side as more guests welcomed her to the party. Frank Sinatra kissed her on the lips and introduced her to Cary Grant. Studio head Jack Warner gave her a warm hug. "I was wrong about you, girl," he told her, grinning widely. "I thought you didn't have what it takes to make it, but you've made it, baby!"

Louis B. Mayer, her boss at MGM, approached her quietly with some advice. "You should be home getting your beauty rest," he told her. Mayer now had a small fortune tied up in the twenty-year-old and was doing his best to protect the studio's investment.

Lana and Siegel continued to mingle separately for the next few hours before finding a moment alone under moonlight on the back brick-laden terrace, which led to a sprawling garden, shimmering swimming pool, and a gazebo. Siegel wrapped his muscular arms around her narrow waist. They kissed and made plans for a proper date a few days later.

On that night, he picked her up in a bulletproof limousine. She slipped into the back seat wearing a champagne-colored gown and matching shoes. They had dinner at Siegel's home. As if he could read Lana's mind, Siegel had bottles of champagne at the ready to wash down their catered supper. They spoke about doing business in Hollywood. Lana performed in front of the camera while Siegel flexed his muscle in the executive suites.

"Mayer and Warner pay me off so I won't cause problems at their studios," he told her. Siegel also explained how he took sizable loans from stars like Gary Cooper, Clark Gable, and Cary Grant. "Although they know that I'll never pay them back, they come through for me."

When they finished dinner, Lana's head was light from the sparkling bubbles after swallowing her last sip of champagne. Siegel took her to his bedroom, and she followed willingly. As Siegel stripped before her, she noticed that he was wearing silk underwear with his monogrammed initials stitched into the fabric.

"He looks better with his clothes off," she told her close friend Virginia Grey later. "He was one of those men that wives dream about when their dull husbands are screwing them."

Surprisingly, Siegel was a gentle lover. He did startle Lana though when he slept with a chin strap to keep his movie star-like profile in place. Unbeknownst to her, Siegel was taking acting and elocution lessons. His dream was to leave gangland behind and become a motion picture star just like his childhood friend George Raft.

The next morning, as Lana strolled into the breakfast room, she overheard Siegel on the telephone with his attorney Jerry Giesler, who had successfully defended him in the gangland slaying of Murder, Inc., hit man Harry Greenberg in 1939. Siegel and two members of his gang had shot and killed Greenberg outside his Los Angeles apartment. Giesler won an acquittal for Siegel after destroying the credibility of the prosecution's star witness.

Siegel finished the call and invited Lana to join him at the breakfast table. "This Giesler's a great guy," he told her. "He's the best lawyer in Hollywood." Siegel then bit into a buttered roll and continued. "If you ever commit murder, call Giesler. He'll get you off," he added jokingly.

CHAPTER TEN

THE HOME FRONT

With the Joan Crawford rivalry now in Lana's rearview mirror, she still had to fight each day to stay on her top perch at MGM. War was now raging in Europe and the Pacific, and America's fighting men needed inspiration beyond the love letters penned by their hometown sweethearts.

Sailors aboard the battleship USS *Idaho* were asked to vote for their favorite female movie star. Lana's name dominated the balloting, with Betty Grable and Rita Hayworth far behind.

Lana decided to volunteer at the Hollywood Canteen on Cahuenga Boulevard. The canteen was founded by Bette Davis and was a place where servicemen got the opportunity to dance with Hollywood stars. Lana worked at the grill in the kitchen alongside German screen siren Marlene Dietrich. When Davis discovered that two of her most alluring celebrities were making hamburgers and cleaning up after the GIs, she flew into a rage. "Get that Kraut [Dietrich] and Turner out front dancing with the men," Davis ordered. "We can always get Ethel Barrymore and Cecil B. DeMille to wash the dishes."

Like many celebrities, Lana was also recruited by the U.S. government to help sell war bonds. "When I had time between pictures, I boarded that long train that rolled into cities where munitions plants were located," she wrote later in her memoir. "At every stop, we were greeted by wildly cheering crowds, often mostly women. That sea of female faces—you knew the men had gone to war."

Those who were either too young or too old to fight received a special incentive from Lana to help support the war effort at home. "When there were men in the crowd, I promised a sweet kiss to anyone who bought a $50,000 bond," she later recalled. "And I kept that promise—hundreds of times. I'm told that I increased the defense budget by several million dollars."

Most films produced in Hollywood during the war were either escapist fantasy, song-and-dance pictures, or movies about combat or the extension of war and its impact on the daily lives of Americans and allies overseas. Lana landed a starring role opposite Clark Gable as war correspondents in the romantic drama *Somewhere I'll Find You*. The pair had worked together a year before on the western *Honky Tonk*. Gable was newly married to actress Carole Lombard at the time. Lombard had been acting professionally since she was twelve years old and had made a name for herself starring in screwball comedies where she always played the wisecracking blonde.

Lombard knew her husband could not resist a beautiful blonde, so when Lana was hired for *Honky Tonk*, Lombard stormed into the office of Louis B. Mayer and demanded that he tell the twenty-year-old Lana to keep her hands off Gable. Lombard hovered around the set so often that Lana became flustered and had to flee to her dressing trailer. Between takes, Gable grumbled about Lana's lack of acting talent. But when the two embraced in front of the cameras, their chemistry was pure dynamite, and Mayer knew he had a hit on his hands. Moviegoers flocked to *Honky Tonk*, making it the highest-grossing MGM film of 1941. It only made sense that the studio would pair them again in *Somewhere I'll Find You*.

Carole Lombard was not keeping a close eye on Gable and Lana on the set of the new film. Instead, she was selling war bonds in her home state of Indiana, where she raised more than $2 million for defense production.

Before leaving on her trip, Lombard accused Gable of having an affair with Lana, whom she referred to as "that blonde whore." Gable did not readily deny it.

Lombard and her entourage were supposed to travel home from Indiana to Los Angeles by train, but the actress was unnerved by the fact that her husband was working with Lana again, so she decided to fly to LA instead. She boarded TWA Flight 3 and headed west with a refueling stop in Las Vegas. When the plane took off again, it traveled just thirty-two miles before crashing into a nearby mountain, killing everyone on board, including Lombard, her mother, and fifteen soldiers. Gable was devastated. MGM considered shutting production down on *Somewhere I'll Find You*, but Louis B. Mayer had sunk a lot of money into the picture already. The studio head called Lana into his office in an effort to save the movie and MGM's most popular male star.

"Now, Lana, here's where you come in," he told her. "You're going to be very patient with him. If his mind should wander, don't be upset. You just be ready at all times. If he wants to come in earlier, you be there before him... A lot of pressure on this picture is going to be riding on your shoulders. We're trying to arrange for people to go home with him for dinner. If he should ask you, go. Agreed?"

The subtext was obvious. If Gable needed sex and companionship while grieving over the shocking death of his young wife, Lana would have to submit herself for the sake of the picture and the movie studio. She joined Gable for a private dinner at the home he had shared with Lombard. An MGM limousine brought her there. Gable was pale and distraught. He was in no mood for sex. Instead, he showed Lana his gun collection and then called for the limousine to take her home.

Lana attended Lombard's massive funeral along with Louis B. Mayer. Gable sat speechless in the front pew, tearing a handkerchief to shreds. Production later resumed on the movie, with Gable numb and virtually sleepwalking through the role. When the film opened, it was a hit for MGM, but critics were not so kind. In its review, the *New York Times* wrote, "For those whose pulses throbbed violently to the Gable and Turner osculations in 'Honky Tonk'...the new film provides even more of the same." But despite the lukewarm reviews, Lana maintained her reputation as Hollywood's most alluring female star. *Variety* called her "the modern Jean Harlow of cellu-loid—a sexy, torchy, clinging blonde who shatters the inhibitions of the staidest male."

Clark Gable did not read reviews of the film. He joined the U.S. Army Air Services and was eventually stationed in England, where he flew several missions with the 351st Bomb Group, including a raid on Germany. Lana was sent back on the road to support the war effort, traveling with her mother by train to San Francisco, their first trip back since the murder of Virgil Turner, and then on to Portland and Seattle before heading east. While stumping for war bonds in Chicago, Lana met a friend of Howard Hughes, who told her the reclusive billionaire enjoyed her movies and was excited to meet her.

Hughes followed up with a personal phone call and invited her to dinner. Lana found him to be a peculiar suitor. Normally, she gravitated toward handsome, well-dressed men. Although Hughes was considered to be good looking by some, his personal hygiene was atrocious. Lana found him "likable enough but not especially stimulating." During their dates, America's richest man usually wore the same pair of tattered gray pants and a white shirt with missing buttons. He had a weathered fedora and raggedy black shoes, and he never wore socks or underwear. Hughes, an extreme germophobe, also confessed to Lana that he preferred oral sex over intercourse.

"Howard was brilliant, but in all honesty I found him boring," she wrote years later. "It was obvious to me that it wasn't my mind he was after."

An aviation and real-estate tycoon, Hughes was also a major force in

Hollywood. He had produced several films, including the 1930 war epic *Hell's Angels*. Hughes also had affairs with several famous actresses, including Bette Davis and Joan Crawford. While Lana may have appeared tepid to his sexual advances, he adored her, along with her mother, Mildred, who stitched his ripped trousers before a dinner date with her daughter. Hughes also taught Lana how to fly and took her cross-country on his fleet of aircraft. She dated other men who were more physically attractive to her, including musician Gene Krupa and actor Robert Stack, but Hughes had a special place in Lana's heart. Their intimacy went beyond the bedroom, and Hughes would remain Lana's staunch defender and protector in the years to come.

The pair also shared a mutual friend—Benjamin "Bugsy" Siegel. When Hughes launched his new airline, TWA, he invited Siegel on the inaugural flight from Los Angeles to New York. Siegel graciously declined the offer, as he was now shifting his focus away from Hollywood toward a dusty thirty-three-acre lot along Highway 91 in Las Vegas, Nevada. Built on the property were more than a dozen ramshackle cottages that would be bulldozed to make Siegel's dream of developing the "god damnedest biggest hotel and casino you ever saw."

Siegel's partner, Mickey Cohen, also showed his patriotism during the war, at least at the beginning. He was now married to part-time fashion model LaVonne Norma Weaver. LaVonne was an attractive, petite redhead whom he had met at a place called the Band Box in Los Angeles. "She was strictly a lady, a great lady, and you could take her anywhere," Cohen wrote admiringly about her in his memoir. "She appeared in homes ranging from top hoodlums to respected businessmen."

He told her that he wanted to join the U.S. Army, but the draft board was worried about his lengthy arrest record. Siegel tried to vouch for his friend with Abe Roth, Cohen's former boxing coach, who now had a position on the draft board. "Look, the guy's probably gonna get drafted anyway," Siegel told Roth. "Why don't you see if you can get him in the army. He wants to go!"

Siegel reminded Roth that Cohen was a fellow Jew and wanted nothing more than to kill Nazis. But Roth could not be persuaded, so Cohen went to the draft board in Boyle Heights and tried to sign up. He was asked to leave the recruitment office after a judge involved in one of Cohen's many court hearings declared him unfit to serve in the military. He was ashamed to tell his wife. On the way from the recruiting office, Cohen bought a beautiful raincoat with epaulets for $150. He looked like a field general when he tried it on and marched home to break the news to LaVonne. It was Cohen's idea of a joke, but his young wife took one look at him and immediately telephoned a friend. "He's in the army!" she exclaimed.

But instead, Cohen was relegated to fighting the war at home. Like Meyer Lansky, Cohen was recruited by an LA judge to terrorize German Bund meetings in the city.

"We went over there and grabbed everything in sight, and smacked the shit out of them, broke them up the best we could," Cohen recalled. "Don't forget, we had to fight the coppers too because a lot of them were Nazis themselves in those days."

Cohen did not stay on the right side of the law for long. He jumped into the deep end of the exploding black market in Los Angeles, stealing and reselling ration stamp booklets as well as silk stockings, which fetched top dollar due to the fact that all silk imports from Japan had been suspended. He also opened a restaurant called the La Brea Social Club, a private two-floor casino that operated out of a beautiful, Venetian revival building on La Brea Avenue near Beverly Boulevard. The casino earned hundreds of thousands of dollars and attracted violent competitors. One night, a rival gangster named Maxie Shaman burst into Cohen's office to settle some minor score involving a friend of Cohen's. Shaman, who was accompanied by his brother Izzy, began shouting obscenities at Cohen.

"I'm gonna tell you right now," Cohen responded in a soft voice. "If you open your fucking mouths one more time in a belligerent tone, I'm gonna kick the both of you outta here."

Maxie Shaman then lunged toward Cohen with his pistol. Cohen blasted him with a gun that he had hidden in his desk. Shaman stumbled to the floor. Cohen approached the wounded man and stood over his body.

"Are ya dead?" Cohen asked. There was no answer. Still, Cohen fired another shot at close range just to make sure.

Cohen was arrested for the murder but claimed that he had acted in self-defense. Izzy Shaman, the dead man's brother, refused to testify, and the case was dismissed. Cohen was released from jail, and the district attorney gave him back his gun. He then moved his operation over to nearby Burbank, which had become a boomtown for defense contractors, especially the Lockheed Aircraft Company. He took control of the Dincara Stock Farm, a horse stable on Mariposa Street. He started out with a one-game craps table in one of the stalls and soon expanded to four, along with five blackjack tables and slot machines. Cohen hired the chief of police at Warner Brothers to guard the place. Cohen also paid off Burbank's police chief, Elmer Adams, to turn a blind eye to the illegal gambling operation. Along with defense contractors, Cohen's casino was also popular with actors and extras pouring in from Warner Brothers.

"You'd come in there in the afternoon and think you were on a movie set," Cohen recalled. "There'd be guys in Indian suits or dressed up like cowboys... this joint ran good for ten years."

CHAPTER ELEVEN

ALONG COMES MR. CRANE

Bugsy Siegel had information that he wanted passed along to Louis B. Mayer about his reigning screen queen. The gangster thought the studio head should know that Lana was getting mixed up with another lover with underworld connections. His name was Steve Crane, and he had been recently introduced to Lana at Mocambo, a Latin-themed nightclub complete with live squawking parrots, macaws, and cockatoos in West Hollywood. Smart, handsome, and well dressed, Crane told Lana nonchalantly that he was in the tobacco business. After her miserable marriage to Artie Shaw and flings with Gable and actor Robert Stack, Lana was ready to fall in love again. But as with her whirlwind romance with Shaw, she threw herself into her new relationship without recognizing the warning signs. Crane had gone around town selling the story that he was the heir to a big tobacco fortune when in reality, his father ran a cigar store attached to a run-down pool hall in Crawfordsville, Indiana. But Hollywood was the place of make-believe, so no one ever dug too deep to authenticate anyone's origin story.

Lana did not seem to care where Crane's money came from. They danced closely at Mocambo that first night, with his body pressed tightly against hers. They sat and drank and talked for hours until closing time, when Crane drove Lana home. Just three weeks later, he proposed, asking

Lana to elope with him to Las Vegas. Mayer warned Lana against getting in too deep with Crane and said that she should drop him because of his reputed mob ties. But this time, Lana refused to listen. She was not a scared teenager anymore and would no longer cower to Mayer, the great Oz of Hollywood.

Lana held firm to her love for Crane and jetted to Las Vegas for a quick marriage ceremony.

During their honeymoon, Lana confided to a friend that she was "heels over chin, pinwheels on fire in love." When first asked by a reporter about the elopement, Lana told him, "I'm lonely unless I have someone to love. Along came Mr. Crane."

Lana was blissfully happy with Steve Crane over their first five weeks of marriage, until Crane made a stunning revelation to her—he was still married.

"I got this paper," he told her. "I thought it meant I was free, but it appears I wasn't."

Lana knew Crane had been married before. What she did not know was that his divorce decree stipulated that he had a one-year waiting period before he could remarry.

"Please understand, it's just an awful mistake. But it's probably going to cost us some money."

"You mean you want to give her money—my money?" she asked, fuming. "My money?" Until that moment, Lana had been paying all the household bills despite Crane's promise to split the costs with her.

Lana felt betrayed and sick. Coupled with this troubling development was news that Lana was now pregnant.

"I wasn't legally married," she later recalled. "Here I was expecting a child of a man who wasn't my husband. My head started spinning and I just made it to the bathroom, where I leaned over the sink for a long time."

Lana demanded to meet Crane's wife, a woman from Indiana named

Carol Ann Kurtz, who was now living in Los Angeles. They drove to her apartment and sat down with the attractive, petite brunette. Kurtz confirmed what Crane had told Lana about the divorce decree.

"He will not be free to marry for a couple of months," she said, smiling.

Lana lost it. She screamed at Kurtz, accusing her of setting up the entire charade for fame and money. Kurtz had waited until Lana announced her pregnancy to the press before raising the issue about the divorce decree. Kurtz then reportedly blackmailed her with a demand of $5,000 for her silence. Lana agreed to the terms and was shocked when she learned the following day that Kurtz had sold her story to the press.

Lana immediately threw Crane out of their new home in Brentwood and consulted Greg Bautzer, who warned her that unless she sued for an immediate annulment, she would face bigamy charges. Louis B. Mayer also threatened to fire Lana from MGM for violating a morals clause in her contract.

Lana sued for an annulment while Crane fell on his sword in front of the press, telling them that she had no prior knowledge of his legal entanglement with Kurtz.

The trauma over her marriage and the media onslaught that followed weighed heavily on Lana and impacted her pregnancy. She passed out, and her mother, Mildred, found her lying on the floor. Lana was rushed to the hospital where she spent ten days slipping in and out of consciousness. Doctors determined that her white blood cell count was dangerously high and that she had become anemic. Her physician recommended what he called a "therapeutic abortion," as he did not believe Lana could bring her baby to term. The idea of another abortion sickened Lana even more. She was determined to save her baby, despite her doctor's warning about her own survival.

"Whatever we try will be dangerous for you," the doctor told her. "You will probably lose the child anyway."

"Go ahead," Lana replied defiantly. "I'm going to keep this child."

As Lana discovered a new resolve and strength for her unborn baby, Steve Crane descended into despair. His divorce to Kurtz was now final, but Lana had no intention of taking him back.

"Please, you're carrying my child," he pleaded. "Don't deny me the right to be a father."

She finally agreed to meet with Crane face-to-face and told him that although she needed him to help her get through a difficult and dangerous pregnancy, he had destroyed her dreams of having a normal family. Disillusionment had replaced love in her head and heart.

"My answer is no. I will not remarry you," she said emphatically.

But the idea of carrying an illegitimate child was too scandalous for the studio. Louis B. Mayer called Lana to his office and begged her to reconsider. "I demand that you remarry that whore-mongering bastard," he told her.

Once again, Lana refused. A short time later, she heard a loud crash outside her bedroom window. Crane's Lincoln coupe had plowed into shrubbery near her home, and the vehicle was perched on the edge of a steep cliff top. He had swallowed nearly a full bottle of barbiturates and planned to commit suicide within earshot of Lana's house. Crane was rushed to the hospital, where he tried to commit suicide a second time by overdosing on sleeping pills. He was placed on suicide watch, and Lana joined his side. During his recovery, he convinced Lana that their baby would need a father. Crane's pleas eventually wore her down.

On Valentine's Day, 1943, the couple drove to Tijuana, Mexico, for a quickie wedding. The tropical air was oppressive, and Lana, now six months pregnant, nearly fainted from the heat. Crane found a random guy on the street, slipped him some cash, and brought him into a small office to serve as a witness before the justice of the peace. The entire wedding ceremony took only a few minutes. Lana Turner was now Mrs. Stephen Crane once more.

His wedding present to her was a pet lion cub. The cub was eight weeks old and adorable, but Lana was rightly concerned about how quickly the animal would grow and how unsafe it would be for them and their new baby. Crane figured that the queen of MGM should have a roaring lion of her own, but his wife demanded that they donate the cub to the studio. She won the argument, and soon after, Crane answered his draft notice and reported for duty at Fort MacArthur in Los Angeles.

Crane was assigned to Special Services at Fort MacArthur and slept in their bed most nights. It was a cushy gig, and he drove Lana's blue Lincoln convertible back and forth to the base each day. Occasionally he would invite army officers home for dinner and urged his pregnant wife to invite her movie star friends over in an effort to build up his reputation on base.

When Lana was seven months pregnant, she experienced early contractions and was rushed to the hospital where doctors stuck a needle in her spine. She feared that if she gave birth while lying there on the surgery table, the infant would have been stillborn. Lana fought through the painful contractions and was released after twelve hours.

In late July 1943, while on a walk with her mother, Lana felt her water break, and she was whisked back to Hollywood Presbyterian Hospital, where she remained in labor for eighteen hours. She had been driven to the hospital by her husband, who quickly grew bored with all the waiting around. Crane slipped out to watch a boxing match while Lana struggled mightily to give birth to their child.

"It's a her, it's a her!" she said, weeping with joy.

Lana named the girl Cheryl. She had a head of curly black hair and delicate ivory skin.

However, the excitement over the birth of her daughter quickly turned to concern. Lana's doctor was worried by the baby's porcelain skin color and immediately ordered a blood transfusion. The baby was suffering from erythroblastosis fetalis. While Lana was pregnant, Cheryl's Rh-positive blood cells had entered her mother's circulatory system. To fight them off, Lana's body produced antibodies that were now killing her child.

If doctors did not act quickly, Cheryl would die.

The infant was taken by ambulance to Los Angeles Children's Hospital, where a complete blood exchange was ordered. Cheryl's life was saved, and she remained at the children's hospital while Lana recovered at a different facility. The separation was torturous for the new mother.

"I could hear the other babies crying, but I couldn't even give milk to my baby," she later recalled. "I could hear the other doors open, and then the peaceful silence as the babies nursed. But my arms were empty and no nurse ever wheeled a tiny crib into my room... Not seeing my baby, not touching her! Aching to hold her knowing that she was gravely ill. It was driving me crazy."

Mildred Turner kept watch over baby Cheryl and then visited Lana to update her on the infant's condition. Lana quizzed Mildred about whether her child had all her fingers and toes.

"Tell me, Mother, does she have rosy cheeks?"

Mildred sadly reported that the baby's skin was still pale. Lana could not take being separated from her daughter any longer, so she won permission to travel three blocks by wheelchair to Cheryl's crib side. A nurse picked up the infant and placed her in Lana's arms.

"I can't find the words to describe the intense joy I felt when I first held my little girl," she wrote decades later. "She weighed almost nothing. She was so fragile, so delicate."

Her baby would remain hospitalized for two agonizing months before Lana could bring her home in late summer 1943. Lana was now buried under a mountain of hospital bills and got no support from her husband, who was still in the army. MGM booked Lana on a radio series in New York just two weeks after she brought Cheryl home from the hospital. The money, $5,000, was too good to turn down, and Lana was in dire straits financially. Steve Crane somehow got a leave from the army, but instead of staying home with baby Cheryl, he tagged along with Lana on the trip to New York City.

En route to the Big Apple, they visited Crane's hometown in Indiana. Crane had filled his wife's head with lies that he had come from wealth, and Lana kept looking for a "handsome family residence" as they sat in the back of a chauffeured limousine on a drive through the small town of Crawfordsville. Instead, Lana saw men in work clothes and women in faded housedresses sitting on the front stoops of dilapidated row houses as children in hand-me-down britches zigzagged back and forth across the street. Crane's ancestral home was no mansion—far from it. It was a weather-beaten two-story house, similar to all the others in the low-income neighborhood. After meeting Crane's mother and grandmother, they drove ahead to a storefront that advertised beer, tobacco, and pool.

"It was only then that I realized that this was the tobacco business that [he] had mentioned so casually when I first met him," she recalled. "From then on, I couldn't help seeing [him] with different eyes."

Lana had come from humble stock herself, but she had never lied about her background to her husband or anyone else. At that moment, she knew she was headed for trouble with her new husband.

When the couple returned to Los Angeles, Crane went back to the army base, and Lana resumed her motherly duties while still performing for MGM. When Crane wasn't trying to impress his superiors at Fort MacArthur, he was gambling heavily at casinos owned and operated by Mickey Cohen and Bugsy Siegel.

One day, Lana heard a knock on the front door. Standing outside on the steps of their Brentwood home was Virginia Hill, Siegel's mistress.

"Is Mr. Crane home?" Hill asked Lana as she opened the front door. Hill barged into the home. "I haven't heard from him in days," she told Lana. "And I'm getting worried."

Lana was both angry and confused. Virginia Hill provided some clarity in her usual gruff tone.

"I'll get right to the point," she said. "Your husband is my boyfriend, that is, whenever Ben isn't around."

"That can't be," Lana protested. "He's married to me."

Hill then explained that she had been covering Crane's huge gambling losses with her own money. She also claimed that she had paid for Crane's nose job when he first arrived in Hollywood. This meant Hill had been sleeping with Crane years before he met Lana.

Lana did not know whether to believe Virginia Hill, but it seemed both odd and suspicious that Siegel's moll would show up at her house claiming to be in love with her husband.

For Lana, it was the last straw. She could take Crane's deceit no longer. When he eventually arrived home, Lana told him their marriage was over and she wanted a divorce. Once again, he protested tearfully. But this time, she offered him a lie of her own.

"I'm in love with another man," she said. "His name is John Hodiak."

Hodiak was an actor friend who had just signed a contract with MGM. There was no romance between them, but his name just popped into Lana's head. She proceeded to tell Crane details of their illicit affair. At first, her husband did not believe it, but Lana put on her best acting job to convince him it was true.

Steve Crane would eventually agree to a divorce, leaving Lana free to scale the Hollywood mountaintop all on her own.

CHAPTER TWELVE

THE POSTMAN RINGS

Louis B. Mayer had a steamy project that he had been sitting on for more than a decade, a film adaptation of a novel and later Broadway play called *The Postman Always Rings Twice*.

MGM had paid $25,000 for the option rights in 1934 but could not propel *Postman* into production because the sex scenes depicted in the movie violated Hollywood's Production Code due to its themes of adultery and murder. The script was overhauled to satisfy censors and became a hot property at MGM, especially after James M. Cain, the author of the novel, had a smash Hollywood hit with a similar noirish film, *Double Indemnity*, starring Fred MacMurray and Barbara Stanwyck.

Lana was offered the role of Cora, the wife of a diner owner who falls in love with a shady drifter named Frank Chambers, played by John Garfield, a New York actor on loan to MGM from Warner Brothers. Together, their characters hatch a diabolical plot to kill Cora's husband. Unlike with her previous movies, there was no competition for the lead role. Lana was now earning $4,000 per week at the studio, making her one of the highest-paid actors in Hollywood. She was also fearless in her approach to the character. Lana had grown as an actress since turning down a role in *Dr. Jekyll and Mr. Hyde* because it was too demanding. Like her character, Cora, she knew what it was like to be young, beautiful, and trapped in a loveless marriage. It was a role that she had lived and was born to play.

Still, there was a great deal of sex in the script, and the censors were looking for any excuse to halt production. But director Tay Garnett had a work-around in mind. He would dress Lana in white, almost virginal, hoping the angelic tone would make her less sensual. MGM's head costume designer, Irene Lentz, went to work creating a white halter top, white shorts, white turban, and white high-heeled shoes for Lana to wear in a pivotal scene with Garfield, her leading man. In it, Lana's character, Cora, rolls her lipstick across the floor of the diner in Garfield's direction. The camera then follows Garfield's point of view across the floor toward Lana's toes and up to her shapely legs. The next shot is a close-up of Garfield's stunned face as he drinks in Lana's beauty. Finally, the camera captures Lana's full body and bare, toned midriff. Garfield fetches the lipstick and offers it back to Lana. She applies it to her lips and closes the door behind her. The scene is brief but smoldering. Lana is perfectly outfitted in Lentz's design.

Director Garnett, a war veteran and former MIT student, demanded authenticity in every scene and tried to film outside the studio in places like San Clemente and Laguna Beach. Lana and Garfield both recognized Garnett's talent, but they feared his heavy drinking would derail the production. Rumors spread on set that Garnett was about to be replaced. With Lana's urging, Garfield confronted the director about his alcohol use. On that particular day, the director was on a real bender and did not even recognize his leading man. Garnett attacked Garfield with a cane and threw him out of his hotel room. Instead of giving up, Garfield and Lana called for a nurse to help settle the director down, and they later got him treatment for his alcohol addiction in Los Angeles. Garnett returned to the set a week later and finished the film without any further incidents.

The director had drawn out the best performances from each of his lead actors, and they both knew it. At first, Lana protested the casting of Garfield, whom she did not find attractive. But the five-foot-seven-inch actor possessed a raw sexual energy that penetrated Lana's defenses. The two became lovers while filming scenes at Laguna Beach. Crew members averted their eyes each morning as Lana slipped out of Garfield's hotel room after a night of sex.

Although Louis B. Mayer hated the movie and called *Postman* an "evil film" because of its lurid subject matter, he predicted that it would be a hit and praised Lana for her Oscar-worthy performance. The studio did not shy away from Lana's seductive figure in its promotion of the film. The official trailer for *The Postman Always Rings Twice* opened with a full-length shot of Lana in her white halter top and shorts before a caption that read "He Had to Have Her Love…If He Hung For It." It was touted as a sensational, sultry story of love and violence, and it struck a chord with young GIs who had come home from the war hungry for love and romance. The movie was a towering success for the studio, earning more than $3 million at the box office, close to $50 million today. For the first time, critics did not judge Lana on her looks alone. The *New York Times* called *Postman* "a tremendously tense and dramatic show" and praised Lana for her "remarkably effective" performance in the best role of her career.

The former studio "sweater girl" had grown into the influential female star in Hollywood and would ride the crest of that wave for many years to come. The same cannot be said of her costar, John Garfield, and her instinctive costume designer, Irene Lentz. Garfield would die from a heart attack six years later at age thirty-nine after getting blacklisted in Hollywood for refusing to name names during the Red Scare. Lentz would end her life tragically in 1962 after jumping out of the bathroom window of the Knickerbocker Hotel, near the corner of Hollywood and Vine. Lentz had checked into Room 1129 under a different name. She was apparently distraught over the death of actor Gary Cooper, whom she was madly in love with. Before throwing herself out the window, Lentz left a suicide note apologizing to hotel staff for any inconvenience she may have caused.

After the release of *Postman*, Lana's fan base continued to grow. While men wanted to sleep with her and even marry her, women began to dye their hair platinum blonde in an effort to look like the movie star. This fashionable hairstyle swept through big towns, small hamlets, and major cities, including Buenos Aires, the capital of Argentina, where the country's First Lady, Eva Perón, clamored for an introduction to her favorite Hollywood actress. Coincidently, Lana had just booked a tour of South America with her good friend, a magazine writer named Sarah Hamilton. MGM loved the idea of a South American tour and made sure that a studio publicist was at every stop to meet the leading lady and her travel companion.

"Latins, I quickly learned, love blondes," Lana recalled of the trip. "Blonde movie stars above all."

Hundreds of screaming fans awaited her when her plane touched down in each city. In Buenos Aires, a woman grabbed Lana's pearl necklace outside the terminal, but she fought her off as more people pushed and shoved one another in a desperate attempt to get closer to the Hollywood star. Customs agents rifled through Lana's luggage and confiscated her jewelry case. They did so on orders from Eva Perón, who wanted her own jeweler to duplicate Lana's jewelry designs.

The First Lady, known as Evita to her adoring fans, was a former actress, radio host, and model who had married Colonel Juan Perón, a Nazi sympathizer and recently elected president of Argentina. While at his side, Evita was determined to bring grace and style to Casa Rosada, Argentina's pink-tinted presidential palace. She collected photographs of Lana from magazines and mimicked her favorite actress in a way that was downright scary.

"Eva Perón wanted to be Lana Turner," said actor Fernando Lamas. "She modeled her wardrobe, her makeup, even her hairstyles to emulate Lana."

When a friend of Lana's hosted a lavish party in her honor, Evita made sure she was at the top of the guest list. She sat in a golden chair in the corner of the room while Lana was introduced to members of Argentinian high society. When Lana reached Evita, she did not know whether to curtsy or extend her hand. Instead, Evita reached for Lana's hands and whispered a few pleasantries. Lana was speechless. As she looked down at Evita, she thought she was staring into a mirror.

"It struck me that she had gone blonde," Lana wrote in her memoir. "Her hair was then the same pale color as mine. Her hairdo resembled mine too!"

As Lana mingled with the other guests, she could feel Evita's eyes trained on her.

"Those eyes were like narrow slits, and they fixed on me all night."

Evita also had Lana followed by the secret police everywhere she traveled in Buenos Aires. It was election time in Argentina, and Juan Perón scattered his soldiers and secret police across the capital city to suppress opposition. Peronista guards broke up protests by slashing picketers with their sharpened sabers. Lana witnessed it all. "It terrified and sickened me to see [the] battered victims, with blood streaming down their heads."

One night, Lana and her friend Sarah Hamilton were startled awake by a bomb blast in the service entrance of their hotel.

Lana finally left Evita and the Argentinian nightmare behind and traveled on to Rio de Janeiro and then up the east coast of South America before boarding a flight to Miami and then to New York, where, once again, she was followed, not by the secret police but by the FBI.

J. Edgar Hoover had opened a file on Lana beginning the previous year in 1945 when she and her mother, Mildred, were the victims of an extortion plot. In that case, a deranged fan in San Francisco wrote letters to Lana demanding money so that he could buy a truck. According to the FBI report dated March 12, 1945, "it is to be noted that Lana Turner has recently purchased a gun which she maintains at her residence." The extortionist then wrote to Lana that "he would have to get himself a gun in order to get his, and if people have to be hurt, they'll be hurt."

A second FBI memo described a conversation overheard in a bar involving the alleged extortionist. "My God, if the dirty bitch doesn't treat us like human beings, I'll get her," the man told a friend. "If I can't get her, I'll get at her through the kid [Cheryl]." The extortionist then zeroed in on the eavesdropper. He grabbed a cocktail napkin off the bar and scribbled a note and handed it to the witness. The note read "Keep quiet if you know what's good for you!"

The note was later analyzed in an FBI laboratory and dusted for fingerprints, but the perpetrator was never found. Director J. Edgar Hoover became personally involved in the case and maintained surveillance on Lana, not in an effort to protect her but to gather any dirt he could to use against her, much like her extortionist had done. While Lana was visiting New York in 1946, an FBI agent wrote to Hoover that "Turner visited a 52nd Street Boogie-Woogie swing club and while there, met one of the members of a colored orchestra. She made a date to meet this negro late the same night in Harlem."

Hoover must have thought, *Why is America's sultry sweetheart meeting with a Black man in Harlem? Sex, drugs, both?* In either scenario, it was juicy information that the FBI director could use against her.

Hoover's agent went on to describe what he learned during the rest of the night. "She kept this appointment and when the negro showed up and entered her car, they were stopped and questioned by a police detective who demanded to know what was going on. After explanations, this detective, probably to check the story, drove with Lana Turner and the negro to the Waldorf Astoria Hotel." The agent then painted a picture of "a wild scene with hotel people, who vigorously protested Lana Turner's efforts to have her negro companion allowed to accompany her to her suite."

Racist staff members at the Waldorf Astoria then kicked Lana out of the hotel, and she was forced to move over to the Sherry-Netherland Hotel on Fifth Avenue. Hoover shared the memo with Louis B. Mayer, who threatened to cancel Lana's contract with the studio, citing a violation of her

morality clause. Later, the feds accused Lana of being involved in a prosti-
tution ring in Hollywood. "Our LA Office advised that two successful 'call
house madams' were arrested separately by the LA Police Department and
LA County Sheriff's office recently," an FBI agent wrote in a memo to the
director. "A 'call book' in the possession of one of the madams revealed the
name of Lana Turner among other nationally known names as one of the
choice clientele."

Despite the Bureau's attempt to destroy Lana's reputation, she kept her
job and status at the movie studio.

CHAPTER THIRTEEN

THE FLAMINGO

Benjamin "Bugsy" Siegel had stolen just about everything he had accumulated in life, including his dream. He was not the first man to envision what would eventually become the modern-day Las Vegas: *Sin City*. That concept was created and developed by Billy Wilkerson, the man who had discovered Lana at the soda fountain years before. It was Wilkerson who had turned Hollywood into a glamorous hotspot with nightclubs like the Trocadero, Ciro's, and the Vendome. Wilkerson had been gambling at Las Vegas's backwater Wild West–themed legal casinos for years, and he always lost big. He had wasted more than a million dollars at the betting tables, and friends suggested he build his own casino where his lost bets could be reimbursed by the house. Wilkerson purchased the thirty-three-acre property from a former brothel owner for $84,000, with attorney Greg Bautzer negotiating the deal. Since Wilkerson had no experience building or running a casino, he brought in two partners, Gus Greenbaum and Moe Sedway, as cooperators. Greenbaum and Sedway were both notorious gangsters who had run the Trans America race wire in Phoenix, Arizona, for Meyer Lansky. Decades later, their names would be mashed together for the doomed character Moe Greene, played by Alex Rocco, in *The Godfather*.

Wilkerson began construction on the casino in December 1945. After tearing down the dilapidated shacks on the property, he laid plans to build the Hotel Wilkerson, which would consist of six buildings, a health club, a beauty parlor, and several luxury retail shops. He also decided that the casino would have no windows and no clocks. Wilkerson was a gambling addict and understood that distractions like those might lure chronic bettors like him away from the tables.

Siegel made his first visit to the construction site in March 1946, accompanied by Greenbaum and Sedway. Siegel had known Wilkerson for years. When Siegel was detained at LA County Jail after the murder of Harry Greenberg, Wilkerson sent him lavish meals from the kitchen of Ciro's. By this time, the foundation for the hotel had been built and work was ongoing to construct as many as 250 rooms, along with a nine-hole golf course and a large horse stable and swimming pool.

Wilkerson was already in over his head. Howard Hughes loaned him $200,000 in exchange for twelve months of publicity for Hughes's movies in the *Hollywood Reporter*. But Wilkerson needed much more. Meyer Lansky gave him $1 million for two-thirds interest in the hotel and casino. The Hotel Wilkerson was a mob front now, and its namesake was about to get squeezed out. With the Syndicate's blessing, Siegel took over day-to-day operations for the hotel. First, he changed the name to the Flamingo, in honor of his mistress Virginia Hill. He personally checked all the supply trucks and deposited $1 million in cash at a local bank. Siegel was a top-echelon killer and robber, but he was a lousy project manager. Soon, construction costs escalated because Siegel had decided to change the architectural plans by having walls pushed out and the penthouse redesigned. The Flamingo was losing money before it even opened. Siegel had to ask his ex-wife Esther for a $46,000 loan to keep building.

Mickey Cohen, one of Siegel's closest advisers, stayed clear of the project but warned him against getting involved in the risky venture. "What the hell? Are you out of your mind?" Cohen asked Siegel.

Cohen also had an obsessive compulsive disorder when it came to cleanliness and hated the windstorms that kicked up every few hours in the Las Vegas desert. "You're outside three or four minutes and you feel like you've just come out of a goddamn coal mine," he later recalled.

The FBI had expanded its investigation into Siegel's activities, hoping to catch him when he slipped up. "We have ascertained that Benjamin 'Bugsy' Siegel, notorious racketeer with underworld connections on the west and east coast, and Las Vegas, Nevada, will again visit the latter city within the next few days," FBI director J. Edgar Hoover wrote in a July 1946 memo requesting authority to place a wiretap in Siegel's hotel room from the U.S. Justice Department. "I also point out that Siegel, because of his far-flung interests, is in almost constant travel status, thereby making it extremely difficult to follow his activities and anticipate his movements."

Until this time, Siegel's involvement with the Flamingo Hotel project had been kept out of the newspapers. But Hoover was determined to draw Siegel out of the shadows. The FBI director reached out to nationally syndicated gossip columnist and radio commentator Walter Winchell with a scoop for his radio show. In late July 1946, Winchell took to the airwaves and told his huge, nationwide audience, "According to the FBI, a prominent West Coast racketeer is endeavoring to muscle a prominent West Coast publisher out of his interest in a West Coast hotel."

When word reached Siegel's ears, the gangster went bug-eyed. He knew bad publicity like this would jeopardize his casino license. "All my money and my friend's money is tied up in the Flamingo Hotel," he told Virginia Hill in a conversation that was captured on a wiretap inside his room at the Last Frontier Hotel, just a short distance from the Flamingo construction site. Siegel then confided to Hill that he was going to fly to New York to demand that Winchell bring J. Edgar Hoover to him. The gangster envisioned interrogating America's top G-man to give up information on those who had leaked him the information.

"We'll make [Winchell] bring Hoover in front of me and let that cock-sucker tell me where he got it from," Siegel shouted. He then turned his rage to Winchell and promised to "knock his fucking eyes out."

The press had already turned on Siegel. The *Las Vegas Tribune* splashed an editorial across its front page criticizing the construction of the Flamingo at a time when building materials were badly needed to construct homes for local veterans returning from World War II.

Siegel opened the doors of his desert oasis the day after Christmas in December 1946, despite the fact that many of its rooms still lacked furniture and had holes in the floor where the toilet should be. The total cost for construction of the hotel and casino had ballooned to $6.5 million. Siegel planned to charter two planes from Los Angeles and pack them with Hollywood stars for the grand opening celebration. But unbeknownst to Siegel, publisher William Randolph Hearst was applying pressure to celebrities to decline the invitation. Hearst had considerable power at the studio level, especially at MGM, which ran his newsreels before the screening of every movie.

"I don't like to tell you this, Ben, but old man Hearst has passed word around the studio that he's against the idea," George Raft reported to Siegel. "And everybody's been told to stay away."

Hearst was influential, but he did not hold sway over the queen of MGM. Lana decided she would support her old friend and lover on the most important night of his life. She climbed aboard a chartered plane with Clark Gable, Judy Garland, and Barbara Stanwyck and flew 270 miles from LA to Las Vegas. Siegel, with help from Billy Wilkerson, had signed top entertainers to sing, dance, and tell jokes in front of this exclusive crowd. Frank Sinatra backed out of the grand opening, not out of pressure from Hearst but because he was now interested in opening his own casino. Singer and comedienne Rose Marie, who would later find television stardom on *The Dick Van Dyke Show*, was one of the headliners.

"On the morning of [December] 25th, everyone was on the plane; Jimmy [Durante], Xavier Cugat, everybody that was in the show," Marie later recalled. "We went to this place [Vegas]. It was nothing but sand… We walked into the Flamingo, and this man greeted us. And I looked at him and said, 'What the hell is this?' Because it was neon and lights. It was Monte Carlo. It was absolutely gorgeous. That was the whole idea."

Lana was greeted by a smiling Siegel and an ice-cold Virginia Hill, who wore a white crepe floral gown for opening night. Lana was escorted from the front entrance, filled with subtropical shrubs and palm trees, into the casino itself, which was adorned with green leather walls, tomato-red furniture, and a black ceiling. Siegel was elated to have Lana at the hotel opening, as *Postman* had made her Hollywood's biggest star, and her presence would legitimize his desert Monte Carlo.

One reporter noted that the Flamingo looked "like a set that MGM wanted to build but couldn't because of budget limitations."

Lana and other guests paid $15 each for dinner and a show, the equivalent of around $230 today. The Hollywood elite were treated to dazzling performances by Cugat, Spanish bandleader Jimmy Durante, and Rose Marie, but the house was losing money hand over fist. Expert card counters had descended on the gaming tables to outwit the inexperienced dealers, and the casino lost an estimated $300,000 in its first two weeks, forcing a brief shutdown of operations.

A closer look at the books also showed that Siegel had been overpaying for construction materials. This mistake did not sit well with the Syndicate. A summit of America's most powerful mobsters was hastily organized at the Hotel Nacional in Havana, Cuba, more than two thousand miles away from the Flamingo. The Syndicate chose to meet in Cuba because its leader, Charles "Lucky" Luciano, had been deported from the United States and was subject to arrest if he returned to America. Gangland heavyweights like Frank Costello, Vito Genovese, Albert Anastasia, and Siegel's closest friend,

Meyer Lansky, traveled by boat and by airplane to Havana to discuss what to do with Siegel. The Syndicate had sunk millions into his pet project, and Lansky tried to assure them that the hotel and casino would soon turn a profit. Despite Lansky's pleas, he could not save his best friend's life. A decision was made at the Hotel Nacional that Siegel had to go.

The mobsters gathered later that night to hear their friend Frank Sinatra croon in the hotel ballroom. Luciano understood that Lansky was distraught over Siegel's pending fate.

"I know you love him as much as you love your own brother, even your sons," Luciano whispered to his partner. "But, Meyer, this is business and [Ben] has broken our rules... He is betraying us. He is cheating us and you know it. If you don't have the heart to do it, I will order the execution myself."

Still, Luciano gave Siegel a chance to save himself. He made three calls to Siegel, warning him to turn things around quickly, or he would not survive the year. But Siegel did not have the money, and now his silent partner Billy Wilkerson was demanding $2 million to sell off his shares. In May 1947, the Flamingo slowly began turning a profit, and Siegel figured he was finally in the clear. He should have recognized the warning signs. First, his mistress Virginia Hill announced abruptly that she was leaving for Paris. He refused to let her go.

"You don't own me, Ben Siegel!" she responded. Hill flew off to France but allowed him to stay at the Spanish Colonial-style mansion he had leased for her on North Linden Drive in Beverly Hills. Her brother Chick would be staying there also.

Before returning to Los Angeles, Siegel received a surprise visit from Lansky at the Flamingo. Siegel failed to recognize it for what it was—Lansky's bid to say goodbye.

When Siegel arrived back in LA, he telephoned Mickey Cohen and asked to meet him at a friend's apartment. Siegel appeared calm and collected as the two men took a walk down and sat down by the pool.

"You got armament?" he asked Cohen. "What kind of equipment do you got?"

"Whatever you want, I got whatever you need."

"Who's the best you got?"

Cohen gave Siegel the names of two of his most trusted triggermen. Siegel asked his friend to set up a meeting with the muscle the following day. Cohen had an uneasy feeling that he would never see Siegel alive again.

Siegel then met with his actor friend George Raft. "I'm tired, Georgie," he said in a fidgety manner.

The next day, June 20, 1947, Siegel stopped into Harry Drucker's barber shop in Beverly Hills for a haircut, shave, manicure, and shoeshine. When he arrived back at Hill's home, he failed to notice that the living room drapes had been opened. Siegel had always kept the curtains closed to prevent prying eyes from seeing inside the house—or worse. He was in a good mood and invited three friends to dinner at a new restaurant called Jack's at the Beach on the Ocean Park Pier in Santa Monica. Siegel laughed with his buddies, including Chick Hill, and gladly picked up the tab. They drove back to the house, and Siegel opened the front door with the gold key that Virginia had given him as a present. Chick Hill retreated upstairs while Siegel turned on the lights. He noticed a strong aroma of jasmine wafting in from an open window. At that moment, Siegel may have reflected on an old southern saying that Virginia had once mentioned to him: "When someone smells flowers and there aren't any in the house, it means they're going to die."

Siegel grabbed a copy of the *Los Angeles Times* and sat down on the living room sofa. At approximately 10:45 p.m., an assassin with a carbine took position near the rose trellis that divided Hill's house from her neighbors. The hit man stood about fifteen feet away from the living room window and had a clear shot. He pulled the trigger, and the explosion sounded like a brick of firecrackers going off. The first bullet fired struck Siegel through the right eye, dislodging it and sending it several feet into a nearby wall. The second shot tore through Siegel's brain and neck. The killer fired three more bullets, all hitting their mark.

Benjamin "Bugsy" Siegel was dead.

And the Mickey Cohen era was born.

CHAPTER FOURTEEN

COHEN'S WORLD

If there was an Academy Award handed out for gangland slayings, Bugsy Siegel's murder would have been a front-runner. It was audacious in its planning and bold in its execution. Police were called to the ghastly scene and took crime scene photos of Siegel's bloody body sprawled on the couch with a gaping wound in his right eye socket. Florabel Muir, a correspondent for the *New York Daily News*, arrived while the scene was still active and unsecure. Muir lifted the newspaper from Siegel's cold lap to see what he had been reading. She then walked across the living room and picked up his eyeball, along with a sliver of flesh from which his long eyelashes extended. A photo of Siegel's foot with a toe tag that read *Homicide* was splashed across the front page of the *Los Angeles Herald-Express* the next day.

On June 25, 1947, Siegel was laid to rest in a $5,000 silver-plated casket, clothed in a blue suit, white shirt, and blue tie with a white handkerchief tucked into his breast pocket. The service took only four minutes and was attended by Siegel's ex-wife and their two children, his brother and sister, and an unidentified business associate. Siegel was interred in the Jewish section of Hollywood Forever Cemetery. No one would ever be charged with Siegel's murder.

Meyer Lansky had paid Mickey Cohen to keep a close eye on Siegel and protect him if he could. Suspiciously, Cohen was nowhere in sight when the assassination took place. He was questioned by authorities and denied any knowledge about the hit. When asked by the Beverly Hills police chief who killed Siegel, Cohen replied, "I wish I knew."

No one believed him, as he had the most to gain from Siegel's murder. Cohen admitted as much in his memoir. "Naturally, I missed Benny. We were real close and he taught me many things. But to be honest with you, his getting knocked in was not a bad break for me. Pretty soon, I was running everything out here."

But this was Hollywood, and Cohen had to make a show of finding Siegel's killers. He drove his Cadillac to the Hotel Roosevelt and walked in waving a pistol as he claimed he had heard that Siegel's assassin was hiding there. He reportedly fired two shots in the ceiling of the foyer before driving away. Later, a police wiretap on Cohen's telephone picked up a conversation about collecting $50,000 in bail money for the release of a prisoner in Fresno, California. Investigators for the Los Angeles district attorney's office believed the bail money was for Siegel's killer.

The Hotel Roosevelt on Hollywood Boulevard as it looks today (photo by Casey Sherman)

But Cohen had the state's attorney general in his back pocket. He supported Republican Fred N. Howser's bid for the office, and in return, California's top cop told police to lay off Cohen as he was a key witness in a grand jury investigation of sustained corruption in the Los Angeles Police Department (LAPD).

With little concern now

about the local cops, Cohen continued to consolidate his strength as LA's most powerful and ruthless gangster. By this time, the FBI had fingered him for at least seven murders, although there was not enough evidence to support criminal charges against him.

Cohen also preyed on young Hollywood actresses, setting them up to have sex with his underlings and then surreptitiously filming them in the act. He would then sell the movies on the black market or hold them over a starlet's head as blackmail. Occasionally, Cohen got romantically involved with aspiring Hollywood hopefuls, including Elizabeth Short. Originally from Medford, Massachusetts, Short had arrived in Los Angeles in 1946 and found work as a waitress while trying to secure film auditions. She was not "movie star beautiful" in the way that Lana was, but Short's pouty lips, powder-blue eyes, and brown, curly hair made her alluring, especially to Cohen. They met at the Spanish Kitchen, a popular celebrity haunt on Beverly Boulevard. Cohen's relationship with Short was brief. In mid-January 1947, months before Siegel's murder, Elizabeth Short was found dead, her naked body cut in half at the waist and left in a vacant lot in LA's Leimert Park neighborhood. No one would ever be charged with her murder, but Short found her celebrity in death. She became known around the world as "the Black Dahlia."

As with the hit on Siegel, Cohen never asked questions about the gruesome murder of Elizabeth Short, even though her body was found near the home of his emerging rival Jack Dragna. Instead, Cohen was focused on his future. He opened a men's clothing store at 8800 Sunset Boulevard called Michael's Exclusive Haberdashery. It was the perfect front for the dapperly attired Cohen, who loved wearing expensive pastel suits.

He got word that police had hidden a bug in his home, so he ordered a meeting with the LAPD's electronics expert, James "Big Jim" Vaus. Cohen invited Vaus to his clothing store, which had been decorated with walls of polished chestnut and merchandise behind sliding glass doors. The door to

Cohen's office was reinforced with steel plates. When Vaus entered Cohen's inner sanctum, he found the diminutive crime boss sitting at a large wraparound desk under a framed portrait of Franklin Delano Roosevelt. Cohen spared no time with pleasantries and immediately got to the matter at hand.

"Vaus, I understand that you're the man who planted a microphone at my home for the police department. Is that right?"

"I don't even know where you live," Vaus replied.

Cohen waved off the obvious lie. "If there were a microphone in my home, do you think you could locate it and take it out for me?"

"Mr. Cohen, you've got me all wrong," Vaus said. "I'm in the business of putting them in, not taking them out."

Cohen pulled out a large bankroll and peeled off several hundred-dollar bills. Vaus quickly made a deal to moonlight for Cohen while continuing his work with the LAPD.

Vaus was paid handsomely for his work, but it turned out to be a better deal for Cohen, as it also saved his life. While searching Cohen's Brentwood home for bugs, Vaus noticed an odd-looking wire running along a window frame and sticking out several inches from the screen.

"Is that another bug?" one of Cohen's henchmen asked.

Vaus then examined the wire and realized that it was not connected to any telephone. He began pulling the wire slowly, and a thick fourteen-inch pipe came out of the substructure of the wall. Vaus recognized it right away. It was a pipe bomb known as a "Bangalore torpedo," and it was packed with dynamite. The bomb had been placed directly under the bedroom where Cohen and his wife slept. Vaus kept the explosive and did not turn it over to his colleagues at the LAPD. Cohen had another plan in mind. The crime boss then offered a sensational scoop to reporter Florabel Muir for her column in the *New York Daily News*, that the LAPD had bugged his home for two years without a court order. Muir ran with the story and added that detectives in the department's infamous Gangster Squad had attempted to shake Cohen down with transcripts of his telephone conversations. Muir's story sparked a scandal within the police department, and now Cohen had enemies gunning for him on both sides of the law.

With Siegel now out of the way, Jack Dragna and his crew were ready to wage battle with Cohen for control of the Sunset Strip. Dragna associate Jimmy "the Weasel" Fratianno was true to his nickname. He befriended Cohen and bonded over their mutual love for the theater. Fratianno had recently been released from prison and suffered from tuberculosis. Cohen paid for his hospital bills. Cohen had just seen the stage musical *Annie Get Your Gun* at the Greek Theater in LA. He enjoyed the performance so much that he recommended it to Fratianno and offered him complimentary tickets for his family. Fratianno showed up at Cohen's clothing store in mid-August 1948 with his wife and daughter in tow. Cohen smiled as he greeted Fratianno and his family with theater tickets.

"Be my guests. They don't cost me nothing," Cohen told Fratianno. "I can get all the free tickets I want. Best seats in the house, too. I got you third row, center aisle."

Fratianno grabbed the tickets and shook Cohen's hand. A germophobe, Cohen immediately retreated to the bathroom to scrub his hands. As Fratianno left the store with his wife and their young daughter, he nodded to a hit squad waiting outside. He then got his family out of harm's way, while the killers, Frank DeSimone and Frank "the Bomp" Bompensiero, readied themselves for the attack. Dragna had chosen his men wisely. Bompensiero was a seasoned triggerman, who mob admirers claimed had "buried more bones than could be found in the brontosaurus room at the Museum of Natural History."

While Cohen was washing his hands, Hooky Rothman, his trusted bodyguard, noticed the gangsters assembling outside. Rothman rushed out to confront the pair and tried to grab Bompensiero's sawed-off shotgun. Bompensiero fired a shell that ripped off half of Hooky's face. Rothman stumbled back and was struck by another bullet and collapsed dead at the entrance of the store. The killers fled in a yellow convertible. Cohen managed to escape but was later arrested for suspicion of murder. Understanding that he was the intended target of the assassins, police soon let Cohen go.

He drove to the hospital where Rothman's body was taken. A gaggle of reporters met Cohen in the lobby. "I have no idea why anybody would want to bump Hooky or me off," he told them. It was an obvious lie.

At the funeral, a distraught Cohen attempted to console Rothman's family and was greeted with a response befitting of the gangster's code.

"You don't have to say nothing," Rothman's brother told Cohen. "Hooky died the way he wanted. He lived for you and died for you the way he wanted."

Rothman was buried in a $5,000 casket and interred near the crypt that held Bugsy Siegel's remains. Rothman had taken the bullet meant for his boss, and the LAPD braced for more violence.

"Mickey's going to get his and he knows it," Norris Stensland, chief detective with the Los Angeles County Sheriff's Department, told reporters. Stensland added that he hoped Cohen would stay alive long enough to appear at the official inquest regarding Rothman's murder.

Columnist Florabel Muir also knew it would only be a matter of time before Dragna's goons struck again. She turned up at just about every nightclub that Cohen was known to frequent. "I was following Mickey Cohen around the nightspots on the famous Sunset Strip," she recalled years later. "Watching and waiting for someone to try to kill him and hoping I would be there when they did."

In July 1949, Muir met Cohen for a late-night cup of coffee at a restaurant called Sherry's on the Sunset Strip. Two LA police detectives were stationed out front. They were working undercover for the state's attorney general in an effort to protect Cohen, as word had spread that gangsters from New York were coming to town to put him out of business—permanently.

"What are you standing out here for?" Muir asked the officers as she passed by. "Trying to get yourself shot?"

She stepped into the restaurant and saw Cohen eating ice cream and holding court at a table with a reporter and photographer from the *Los Angeles Times*. Cohen motioned for Muir to join them. She took a seat and dove into their topic of conversation—who was trying to kill him? They pointed to the police detectives now serving as his bodyguards as proof that Cohen had a bull's-eye on his back.

"I don't need protection." Cohen shrugged. "Not as long as you people are around. Even a crazy man wouldn't take a chance shooting where a reporter might get hit."

The conversation flowed and the coffee continued to pour, and soon Cohen invited another man to join them. "This is my jeweler friend," he told everyone.

At 3:55 a.m., Cohen and his entourage left the restaurant. Florabel Muir was standing in the foyer of Sherry's when she heard the sound of smashing glass outside. She thought someone was throwing rocks. Instead, gunmen were riddling Cohen's Cadillac with bullets.

Seconds later, the reporter saw a spent slug on the floor. Muir tried to move but was hobbled by intense pain as she had been struck in the hip by shrapnel. A second bullet sailed past her head and struck a glass door. Outside, a member of Cohen's police detail, LA detective Harry Cooper, screamed, "I'm hit," as three bullets penetrated his stomach. Former MGM actress turned nurse Dee David, another member of Cohen's entourage, was also shot. Four bullets ripped through her intestines and sliced her kidney. David screamed as she fell to the ground in intense pain. She could not feel her legs. She tried to move them but was temporarily paralyzed on the street.

The gunmen then fired at Cohen, hitting him once in the right shoulder. As blood dripped down his arm, Cohen fought to maintain his balance out of fear that if he fell on the street, he would ruin his new suit. Neddie

Herbert, one of Cohen's top lieutenants and an expert marksman, was also shot and then rushed to nearby Citizens Emergency Hospital, where he later died. Cohen dragged Detective Cooper into his car and sped away to another hospital where he had the bullet removed from his shoulder. The slug had just missed his lung.

Newspaper reporters camped out in the hospital corridors. The headline in the *Los Angeles Mirror* screamed, "Mickey 'Gets His' Surrounded by Heavy Bodyguard." The *Mirror* also reported that the hit squad had tossed two twelve-gauge shotguns from their getaway car. The weapons were recovered near the scene and "glove prints were found on both guns and on ten empty shotgun shells found at the scene. Two live shells remained in each gun." A *Mirror* reporter speculated that "underworld gossip is [that] the outburst of gang violence results from the decision that the midwest mob with Italian Mafia connection to move in on Los Angeles rackets."

While Cohen was under sedation at the hospital, a call came in to the nurses' station.

"Be on your guard," the caller warned. "We're going to come down and get Mickey tonight!"

The caller almost made good on his promise. A sedan pulled up to the hospital a short time later carrying gangsters with guns. They went room to room, searching for the wounded Cohen, but he was already gone. The groggy crime boss had been pulled out of his bed and escorted out of the hospital through a side entrance by his new jeweler friend—a combat veteran named Johnny Stompanato.

CHAPTER FIFTEEN

ENTER STOMPANATO

Johnny Stompanato was born into death. The youngest of four children, he grew up without his mother, Carmela, who was stricken with peritonitis and died just six days after giving birth to him by cesarean section on October 19, 1925. Born in Italy, his father, John Sr., had met his wife, Carmela

Mickey Cohen hired Johnny Stompanato as a bodyguard and partner in a lucrative Hollywood extortion scheme (Courtesy: Associated Press)

Truppa, in Brooklyn, New York, before moving to the Midwest and opening a barbershop and beauty parlor in the idyllic small town of Woodstock, Illinois, forty-five miles northwest of Chicago. The couple was well respected in Woodstock, and Carmela's death was reported on the front page of the town's two local newspapers, where she was described as the "favorite Italian mother of Woodstock."

Their son Johnny, or Jack as he was then known, had a typical Depression-era upbringing. Although he was watched over closely by his sisters Grace and Teresa and his big brother, Carmine, the boy ran freely around town, playing marbles with friends in front of the courthouse and tossing a baseball around in the town square, just a stone's throw from the family barbershop on Main Street.

The Stompanatos lived in a large, comfortable home on Blakely Street in Woodstock, and although they were one of just a few Italian families in a town of six thousand residents, they did their best to assimilate in their community. Raised Roman Catholic, John Sr. joined the Presbyterian church. After the death of his wife, the elder Stompanato remarried four years later to a woman from Wisconsin named Verena Freitag. Contradicting the wicked stepmother trope, Verena adored little Jack.

"I used to get confused as to whether she was my real mother, and my father was my stepfather or vice versa," he later told a friend.

As a boy, Stompanato had his hands in plenty of mischief. He was called a "devil" by some neighbors who knew him from church, but he also had a soft side when it came to his friends.

Stompanato was big, strong, and willing to stand up to local bullies.

"He was my protector—nobody fooled around with me as long as I was with Jack," his childhood friend Casimer Polizzi recalled. "He was tough, but he liked people."

Stompanato's classmates snickered behind his back, claiming that he was in the Mafia. Although tiny Woodstock was a short drive from Chicago, it was a world away from the killings and corruption triggered by Al Capone and his successor Frank Nitti. Stompanato paid little or no attention to roaring headlines of gangland shootings and rubouts in Chicago and enjoyed an ordinary upbringing in sleepy Woodstock.

Stompanato attended Woodstock Community High School for one year before John Sr. and Verena sent him to Kemper Military School in Boonville, Missouri, in 1941. His parents had little choice; their son had impregnated two local girls, and the growing scandal threatened to destroy their family business. With Johnny out of sight, he would be out of people's minds.

Kemper, dubbed "the West Point of the West," had five hundred cadets enrolled when Stompanato arrived just as America was preparing to enter WWII. Spread out on forty-six acres and surrounded by beautiful antebellum homes, Kemper had a rigid training curriculum that was supposed to instill discipline in Stompanato, who was growing exceedingly wild as a teenager. Standing six feet tall and weighing 180 pounds, he had the makings of an ideal soldier. But Stompanato's passions were elsewhere. He earned a reputation as a local lothario who drove teenage girls in the small southern town crazy. Like those of most boys his age, his thoughts were dominated by dreams of the fairer sex. According to Stompanato's instructors at Kemper, he had "better than average intelligence" and was a "quick learner when he wishes, but [is] interested in little but salacious literature and women."

When Kemper cadets, including Stompanato's roommate Hugh Krampe, who would later break into Hollywood with the name Hugh O'Brian as television's Wyatt Earp, were ordered on five- to ten-mile marches, Stompanato routinely faked an injury or stomach ailment to get sent to the nurse's office. His fellow cadets all believed the teenage Stompanato was having sex with the school nurse. According to O'Brian, he also liked to parade around naked in the shower in front of his fellow cadets and pull dangerous pranks on campus. During one incident, Stompanato stuffed a dynamite cap into a soda bottle and tossed it from an upper window of the barracks. The explosion caused a tremendous roar and shattered several windows. He was almost kicked out of school for the stunt.

Stompanato survived the infraction and spent two years at Kemper Military School before graduating and joining the U.S. Marine Corps, where he was assigned to the First Marine Division in the Pacific theater. Stompanato worked as a clerk during the massive Allied campaign to seize islands fortified by the Japanese, which was critical to the overall war effort. For Stompanato, days of boredom aboard a ship were broken up by moments of unfathomable terror. As he wrote in his hometown newspaper on August

10, 1944, "We have a wonderful bunch of fellows in our outfit and everything is pretty much O.K. Of course we would rather be home but that is besides the point. But when the outfit isn't in the combat zone we have movies most every night. It is a grand thing, the motion picture industry is doing by seending [sic] the movies over here to us."

As a member of the First Marine Division, Stompanato saw combat during the Allied invasion of Peleliu, beginning in September 1944. The small coral island was supposed to be captured in four days, but the eleven thousand Japanese troops stationed there dug in and fought for nearly three months. The First Marines landed on the north side of the island and were immediately barraged by heavy fire. In all, American troops would suffer three thousand casualties in their attempt to secure Peleliu's lone airstrip. Months later, Stompanato fought in the desperate kill-or-be-killed battle to take control of Okinawa. While he managed to dodge a Japanese bayonet, he could not steer clear of trouble in his own outfit. After securing the island, Stompanato was reprimanded for impersonating an officer by sneaking into the mess wearing a Marine lieutenant's uniform.

He was discharged from the Marines in March 1946 but decided to stay in the Far East. He traveled to the city of Tianjin, China, located on the coast of the Bohai Sea. Stompanato later told mob friends that he ran several nightclubs that catered to American and British GIs. He reportedly sold off underage girls for five dollars.

While working in Tianjin, Stompanato met a darkly attractive woman while browsing in a local dress shop. Her name was Sara Utush, and her parents were born in Turkey but had emigrated to China, where Sara was raised. Stompanato fell quickly for Sara, and she soon fell in love with him, but there was a problem. She was Muslim, which meant Stompanato would have to convert to Islam if the pair wanted to marry. But he did not hesitate for a minute. He changed his religion as quickly as he would change a shirt, and the two were wed in a traditional Muslim ceremony in May 1946.

Stompanato got in some trouble with police in Tianjin and eventually brought his new wife back home to Woodstock, Illinois. While filling out paperwork for their journey to the states, Sara noticed that Stompanato had lied about his age. He was only twenty years old, five years younger than she was, and she saw that as a bad omen. In Woodstock, Stompanato found work as a truck driver and on the factory floor at an auto manufacturer while his wife got a job as a seamstress at a local textile factory. Sara did her best to assimilate to a new country and culture, and Stompanato's parents and siblings accepted her graciously into the family.

But like many combat veterans, Stompanato had difficulty adjusting to life back home. He was fidgety and experienced post-traumatic stress disorder and wanderlust. Sara got pregnant and delivered their baby in the same hospital where Stompanato was born and where his mother had died many years before. Unlike his own father, Stompanato was no doting dad to his infant son, John Stompanato III. Soon after Sara's delivery, her husband fled to Los Angeles. Stompanato had always been fascinated by Hollywood, especially the film industry, which he gushed about in his letter to the newspaper while he was serving overseas during the war. Working two jobs, he was barely scraping by, and a trip out to California would cost big money. His wife certainly would not cover his travel expenses now that she was the sole supporter of their infant child.

Stompanato took a train to Chicago where he met a rich, lonely man named Charles Hubbard in the bar of a hotel. As he had done back at Kemper Military School, Stompanato showed off his powerful physique for Hubbard and then smooth-talked him into funding a trip out west. Hubbard had plenty of money. He was the titled heir to a British fortune and eager to see where the friendship with Stompanato might lead. Over the course of their relationship, Hubbard gave Stompanato more than $65,000. Stompanato later told the IRS that he had borrowed the money from his British friend, but there was no indication that he ever paid him back.

When he got to Hollywood, Stompanato bought a bikini swimsuit and took up position poolside at the Beverly Hills Hotel. He quickly became popular with entertainers like Merv Griffin and Liberace. Griffin reportedly propositioned Stompanato the first day he met him and soon became a weekly customer, while Liberace was rumored to have paid Stompanato as much as $1,000 for one night of sex. But Stompanato did not consider himself a homosexual; he loved women and figured that he was only paying his dues in Hollywood like so many actors had before and since. He knew that his good looks and combat experience would open the doors of opportunity in Los Angeles. Stompanato played male gigolo at the Beverly Hills Hotel pool by day and Sunset Strip tough guy by night. He had read stories about Bugsy Siegel and his takeover of LA, and it gave him inspiration. He just needed the right mentor.

"Someone sent him to me and he was looking to get started in something," Mickey Cohen later recalled. "He had been in the Marines and had a couple of nightclubs in China. I put him on the payroll and worked him into a couple of things in my gambling business."

After the attempted hit on Cohen at Sherry's restaurant, the pugnacious crime boss knew he needed better protection. He admired how Stompanato, his new jeweler friend, carried himself at the hospital and had acted swiftly when Cohen's would-be assassins rushed in to finish the job. When Cohen returned to the hospital for more treatment, Stompanato decided to bring him a gun for protection. He was pulled over by Beverly Hills police on the way to the hospital and arrested on the spot. Recuperating in his hospital bed, Cohen called his lawyer and got the gun charge reduced to a vagrancy violation. Stompanato was fined $250 and sentenced to sixty days in county jail. His conviction would be overturned on appeal as a judge declared that Stompanato's idleness did not necessarily make him a vagrant. The headline in the next day's newspaper read "High Court Rules Stompanato No Bum."

The botched hit at Sherry's was just the latest attempt by Jack Dragna's men to kill Cohen. Gunmen had also shot at him as he was getting ready to pull into his driveway at his house in Brentwood. The next day, Cohen bought himself a custom-built bulletproof car for $15,800. The vehicle was built with a curved bulletproof windshield, eight-inch-thick armor-plated doors, bombproof flooring, and bulletproof tires. It was also outfitted with a custom-built bar.

He had Stompanato, a fighting Marine, protecting his blindside and now a bulletproof car that drove like a tank, and still, Mickey Cohen was not safe.

There would soon be another bombing attempt on his home in Brentwood. This time, an explosive device was planted across the street from his house in a neighbor's driveway. The blast, which occurred just fifty feet away from Cohen's bedroom, rattled windows in the neighborhood, but nobody got hurt. Police scoffed at the attack and blamed it on pranksters.

Stompanato also felt the heat. Just after the deadly ambush at Sherry's, he noticed someone tailing him as he drove down the Sunset Strip. Los Angeles police officer Fred Otash, a fellow ex-Marine, combat veteran, and rogue cop, was behind Stompanato in an unmarked car. Otash pulled alongside Stompanato's vehicle and stuck his shotgun out the window.

"Now you've had it, you motherfucker!" Otash shouted.

Stompanato ducked and then lost control of his Cadillac. The car hit a curb and rolled down the hill on Sunset. Stompanato managed to escape, but just barely. He eventually got to a pay phone, called police headquarters, and screamed that Otash had just tried to shoot him. The officer was called to the police chief's office, where he claimed that he was only trying to scare Stompanato. But Otash was a notorious double-dealer with ties to Dragna's gang. It could have been a hoax, a hit, or even an act of jealous rage on the part of Otash, whose girlfriend had told him that Stompanato was "just the cutest thing I ever saw."

Stompanato took the threat seriously. It was time for him and his boss to leave Los Angeles for a while until things died down. They traveled to Chicago together to meet with members of the Syndicate, who were concerned about the escalating battle with Dragna on the Sunset Strip. Cohen needed to square things with Meyer Lansky, New York mafia boss Frank Costello, and others who saw diminished returns coming out of their gambling joints in LA, as celebrities now feared they would get caught in the crossfire of Cohen and Dragna's turf war. Jack Dragna had been questioned about his alleged role in the shooting at Sherry's Restaurant and gave an alibi that police found "entirely satisfactory."

A story from the United Press International (UPI) summed up the fear and loathing in Los Angeles this way in a column titled "Hollywood's Famed Strip Becoming Gasoline Alley." "The Strip, a hunk of county land between Hollywood and Beverly Hills that doesn't belong to any city, is filmville's glamor row of nightclubs, swank shops, restaurants and actors' agents offices," wrote reporter Aline Mosby. "But largely fusillades from sawed-off shotguns have taken the place of one-punch nightclub matches... The Strip that shot to fame the night that somebody almost got Mickey Cohen in front of Sherry's Restaurant was just a poinsettia patch fifty years ago."

The deadly ambush at Sherry's was good for Hollywood business though. A short time later, UPI reported on "A Film to Be Written from LA Headlines" by future Oscar-winning screenwriters Clarence Greene and Russell Rouse called *Dead on Arrival.* "We've been writing the script since the day one headline," Rouse gushed. "When Mickey Cohen got shot at Sherry's, we worked the Sunset Strip and the outside of the restaurant into our script." The film noir, retitled *D.O.A.*, would star Edmond O'Brien and be remade in the 1980s starring Dennis Quaid.

While visiting Chicago, police were tipped off to Cohen's presence and arrested him and Stompanato in the penthouse of the Ambassador East Hotel, where they paid $75 a night for the lavish room. Cohen had booked the room under the alias Michael Cain. Police had nothing to go on, and

Cohen's lawyer won their release from jail. Andrew Aitken, Chicago's chief of detectives, offered Cohen a warning as he left the jailhouse. He believed that both Cohen and Stompanato would get whacked if they did not leave the city immediately. "We don't want your scar tissue messing up the place," Detective Aitken said. "We don't want to find your body on a street here."

Aitken ordered Cohen and Stompanato to leave town. After Cohen fled to Cleveland, Aitken told a reporter, "He's gone and we're glad of it. We don't want him in Chicago. He better stay out of this town. All police have been told to pick him up on sight!"

After visiting Ohio, Cohen and Stompanato returned to Los Angeles, where the city's mayor, Fletcher Bowron, had offered his own warning to the crime boss through the press. "Well, Mickey, I have never met you," Bowron said during his weekly radio address. "You have never picked up a check for me and I have never picked up a suit or other present from your so-called haberdashery. And you never will and I never will. I give you the full warning. You have not intimidated me or the Los Angeles Police Department. We are coming after you, we are going to stay after you, and we are going to put you out of business."

The mayor's sentiments were echoed by California governor Earl Warren, who would later oversee the investigation into the assassination of President John F. Kennedy as chief justice of the U.S. Supreme Court. "The situation is bad," said Warren. "It is giving our state a very bad name throughout the world and it calls for leadership in the suppression of every type of commercialized vice and crime."

Despite the pressure, Cohen did not hide. In fact, he did the opposite. The crime boss began a full-court press with the media. If politicians could use magazines, newspapers, and the radio to spread their message, so could Cohen. He had learned how to cultivate favorable media coverage from his mentors Capone and Siegel.

He cooperated with *Life* magazine for an exposé called "Trouble in

Los Angeles." In the article, Cohen was described as an "exhibitionist hoodlum," but the accompanying photo spread taken by legendary *Life* cameraman Ed Clark, best known for his image of an African American accordion player weeping during the funeral cortege for FDR, showed a lighter side of the gangland killer. During the shoot, Cohen posed wearing shorts in the backyard of his Brentwood home with his wife, LaVonne, and their two dogs. Other photos showed him watering plants and smelling flowers while his wife posed inside their living room with her knitting. The Cohens appeared to be like any other hardworking couple living their dream in postwar America. But one photo belied the gangster's well-crafted image. It showed Cohen standing over his desk in his Sunset Strip office with his so-called business manager Mike Howard, who was just another murderous thug in a finely tailored suit, and the handsome, brawny Johnny Stompanato, who glared menacingly into the lens, looking like he was ready to cut Clark's throat.

Cohen's public relations campaign may have tricked some into believing that he was a law-abiding, domesticated family man, but it had no effect on the legion of killers who wanted him dead. In the predawn hours of February 6, 1950, Cohen was asleep with his wife, LaVonne, in her bedroom and awoke to a high-pitched sound coming from the elaborate warning system that he had installed in their home in Brentwood after the previous pipe bomb attack. With the loud noise ringing in his ears, he and his live-in maid Katherine Jones searched each room but found nothing peculiar. They looked out the windows, and Cohen grabbed a flashlight and raced into the backyard hunting for any prowlers, but again he found nothing. He went back to his wife's bed and tried to fall back to sleep. The couple had slept in separate rooms since the initial attack on their home as Mickey did not want LaVonne hit by bullets or bombs that were meant for him.

Cohen then smelled a lit fuse burning and jolted out of his wife's bed. Seconds later, a deafening explosion rocked the house, tossing Cohen and

LaVonne to the floor. The heavy blast blew out every window, created a six-foot hole near the foundation, and tore off the southwest wing of the house. Cohen placed his body over LaVonne's as smoke billowed into the bedroom. He stumbled to his feet and staggered through the fiery debris to check on their maid. She was unharmed, which was surprising, since the fireball could be seen and felt three miles away. Cohen and his wife were bruised but otherwise okay. The bombing would have destroyed the entire house if he hadn't built a steel vault inside the foundation. Cohen was angry to see his house demolished, his own bedroom ripped apart, and his expensive wardrobe of fifty custom-made suits destroyed.

An army of police and several crime reporters flocked to the address within fifteen minutes. Cohen greeted them wearing monogrammed pajamas and a robe. He laid down newspaper on what was left of the living room floor and ordered police to remove their shoes before entering to prevent them from tracking in mud as heavy rain fell outside. LaVonne appeared calm after the explosion. She made coffee for the cops while wearing a blue dressing gown over a nylon nightie and fluffy slippers. The couple treated the massive bomb blast as just another normal morning in the Cohen household. Investigators searched through the wreckage and told Cohen that he would have been killed if he had chosen to sleep in his own bed that morning, as a bundle of dynamite sticks used in the bombing had been placed against the foundation of the house under his bedroom window.

Cohen was expected to appear in court later that day on a separate issue and joked to reporters that he had nothing to wear. "It's a shame," he told them. "A guy goes into the clothing business and stuff like this happens." When asked if he knew who had targeted them for death, Cohen replied, "Your guess is as good as mine."

Five members of Jack Dragna's gang, including his twenty-six-year-old son, Frank Paul Dragna, were arrested a week later and charged with the attack. Investigators also wanted to bring in Jack Dragna himself for questioning, but the boss fled to Nicaragua after getting tipped off about his impending arrest.

While Johnny Stompanato and the rest of Cohen's crew took to the streets looking for any member of Dragna's gang who had not been busted for the bombing, their boss had to quell an uprising from his neighbors. One resident, described in news accounts as Mrs. Mel Bren, lived one thousand feet away from Cohen and told reporters, "I just got back in bed after feeding the baby. Then we felt the blast. The noise of the shattering of glass was terrific."

Cohen's neighbors feared for their lives, and they wanted him gone. This prompted the crime boss to type up a response in a letter that he mailed to his fellow residents living in the upscale neighborhood, including actor Dean Jagger.

"Guided as I was by the kindly statements of those in the neighborhood who apparently took only into consideration that Mrs. Cohen and I are going through a very rugged and painful period of our lives, I took for granted that if I could expect no breaks from the mad beast who bombed me, I would certainly have no reason to fear hurt from my neighbors, whom I never molested in any way," he wrote. "Let's both stop being victimized. I am a gambler and a betting commissioner, no more, no less. I am not a mobster, a gunman or a thug. I leave such antics to Mr. George Raft and Mr. Humphrey Bogart, who make money at it... I am not in the dynamiting business, the shooting business or in any other varied forms of homicide. I sell shirts and ties and sometimes I make a bet or two."

The stylish gangster was later undressed publicly in the high-profile congressional hearings staged by Estes Kefauver, a crime-fighting U.S. senator from Tennessee. Under questioning by committee member Senator Charles Tobey of New Hampshire, LAPD chief William H. Parker described Cohen under oath as "essentially stupid... He is heavy-set, heavy-browed and quite ignorant." Parker continued, "The private conversations we have been able to pick up do not indicate he is an intelligent or educated man." Kefauver himself would describe Mickey Cohen as "a simian-like figure with a pendulous lower lip, thinning hair and spreading paunch."

Public embarrassment was one thing; getting enough evidence to put Cohen behind bars was quite another. When questioning Cohen about his criminal activities, the committee focused first on Johnny Stompanato. Committee counsel Rudolph Halley asked Cohen if Stompanato was a man of wealth.

"I don't know that," Cohen replied. "I know he got his money someplace."

"He borrowed money from a very rich man, did he not?" Halley asked.

"That is right, yes."

"Isn't it a fact that he got his money by extortion?" the government attorney pressed, alluding to Stompanato's peculiar relationship with British heir Charles Hubbard.

"I don't think so," Cohen countered, trying to protect his bodyguard. "I think that is *not* a fact." Technically, Cohen was half right. He did not want to reveal to the committee his own suspicions that Stompanato had swapped sexual favors for cash from Hubbard.

The Kefauver committee then peppered Cohen about his own finances, particularly $300,000 in unpaid loans from several Los Angeles banks.

"I'm trying to find out how you and Stompanato succeeded in persuading people to loan you large sums of money," Halley told Cohen.

"I can only answer for myself," the crime boss replied. "If you want Stompanato, you can ask him."

Cohen finished his testimony and felt confident about his sparring session with politicians and prosecutors. But Kefauver committee counsel Rudolph Halley had one more card to play. He called Cohen's Beverly Hills accountant, Harry Sackman, to testify under oath. Halley pointed to some vague receipts as large as $10,000 that were filed under "various commissions."

"How do you get away with that?" Halley asked Sackman.

"I've always asked him [Cohen] each year to give me the detail on it," the accountant tried to explain. "I tell him the law, but he says 'Well, here is the figure and that's the only thing I can present to you.' Therefore, on that basis, I file the return with the government."

Stompanato and others defended the boss during his subsequent trial for tax evasion. They all testified that the $156,000 that Cohen was accused of hiding from the government was not income. Instead, they claimed to have loaned the money to Cohen, who was in the process of paying it back. One of Cohen's defenders, a notorious gambler named Hymie Miller, was asked why he did not make a greater effort to get his money back from Cohen.

"People in my business don't sue anybody," he told the court.

Mickey Cohen was convicted of tax evasion and sentenced to five years behind bars.

"I want to begin my sentence now," Cohen told the judge upon learning his punishment.

He was immediately flown from Los Angeles to McNeil Island Federal Penitentiary near Tacoma, Washington, where Robert Stroud, the infamous "Birdman of Alcatraz," had once served time.

Without Cohen to lead them, his gang, including Johnny Stompanato, would need to find other ways to earn a living until their boss was freed from jail. It appeared that Stompanato would drift quickly into obscurity. A few months after Cohen's conviction, gossip columnist Dorothy Kilgallen wrote, "For the Whatever Became of Department: Mickey Cohen's former Los Angeles bodyguard Johnny Stompanato is currently employed selling lovebirds at a pet shop."

CHAPTER SIXTEEN

LANA IN TECHNICOLOR

Lana Turner's hand and footprints memorialized in cement outside of the TCL Chinese Theater in Hollywood on May 26, 1950 (Photo by Casey Sherman)

The IRS was also investigating the finances of Hollywood's biggest stars, including Lana Turner. Like Cohen, she owed a fortune in back taxes. Lana had routinely asked her managers to provide her with what she called a "star's essentials": furs, limousines, a chauffeur, and lavish gifts. Her business managers tried to deduct the items on her tax returns, but the IRS refused to allow it. Lana begged for leniency, reminding agents that her war bond tours had added "many millions to the Treasury." But the IRS still assessed her with a staggering number of financial penalties. Greg Bautzer huddled with his fellow attorneys at MGM to arrange for the deduction of large amounts from her weekly salary, which would be handed over directly to the federal government.

Lana realized that although she had signed a new contract with the studio, she would need a wealthy husband to sustain her luxurious, free-spending lifestyle. She had recovered from a long but disastrous affair with actor Tyrone Power and was ready to fall in love again. Lana traveled to New York to attend the world premiere of *The Bishop's Wife* starring Loretta Young. Her date for the evening was Henry J. Topping Jr.

Overweight with a set of bad teeth, Topping was not a man who would normally attract Lana's attention. But he was a self-declared sportsman and heir to a tin-plate and steel fortune worth more than $140 million. His brother, Dan Topping, was co-owner of the New York Yankees. The actor and the sportsman had never met in person before, but Henry Topping, known as Bob, had flooded Lana's dressing room with boxes of chocolates and bouquets of roses while she filmed *Cass Timberlane*, a romantic comedy based on a Sinclair Lewis novel and costarring Spencer Tracy. Topping picked Lana up at the Plaza on the night of the premiere and presented her with a gift wrapped in tissue paper in the back of their limousine.

"What's that?" she asked.

"Unwrap it and find out."

Lana opened the wad of tissue paper to discover a set of sparkling diamond earrings. She calculated the math quickly in her head. If Topping handed out expensive diamond earrings on first dates, he would surely spend more lavishly on her if they were married.

Lana continued to see Topping while she was in New York and was invited to his family estate, Dunnellen Hall, a Tudor-style mansion in the elite Round Hill section of Greenwich, Connecticut. Built to resemble an English manor, Dunnellen Hall sat on more than twenty-five hundred acres and had twenty-eight rooms, including four large drawing rooms, marble fireplaces, and servant's quarters. It was the exact opposite of the beat-up row house that her second husband, Steve Crane, had shown her in his hometown in Indiana.

"The master hall reminded me of something out of a Gothic romance film," Lana wrote in her memoir. "I was impressed."

Topping was ready to propose with a fifteen-carat, marquise-cut diamond ring. He knew that Lana did not love him, but he assured her that she would eventually. She may not have swooned over him, but Lana loved what he represented: respectability and long-term financial stability for her and her daughter, Cheryl, who was now attending a parochial school in Westwood, California. Lana agreed to marry Topping as soon as his divorce to B-movie actress Arline Judge was finalized. But Lana was eager to announce their engagement beforehand. She and Topping planned for a glitzy affair at Mocambo, where the guest list would include the Duke and Duchess of Windsor.

When Louis B. Mayer received his invitation to the engagement party, he exploded once again. Mayer grabbed one of the many telephones on his desk and got a hold of the studio's publicity department and demanded that MGM's top PR flack convince Lana to cancel the event. "For God's sake, the guy's married," Mayer howled. "Lana's name has been linked to too many married men... She has a morality clause in her contract. I want no more of this lurid publicity about her getting engaged to married men."

Lana listened to the advice and canceled the party, but her animosity toward Mayer and MGM was growing. She was then hired to play a role in the studio's big-budget film *The Three Musketeers*. The film would be made in Technicolor, capturing Lana's natural beauty for the first time on the big screen. Louis B. Mayer promised that it would be the greatest film version ever made of the classic Alexandre Dumas novel.

Lana was eager to read the script, as she knew very little about her character, the villainous Countess de Winter. Given her stature as queen of the studio, Lana thought she would play the meatiest role, with more screen time and lines than her costars Gene Kelly, playing the aerobatic swordsman d'Artagnan, Vincent Price, and Angela Lansbury. But Lana was shocked to learn that she had been relegated to a supporting role in the film. She had worked and sweated so hard to advance her stature in Hollywood from "sweater girl" to leading lady. Taking a supporting role would signal to the entire film-loving world that Lana Turner had been forced from her throne at MGM.

It was time for Lana to draw a line in the sand. She felt that she had leverage over Louis B. Mayer. After all, she was a full-fledged movie star, and she was about to marry one of America's richest men. MGM needed her more than she needed the studio. Lana marched into Mayer's office and turned down the role. Mayer told her that although he could not force her to appear in the film, he would demand that she cover up to $400,000 in preproduction costs. The studio head believed he had painted Lana into a corner, but she held firm.

"Sorry, I still won't do that script," she told him.

Mayer placed Lana on immediate suspension. The news sent shock waves around Hollywood as MGM's publicity machine portrayed Lana not as a steel-backed businesswoman but as a spoiled, petulant child. No major female movie star had ever been suspended by the studio for refusing a role before.

"Metro-Goldwyn-Mayer has just put Lana Turner in the doghouse," wrote gossip columnist Margaret Bean. "A culmination of indiscretions has strained relationships and there was nothing left to do but put her in the doghouse, probably a gilded one with her name scrolled neatly on the front. Her excommunication includes a suspension without salary."

Mayer sat back in his palatial office and waited for his tempestuous actress to give in. But she continued to stand her ground. Lana refused to answer calls from the studio, and she had become a virtual ghost on the MGM lot. She flew to New York with Bob Topping and went into seclusion at Dunnellen Hall in nearby Greenwich. Mayer was forced to recast the picture with Italian actress Alida Valli taking over Lana's role.

"If you care for your movie career, you'd better get your shapely ass out of New York and appear on the set at MGM," columnist Hedda Hopper advised.

Lana finally negotiated her return, and Mayer agreed to have the script rewritten to enlarge her role if she agreed to go back to the set. Valli, Lana's brief replacement, was fired. Despite her initial well-publicized reluctance, Lana had a merry time on the set of *The Three Musketeers* with her costars Kelly, June Allyson, Lansbury, and Price, all decked out in their ornate and colorful seventeenth-century period costumes. By now, Mayer did not hide his hatred for Lana, but he made good on his word and beefed up her role. When the film's trailer debuted in theaters, Lana's giant color close-up appeared first and before Kelly's. The movie would go on to become a gigantic hit for MGM, becoming the studio's second-highest-grossing film of the decade, with much of the success credited to Lana. As critic Bosley Crowther wrote in the *New York Times*, *The Three Musketeers* was a "splendiferous production," and "more dazzling costumes, more color, or more of Miss Turner's chest have never been seen in a picture than are shown in this one." Despite the blatantly sexist comment, Crowther also hailed her as "completely fantastic" as "the ambitious Lady de Winter."

The film's director, George Sidney, also went out of his way to praise Lana. "She's one of the sweetest people and finest troupers in the business," Sidney said in a newspaper interview. "Most feminine stars are temperamental, but not Lana. She has no whims… Lana doesn't pull rank."

Despite yet another major score for the studio, Lana felt like she was under siege. Her relationship with Topping continued to create major waves in the press thanks to his estranged wife, Arline Judge. "He won't get a divorce from me for any amount of money," she told reporters spitefully. "When I divorce the bastard, I'll ruin him, take every cent he has."

Judge had dipped into the Topping family trust once before when she was married and then divorced from Bob's brother, Dan. She also warned Lana that Topping would "sock her in the eye" and that she would be forced to show up at the studio with "a great big shiner." Judge claimed that Topping had beaten her and had called her vile names during their marriage. Topping told Lana that Judge had once broken an expensive bottle of champagne over his head. Judge eventually agreed to the divorce, settling for $100,000, and Topping was ordered to pay her legal fees.

Lana's first marriage to Artie Shaw was an elopement. Her next to Steve Crane took place in a Tijuana lawyer's office. This time, she wanted an extravagant ceremony, and her new husband was willing to oblige. Billy Wilkerson, the man most responsible for Lana's stardom, offered up his mansion in Beverly Hills for the star-studded event with 150 A-list guests including Louis B. Mayer, Greg Bautzer, and his date, Joan Crawford, Albert "Cubby" Broccoli, the future producer of the *James Bond* franchise, and a drunken Errol Flynn, who tried sticking his tongue in Lana's mouth when he offered a kiss to the bride. Her young daughter, Cheryl, served as flower girl, wearing a white lace dress and bonnet. Lana's wedding trousseau cost a reported $30,000, and she wore an elegant champagne-colored lace dress over nude satin, cut low at the neckline, while she and her husband cut into their six-tiered wedding cake. During the three-hour wedding reception, guests feasted on roasted pheasant, smoked salmon, and six-pound lobsters flown in from New England.

Such opulence triggered a backlash from her critics. One detractor wrote a letter to the editor of the *Spokesman-Review* in Spokane, Washington, denouncing Lana for flaunting another marriage in front of the public and calling the wedding "a blot on the character of America, that we have a responsibility to uphold the sacred marriage vows, and at a time when so many millions of people are starving, this waste should not have occurred."

Like most things in Lana's life, her nuptials were marred by even more controversy as the Presbyterian pastor, Reverend Stewart P. MacLennan, admitted that he had violated church rules by marrying Topping before the grace period of one year after his divorce from Arline Judge had expired. Another front-page story focused on the search for host Billy Wilkerson's dog, which disappeared during the champagne toast and had not been seen since.

Lana and Topping escaped the chaos and sailed aboard the RMS *Mauretania* en route to their honeymoon in Europe. As the couple spent more time together, Topping showed no signs of violence toward his new wife, despite the warning from Judge, but he began drinking heavily as he was forced to pay off huge debts incurred from a disastrous investment in a midget racing car team in England that went bankrupt. The boozing continued when the couple returned to the States and settled into Dunnellen Hall. Lana soon realized that her new husband had no real job. Instead, he kept borrowing against his inheritance.

"Our grandfather made the money," he told her cheerfully. "Now his offspring are spending it."

The daily routine at Dunnellen Hall resembled the champagne-soaked antics of an F. Scott Fitzgerald novel.

"At Round Hill, the Toppings would throw parties for a hundred, even two hundred people," Lana later wrote in her memoir. "There were twelve bedrooms (in the main house), some of the couples who slept there were married, and some were not, it didn't seem to matter. Couples who were together in the evening would have changed partners by the next morning, when the ritual Bloody Mary's were delivered to their rooms. A majordomo commanded a staff of butlers, all impeccably trained...not to raise an eyebrow."

Topping also owned a fifty-eight-foot fishing yacht moored in Miami, Florida. He had a large mirror installed over the bed in the master suite and urged Lana to agree to a threesome with his brother, Dan. Topping told her that he and his brother had shared Arline Judge when they were both married to her. Lana flatly refused to encourage her husband's hedonistic lifestyle. She had recognized all the warning signs and contemplated leaving him, but by this time, Lana was pregnant with their child. She carried the baby for six months before going into premature labor. Like Cheryl, the baby had Rh-positive blood cells that had entered her mother's circulatory system. Tragically in this case, the child would not survive. Lana delivered a stillborn baby boy.

The trauma over the loss stretched the divide between Lana and Bob Topping. He began gambling heavily, routinely betting $1,000 per hole on the golf course. His drinking increased and his violent nature was no longer dormant. He broke furniture, toppled lamps, and threw crystal decanters against the wall each time Lana confronted him about his gambling. True to Arline Judge's prediction, Topping gave Lana a black eye during one particularly violent row. "Don't injure my face, you bastard!" she screamed at him.

As in her previous marriage to Steve Crane, Lana was now paying most of the couple's bills despite the fact that the IRS was still garnishing her wages, and she knew any bruising or battering of her legendary profile would cost her acting jobs. Amid all the fighting at home, there was also growing concern over her daughter's safety. The FBI was now back in Lana's life. This time, federal agents were investigating a kidnapping plot targeting Cheryl Crane at their twenty-four-room Georgian-style mansion in Holmby Hills.

"I looked out of the window to see a surprising sight on Mapleton Drive," Cheryl recalled in her memoir. "Policemen were stepping from squad cars and fanning out around the grounds... In a short time, they were joined by security guards in tan uniforms with guns on their hips and guard dogs on leashes. Flood lights were installed at points along the fence that edged our property."

Greg Bautzer also hired his own team of security guards disguised as gardeners to patrol Lana's estate. The culprit later turned out to be a distant relative of Mildred Turner's living in Arkansas who had done time in prison.

Lana then hired her own private detective, not to keep a close eye on Cheryl but to follow her husband around Los Angeles. Topping was staying out at all hours of the night, and she had an intuition that he was cheating on her. The investigator gathered evidence of Topping's infidelity and handed it over to Lana. She confronted Topping once more, and this time he fled their house and caught a plane to Oregon, where he would spend the next several weeks fishing while a distraught Lana wallowed in sorrow over another broken marriage and considered suicide. She had meticulously planned her own death. She bought a bottle of sleeping pills and sent Cheryl to stay with her mother. "I'll show them," she said to herself. "Boy will they miss me when I'm gone!"

Mildred saw that Lana was in a dark mood and that her vulnerability might lead her to do something drastic. She asked Lana's business manager, Ben Cole, to stop by her daughter's home for a wellness check. Lana opened the front door in a trancelike state. Cole prattled on about a number of unimportant, everyday topics while she nodded back without engagement. Lana then excused herself to the upstairs bathroom and locked the door. She stared into the mirror and saw through her outward beauty to the fiery wreckage inside her mind and soul. Lana Turner was still the highest-paid actress in the world and adored and emulated by millions, including the iconic Evita. But there was a flip side to that coin. She was a four-time loser in marriage, including the two unions with Steve Crane. Her fame and even her fortune had led her to deceitful and dangerous men—men like her own father, Virgil Turner.

"This is the life that will be lost," she mumbled into the mirror of her powder room. "It doesn't matter at all. There is nothing left to do."

Lana opened the cabinet and reached for the bottle of sleeping pills. She swallowed each tablet methodically and took hold of a razor blade. Lana did not want to be revived, as she felt that it would be another in her long list of failures. She ran the blade across her wrist. Lana saw the blood gushing from her veins across the sink and onto the mirror. She felt no pain as she slipped into unconsciousness.

Moments later, Cole kicked open the bathroom door and found Lana lying on the tile floor, covered in her own blood. He grabbed a towel, made a makeshift tourniquet, and applied pressure to her open wrist. He then called Mildred and a neighborhood doctor, who rushed Lana to the hospital in his car.

CHAPTER SEVENTEEN

THE BEAUTIFUL AND THE BAD

Lana woke up some time later in a darkened room at Hollywood Presbyterian Hospital. She had failed again.

She winced in agony as the doctor began sewing up her wrist. She had cut halfway through a tendon, and her veins had retreated. The surgeon had to stretch the veins and then reattach them. He would later describe the wound as a "jagged laceration across the lower quarter of her left forearm."

Lana cried out for something, anything, to numb the biting pain.

"It hurts, it hurts!" she screamed. "Give me something!"

"Like hell I will," the doctor replied. "You've had enough!"

Lana's physician admonished her for the suicide attempt, reminding her of her beautiful daughter and her successful Hollywood career. Hearing this, she wept in shame. Lana remained in the hospital for two days. Reporters got wind that Lana was being treated and descended on the hospital like locusts. Ben Cole did his best to mitigate the situation, telling the media that Lana had fainted in the shower and cut her arm on the glass door. The story seemed too far-fetched for some cynical newsmen, who asked Lana if she had attempted suicide.

"That's utterly ridiculous," she replied while leaving the hospital wearing an all-white ensemble and ankle-length overcoat to cover her bandaged wrist. "I plan to live to be the oldest woman in the country."

Despite their doubts, reporters played the story straight. The next day's national headline read "Lana Suffers Slashed Wrist in Shower Fall." Her injury was declared "accidental" and a result of her slipping after taking a bath and plunging through the glass door of her shower and tub stall.

Seven-year-old Cheryl had also been told that her mother had suffered "a slight accident" after falling against the glass shower door and breaking it. When Cheryl returned home with Mildred, she ran upstairs to her mother's bathroom and immediately noticed that the door was not shattered. Totally confused, the inquisitive young girl shook her head in puzzlement.

Lana began filming her next movie, *The Merry Widow* with Fernando Lamas, just days after her suicide attempt. Despite her fragile emotional state, the studio wanted her back to work. The injury to her wrist remained bandaged and hidden under a large sparkling bracelet through most of the production.

Lana still received boxes of fan mail each week from both male and female admirers. Stuffed in the middle of one batch of mail was a letter from a young actress formerly named Norma Jeane Baker, now called Marilyn Monroe. Monroe sent two photos of Lana and asked for each to be autographed on the back. "Your signature will be immortalized in my heart," she wrote to her idol.

Monroe's manager was Johnny Hyde, one of the agents who had helped launch Lana's career. He had managed to get Monroe a small role in MGM's *The Asphalt Jungle*, a film noir directed by John Huston. Hyde hoped it would help catapult Monroe's career at the studio. But Louis B. Mayer did not see her potential. "We're already grooming other blondes to replace Lana," he told Hyde. "We don't need another one."

While the studio head saw nothing special in Monroe, Lana found her letter endearing and called Monroe for a meeting. When the two sat down, Lana did not spend much time on pleasantries. Instead, she offered the young actress some constructive criticism along with some truth behind their cold business.

"First, your makeup is all wrong," Lana told Monroe. "Unless you've been cast as a streetwalker along Santa Monica Boulevard." She ran her eyes up and down Monroe's curvaceous figure. "You've also got to get rid of those unfortunate bulges."

Monroe took the criticism well enough, and Lana offered her more tutelage on how to become a movie star. They became telephone pals, and Lana agreed to help Monroe navigate the rough waters of Hollywood despite her belief that the newbie was trying to steal her act.

"They all copy me," Lana later told her personal assistant Eric Root. "They all have the same toner in their hair like I do, and use the same bleach. But there's only one Lana Turner, and that's *moi*."

During the making of *The Merry Widow*, Lana enjoyed a brief fling with her leading man, Fernando Lamas, who had reportedly also been a secret lover of Eva Perón. While their on-screen pairing did not dazzle critics (the *New York Times* called Lana's performance merely "adequate"), their romance provided fresh fodder for the gossip rags. Paparazzi captured the dashing Latin star escorting Lana to just about every hotspot in Hollywood. Lana introduced Lamas to Cheryl as her new "gentleman friend." The actor began spending much of his spare time at Lana's home, even when she was not there. He especially enjoyed sunbathing and swimming in her outdoor pool. One afternoon, as Cheryl played by the pool, Lamas appeared wearing a terry-cloth bathrobe.

"I don't suppose you've ever seen a naked man before?" Lamas asked the child.

Before she could answer, he dropped the robe and stood bare in front of her.

"Nudity is perfectly natural," he told Cheryl before diving into the pool.

He continued to skinny-dip in front of the seven-year-old, ordering her not to tell anyone, especially her mother, about their "little secret."

Before the disturbing truth could be revealed, Lana broke off the relationship herself after an explosive argument with Lamas at a party hosted by silent screen legend Marion Davies at her beach house in Malibu, where a handsome, blond young actor named Lex Barker approached their table and asked Lana to dance. "I'd love to," she said, smiling. The two took to the dance floor while Lamas sat alone and fumed.

After the song ended, Barker guided Lana back to the table under Lamas's watchful eye. "Why don't you just take her out to the bushes and fuck her?" the Latin star shouted loud enough for everyone in the room to hear. Embarrassed, Lana demanded that Lamas drive her home immediately. When they got there, Lamas dragged Lana inside and beat her mercilessly, leaving her with bruises and scratches.

Based on the moderate success of *The Merry Widow*, MGM had paired the actors again in a film to be called *Latin Lovers*. On the day that she was supposed to report for costume fittings, Lana stormed over to studio executive Benny Thau's office and showed him the purple bruises and scarlet-colored scratch marks caused by her leading man. Thau was shocked by the battering and promised her medical attention and a full report of the abuse.

"And I hope you'll keep him away from me," she pleaded.

"Yes," the executive replied. "We'll take care of that."

Benny Thau made good on his promise. He fired Fernando Lamas and replaced him with another Latin star, Ricardo Montalbán. It was an act of chivalry on Thau's part, and it also made financial sense, as the studio had just signed Lana to a new seven-year contract.

In front of the press, MGM described the casting shake-up as a mutual parting of the ways and said "that Miss Turner had no part in the decision and that it was a stroke of diplomacy for which the executive minds alone were responsible."

Latin Lovers lost money for the studio, but Lana received high marks for her performance as the uberwealthy Nora Taylor. The *New York Times* declared the film "short on originality" but wrote that "Miss Turner, on the other hand, never looked lovelier."

Still by far the studio's most bankable female star, Lana was offered the leading role in Vincente Minelli's 1952 melodrama, *The Bad and the Beautiful* opposite Kirk Douglas. The film was promoted as an exposé about "the private lives of the famous and notorious" of Hollywood. Lana played self-destructive movie star Georgia Lorrison. The role was no stretch for her, but it demanded real acting chops. Director Vincente Minelli did not give her many notes and instead told her to trust her gut. Lana gave a bravura performance, one that she felt was strong enough for the Academy to finally take notice of her work. The film would be nominated for six Oscars, including Best Actor for Kirk Douglas and Best Supporting Actress for Gloria Grahame.

Lana threw a big party the night before the nominations were announced. She was confident that her name would be called as a nominee for Best Actress, but her telephone did not ring. Lana was shut out of the award season hoopla surrounding *The Bad and the Beautiful.* Despondent over the snub, she sought out companionship and quickly fell into the arms of another man.

CHAPTER EIGHTEEN

TARZAN THE TERRIBLE

Lana's new beau was Lex Barker, the handsome man who had spun her around the dance floor at Marion Davies's party in Malibu, which had also triggered her violent beating at the hands of Fernando Lamas. Although she had vowed never to marry again, Lana was trapped by the societal mores of the Eisenhower era, when women were looked down on if they did not have a husband to obey and dote on. Any single female over the age of thirty was considered a spinster, and those who slept with men without a wedding ring on their finger were called harlots and sluts. If Lana was going to be in a serious relationship with any man or cohabitate with one, the idea of marriage would have to be on the table. Otherwise, scandal would ensue.

Barker called Lana for a date, and the two had dinner at her house. Physically, he was the type of man she always found alluring. Unlike Bob Topping, Barker was strikingly handsome, stood six foot four, and weighed two hundred pounds of lean muscle, which made him the perfect choice to become the tenth actor to play Tarzan the Ape Man in nothing more than a loincloth on the big screen. Barker made the role his own for sixteen years beginning with his first movie, *Tarzan's Magic Fountain*, in 1949. He was equally impressive off-screen. Barker came from a wealthy family and had attended Phillips Exeter Academy and then Princeton University. He also had a distinguished military career during WWII, serving as a major in the U.S. Army and receiving two Purple Hearts for wounds he received while fighting Germans in the invasion of Sicily.

But on his first date with Lana, Barker got drunk on four glasses of brandy after dinner and passed out at her home. She called a friend to carry him back to his own apartment. The next day, Barker called Lana and sheepishly tried to explain that he had been fighting an infection and that he should not have mixed alcohol with his prescription medication. He sent her a bouquet of flowers as an apology, and to Lana, he appeared sincere. They began dating just as both actors had signed on to film projects in Europe. Barker moved to Rome, while Lana rented a penthouse apartment in Paris's fashionable sixteenth arrondissement. They saw each other between movie shoots, and Barker began pressuring her to marry him.

"I doubt that in today's moral climate, I would have married Lex," Lana wrote in her memoir. "We could have traveled together and lived together, and very few eyebrows would have been raised. But it wasn't that way then. In those days, when you fell in love, you married."

Barker wore her down until she finally agreed to marry him during a small civil ceremony at a sixteenth-century town hall in Turin, Italy. The couple tried to keep the wedding a secret from the press. Lana sent Cheryl and Barker's two children to the movies with a governess while she and Lex slipped quietly into the town hall. Lana wore a pearl-gray dress under an orange topcoat for her wedding. The paparazzi learned quickly of the pending nuptials, probably getting tipped off by Barker himself, and were waiting with cameras and flashbulbs ready at the ancient town hall. Lana tried hiding her face with a handkerchief. When she saw the assembled media, she flew into a rage.

"If the photographers don't get out of here, I won't get married," she told Barker.

He managed to calm her down and even got her to pose for photos. The next day, the headline "Lana Turner, Lex Barker Wed in Italy Ceremony—Film Couple Exchange Shield-Shaped Rings After Photographers Upset Secrecy Plans" ran in newspapers across the globe.

The news coverage of his marriage to Hollywood's biggest female movie star helped bolster Barker's career, as he was hoping to break out from being typecast in movies like *Tarzan and the Slave Girl* and *Tarzan's Savage Fury*. It made sense for him to leak the story to the press. But Lex Barker could keep a secret when he needed to, including the darkest secret of them all.

"Cheryl, I'm your father now," Barker told Lana's daughter. "Why don't you call me Father…or Daddy?"

"Can I call you Po?" she asked.

"Po it is," he said, smiling.

Cheryl Crane, now ten years old, was desperately seeking a stepfather who could love and nurture her. Bob Topping had showered her with lavish gifts but could also be mean-spirited toward his stepdaughter. Once, when her biological father, Steve Crane, was injured in a car wreck, Topping lied to Cheryl and told her he was dead. She was glad her mother had divorced the drunken, erratic aristocrat and looked forward to a healthier relationship with her mother's new husband.

One afternoon in March 1952, Cheryl was sitting poolside at her mother's Holmby Hills mansion when Barker called her over to the nearby sauna. At first, she was reluctant to join him, as Lana had always forbidden her from entering the sauna.

"Come here," Barker said with a polite smile. "I want to show you something."

Cheryl took her stepfather's hand and entered the steam bath. She sat on a wooden bench while he closed the door.

"Have you ever seen what a man looks like naked?" he asked her.

"Yes," she replied nervously. "Uncle Fernando used to swim without clothes."

"In front of you, huh?"

Cheryl nodded.

Barker then asked if Lamas had ever touched her. Cheryl said no.

He then moved closer to her on the small bench and ran his hands across her small breasts.

"Are you sure he never touched you here?" he whispered before moving his hands to her thigh. "Or here?"

Barker took out his penis and began masturbating in front of the child.

"This is a man's rabbit," he said while stroking himself. "The rabbit's growing up and coming out of his nest. See Mr. Rabbit get big?"

Cheryl was terrified. She gripped the side of the bench with both hands and dug her fingernails into the wood. The girl was forced to sit and watch while the grown man jerked off and eventually ejaculated on the floor of the sauna. Barker wiped himself off with a towel and turned toward the frightened youngster.

"Of course, not everyone would understand what *we* just did here," he warned her. "It's something people just don't talk about… From now on, this is going to be *our* secret, you got that?" Using the words *we* and *our*, the pedophile had pulled the child into his conspiracy of silence.

Unsure what to do next, Cheryl sought her own safe space. She dusted her dolls off the shelves of her bedroom, fetched a porcelain pot, saucers, and teacups, and set them on a table for a teddy bear picnic, her hands shaking and lips quivering as she fought to regain her childhood.

Cheryl never called Barker "Po" again. She did not tell her mother what had happened in the sauna. How could she? Her stepfather had specifically told her that she was not a spectator or victim of sexual assault. He had convinced her that she was an active participant in their dirty little secret.

A month later, as Cheryl was still trying her best to block out what had happened, Barker crept into her bedroom just after 8:00 p.m. He was wearing a Sulka bathrobe as he crossed the carpet in the darkness and sat facing her on the bed.

"Time for another lesson," he whispered.

"What?" she asked, startled by his appearance.

"We're not going to make a sound," he warned her sternly. "Now shut up."

Barker then raped the child in her own bed while muffling her screams.

After committing the crime, the Hollywood Tarzan issued another menacing warning to his ten-year-old stepdaughter.

"You know what they do to girls who tell, don't you? They take you away and you never see your parents again. They send you to a place called Juvenile Hall."

The violent sexual assaults would continue for two more years until Cheryl turned twelve and learned the definition of statutory rape. She realized that she would not be hauled off to some juvenile hall if anyone found out what Barker had been doing during his nightly visits to her room. It would be Tarzan who would get put in a cage for preying on a child.

"I'm not going to do this anymore," Cheryl told Barker when he appeared again at her bedside. "You can't make me."

"What makes you think you can stop me?" he sneered.

"I found out that you can get into trouble for this too!" she cried.

Barker's body tensed. "You haven't told anybody?"

Cheryl told him no but that she was considering such an option.

"Don't get smart with me," he scolded her. "Because you're the one that'll suffer. You little bitch."

Barker slapped the young girl across the face and wrapped his strong hands around her throat and started to squeeze. Cheryl thought she was going to die right at that moment in her bed. But the violence aroused Barker, and the idea of murdering the young girl gave way to raping her again instead. After he finished, he left her battered and bloodied. Despite the torture she was forced to endure, Cheryl knew she was lucky. She was still alive, and her only hope to stay alive would be to finally break the code of silence between her and her monster.

Cheryl first confided to her grandmother Mildred, who was stunned by the allegations. Like everyone else, Mildred Turner had never seen any evidence of an improper, criminal relationship between her granddaughter and her son-in-law. Still, by Cheryl's tone and her descriptions of the attacks, Mildred knew the girl was telling the truth. She immediately dialed her daughter and summoned her to her home.

"Lana, I want you to come down here right away," Mildred declared in an agitated state. "It's about the baby [Cheryl]...and don't bring Lex!"

Lana had just returned home with her husband from a dinner party at Jack Benny's house. After the telephone call, Lana picked up her car keys and rushed out the door to Mildred's. When she arrived, Lana found her daughter sitting on the sofa in silence. Lana sat beside her and gently squeezed her arm.

"Tell me darling, what—"

Cheryl cut her off. "It's Lex."

"What about Lex?"

"He's been coming into my room late at night and doing things to me."

Like Mildred, Lana was shocked. "Oh, my God!" she screamed. But Lana demanded more proof. She told Cheryl she would have a doctor examine her in the morning.

While Cheryl remained at Mildred's, Lana drove back to the house she shared with Barker. With rage building inside her, she walked quietly upstairs and into their bedroom. Lana had kept a pistol by her bedside after the foiled kidnap attempt of her daughter. Barker slept soundly while Lana reached for the gun. She stood over her husband with the weapon pointed directly at his head. One shot and he would be dead. Her finger rested on the trigger. She was ready to pull, but she stopped herself. If she murdered Lex Barker in cold blood while he was sleeping in their bed, she would undoubtedly get the gas chamber herself. And what good would she be to Cheryl then? Lana lowered the pistol and left the room. She stayed up for the rest of the night, smoking, crying, and contemplating her next move.

When dawn broke, Barker woke up and searched the home for his missing wife.

"Why didn't you come to bed?" he asked her after he discovered her curled up on a small couch in her sitting room. Her eyes were swollen with tears, but Barker could recognize the hatred behind them. At that moment, he knew his brutal abuse of Cheryl was a secret no more. "What has your daughter been telling you?" he demanded. "She's lying."

If Lana had had the gun in her hand at that moment, she would have shot her husband where he stood.

"Listen, you," she said coldly. "I want you out of here in twenty minutes, and you know why. Cheryl told me everything and we're never going to discuss it."

Barker tried to defend himself once more, but Lana now threatened to call the police on Tarzan the pedophile. He finally left as Lana then drove off to retrieve Cheryl at Mildred's. The girl underwent a pelvic exam that morning, and the doctor confirmed Lana's worst fears. There was evidence of sexual abuse, and it had happened right under Lana's nose. She felt the unbearable weight of guilt because she had invited a demon into her daughter's life and had not protected her. She wept again until her tears gave way to resolve. At that moment, Lana told herself that she would never let anything happen to her family ever again.

CHAPTER NINETEEN

JOHN STEELE

Like any good hood, Johnny Stompanato carried several aliases. To some, he was Johnny Valentine, while others knew him as Thommie Valen. Eventually, he would introduce himself to Lana as John Steele. She would become his biggest score yet. But a budding thief doesn't start his career planning to hit Fort Knox. Instead, Stompanato would have to start small and work his way up to seducing the silver screen's most glamorous star.

Shortly after he arrived in Hollywood, Stompanato had met an attractive thirty-three-year-old actress named Helen Gilbert. With high cheekbones and blonde curls flowing over her shoulders, Gilbert, a musical prodigy from Wisconsin, was discovered while playing cello in the MGM studio orchestra.

"Why are you behind the camera instead of in front of it?" director Fred Wilcox, known for helming Lassie movies and *Forbidden Planet*, asked her.

Gilbert's first paid acting gig was a small role in another in the seemingly endless series of Andy Hardy movies starring Mickey Rooney. Her career was beginning to take off, and she was cast in the plum and soon-to-be iconic role of Glenda the Good Witch of the North in *The Wizard of Oz*. But the classically trained cellist turned actress had a wild streak. Soon after landing the role, Gilbert disappeared with Howard Hughes for several days.

Frustrated studio executives were forced to recast the role with Billie Burke filling in as Glenda the Good Witch, and the rest is history.

As for Gilbert, she was suspended from the studio and eventually fired. She was down and out when she met Stompanato, eight years her junior, while still hoping to resurrect her Hollywood career. Eager for attention, she used her relationship with Stompanato to garner some much-needed ink in the press. Gilbert's marriage to Stompanato was big enough news to secure a small item from the International News Service under the headline "Actress Weds." Gilbert had called the news service from Las Vegas to announce that she had married Stompanato, whom she described as a "ceramics manufacturer."

Gilbert herself was unsure as to her husband's actual occupation. Their union lasted just five months before she filed for divorce. "During our short marriage, Stompanato had no visible means of support," she told the judge. "I did what I could for him."

But her husband was not destitute. In fact, he had plenty of money but could offer no explanation as to where it all came from. He was arrested in the spring of 1952 due to the fact that, according to a news report, "his pockets had too much jingle, jangle, jingle." Members of the LAPD Intelligence Squad busted Stompanato at his luxurious rented home at 21110 Pacific Coast Parkway on the waterfront in Malibu. He had been under surveillance by police captain James Hamilton after he was seen driving around Hollywood in a shiny new Cadillac. When officers raided the palatial home, they recovered two pistols—a loaded .32-caliber automatic and a 7.65-mm Walther automatic. Stompanato also had $2,689.75 in cash tucked into his wallet. It was a lot of money, too much for a guy who supposedly worked in a pet shop or sold shiny ceramic pottery in a gift shop. He spent a few hours in jail before he was let go, and once again, the charges did not stick.

But to keep the ruse going, he scheduled an interview with Paul V. Coates, whose gossip column, "Well, Medium and RARE," ran in the *Los Angeles Mirror*.

"Yesterday, heedless of the possible peril, I made a meet with Johnny Stompanato, one of Mickey's frat brothers," Coates recounted in his column. "And frankly it was pretty discouraging."

They met in Westwood at another of Stompanato's rented apartments, where the gangster told Coates all about the lovebird business.

"I sell perroquets mostly," Stompanato said. "There's more dough in perroquets. Faster turnover."

Coates scribbled down the information Stompanato shared with him about the colorful, miniature parrots. When he looked up, the gangster gave him a deadly stare.

"And listen, what's all that stuff about me being Mickey's bodyguard?" Stompanato asked. "We were just friends. I never even owned a gun!"

The reporter and the racketeer both lit cigarettes and let them dangle from their bottom lips.

"You ever hear a bodyguard without a rod?"

"I never," Coates replied, shaking his head. The reporter then tried to steer the interview toward a juicer topic. "Johnny, who's the new big man of the rackets out here?"

Stompanato avoided answering and kept talking about his lovebirds. Coates then questioned him about the disappearance of a mobster named Frank Niccoli, another of Cohen's henchmen, believed to have been strangled by a member of Jack Dragna's crew.

"What are you asking me what happened to Frank Niccoli?" Stompanato replied angrily. "What do I know what happened to Frank Niccoli?" Before Coates could press him further, Stompanato picked up one of his lovebirds and showed it to him. "Hello, pretty boy," Stompanato squawked as he petted it gently. "They're easily alarmed. Also, they're monogamous. They don't mess around."

Soon after his divorce from Gilbert, Stompanato set his sights on another older woman, Helene Stanley. Like Gilbert, Stanley was blonde and beautiful and had plans to break big in Hollywood. A veteran of several B movies, Stanley later became a Disney darling, serving as the live model for animators for their drawings of Cinderella, *Sleeping Beauty*'s Princess Aurora, and Anita Radcliffe in *101 Dalmatians*.

Once again, Stompanato's impending nuptials generated media attention with this small blurb: "Helene Stanley and Johnny Stompanato have set the wedding date of April 13 [1953]. She played Gregory Peck's first sweetie in [Hemingway's] 'The Snows of Kilimanjaro.'"

Stompanato stayed married to Stanley for two years, although mostly he was staying away for days and weeks at a time while serving his master Mickey Cohen. Occasionally, Stompanato would take Stanley out on the town to Hollywood hotspots like Ciro's, where both would mug happily for the cameras. One photograph showed tough guy Stompanato smiling with a napkin on his head while Stanley laughed gleefully at his side. But his occasional playfulness was overshadowed by his penchant for violence. When Stanley's mother misplaced his handkerchiefs, Stompanato grabbed her by the neck and nearly choked her to death.

Stanley discussed her marital woes with a friend by mail. "I thought Johnny really loved you?" the friend wrote in a letter.

Stanley wrote a reply. "He doesn't; all he cares about is what he can get out of me."

Helene Stanley filed for divorce in February 1955. By now, Stompanato was a known associate of Mickey Cohen's, and a reporter covered the divorce proceedings. The unnamed reporter wrote that Stanley was ending her marriage to Stompanato, described as a "one time bodyguard for Mickey Cohen and auto salesman," on the grounds that he once knocked her down and choked her mother. At this time, Stanley was a regular on television, playing the wife of Davy Crockett on Walt Disney's hit series. She told a Santa Monica Superior Court judge that Stompanato had used "vile language" against her and that he stayed out all night. "He said I was lucky that he ever came home," she said, sobbing in court. "And he told me that I bored him to death."

Stompanato was now going by the name John Truppa, which was his biological mother's maiden name, and Stanley asked and received permission from the judge to change her last name from Truppa back to her real, nonstage name, Helene Frere.

Stompanato saw Stanley as nothing more than a stepping stone in his climb up the Hollywood mountain. The handsome, brutish bodyguard quickly turned his attention to actress Ava Gardner, a friend of Lana Turner and rival for the position of Hollywood's hottest star. Gardner, a raven-haired beauty, was also married to Frank Sinatra, who was known and feared for his Mafia connections. When the crooner found out that Mickey Cohen's right-hand man was making a play for his wife, he demanded a meeting with the boss, who had recently been paroled after serving just under four years of his five-year prison term.

"I gotta see you on something important," Sinatra told Cohen over the telephone.

"Ya know, why don't you come out here now, Frank," Cohen suggested. "They got [a] twenty-four-hour detail on me."

Sinatra drove out to Cohen's rebuilt house in Brentwood and demanded that the crime boss take action against this underling.

"Look, I want you to do me this favor," Sinatra said, staring at Cohen with his famous blue eyes. "I want you to tell your guy Johnny Stompanato to stop seeing Ava Gardner."

Cohen did not care how famous Sinatra was or what his deep connections to the underworld were. He damn sure wasn't going to play Mr. Fixit for Sinatra's love life. Cohen peered out his living room window and noticed the unmarked police car parked across the street.

"You mean to tell me you came all the way out here where they're recording everybody's name and number that comes near this house?" he asked rhetorically. "This is what you call important? I don't get mixed up with no guys and their broads, Frank."

Sinatra was not accustomed to getting dressed down in this manner. At that point, Cohen took out the proverbial dagger and stuck it in his back.

"Why don't you go home to Nancy where you belong?" he asked spitefully in reference to Sinatra's first and long-suffering wife, Nancy Sinatra.

Later, Cohen offered an olive branch to Sinatra and hosted a dinner in his honor at the Beverly Hills Hotel. But again, he would make one thing clear to the singer: there would be no more talk about Johnny Stompanato. Cohen had great affection for his bodyguard and driver. He truly cared for Stompanato and considered him as something of a little brother.

Cohen was doing his best to stay under the radar after his release from prison, but he knew LAPD detectives still considered him their public enemy number one. Fearing police harassment, Cohen's attorney Morris Lavine warned police chief William H. Parker against any "rousting" of his client and threatened criminal prosecution of any cop who violated any federal civil rights statutes in their treatment of Cohen.

"I'm all washed up with gambling," the gangster told reporters after he returned to Los Angeles. "I want no part of it."

Cohen's wife, LaVonne, did her part to convince the public that he had gone straight. "Mickey's going to be a good little boy from now on," she told members of the press.

As a convicted felon, Cohen could not get a liquor license, so getting back into the nightclub business on the Sunset Strip was impossible. Instead, he and Stompanato rejoined forces for another tried-and-true criminal enterprise: blackmailing Hollywood's biggest stars by filming and photographing them in sexually compromising positions. Reportedly among their blackmail victims were superstars such as Fred Astaire, Lucille Ball, Cary Grant, Rock Hudson, and Spencer Tracy. Stompanato kept all the photo negatives inside a wooden box in his apartment.

"The Stompanato-Mickey Cohen blackmail angles will explode into a new and bigger page-one story involving dozens of Hollywood, Broadway and political figures who have been paying off in fear for years," predicted *Confidential* columnist Lee Mortimer, as reported in an FBI memorandum. "The ring is operated out of Chicago…and the glamor boy and gal affiliates employ gigolos of the Stompanato type, babes and homos, while sleazy, slimy little hoods such as Cohen are the front men." Mortimer called Stompanato a "general stooge" for Cohen and "introducer of gals for visiting mobsters, and dancing escort to the star and would-be's."

Beverly Hills police chief Clinton Anderson was well aware of Stompanato's reputation and routinely called him one of "the Wolves of Hollywood."

CHAPTER TWENTY

THE PLAN

Mickey Cohen had an idea. Hollywood was abuzz over the news that Lana Turner had recently been dropped by MGM despite signing a multiyear contract, and he knew the actress was now vulnerable. He and Stompanato had blackmailed several members of Hollywood's elite, but extorting Lana Turner could result in their biggest windfall yet. Lana was a freelancer now, without any protection from the studio. She had amassed a fortune from her film roles and would pay any sum to safeguard her reputation and save her career.

The two gangsters reverse engineered the classic honey trap scheme, using Stompanato as bait to lure Lana into bed. But that was not enough. They would need to stage a threesome of some kind while Cohen's men surreptitiously filmed the sex act. Another man, or even a woman, would need to be brought into the conspiracy. Both Cohen and Stompanato had heard rumors that Lana was bisexual and that she had enjoyed a brief fling with her friend Ava Gardner. Photographs and film footage of Lana Turner engaged in some raunchy ménage à trois would certainly end her career. They would use that fear, hanging it over the actress's head while siphoning off loads of cash from her bulging bank account.

Cohen had access to all sorts of surveillance equipment thanks to his

LAPD eavesdropping friend Jim Vaus and Fred Otash, the same cop who had aimed a shotgun at Stompanato's car a few years before on the Sunset Strip. Otash had turned in his police badge and was now running his own private eye service in Hollywood. Otash also worked for Robert Harrison, publisher of the notorious celebrity rag *Confidential*, which had a national circulation of 5 million readers. In his new role, Otash dug up dirt on Hollywood's biggest stars and set up sex romps and pot parties involving minor and major league celebrities to be used as currency for extortion plots.

Cohen didn't care if Otash had leaned on Stompanato as a favor to Jack Dragna. That was all in the past now. His focus was on Lana Turner, and with any luck, she would be working for him from now on. Cohen had known Lana for years. He had even hosted a champagne breakfast for her and Steve Crane to celebrate their second wedding at a French restaurant he had owned called the Streets of Paris on Hollywood Boulevard. But business was business.

The question was, how would they make the approach?

Lana had put on a brave face in front of the media and tried to spin the story of her ouster from MGM and position herself in the best light possible.

"I bought six stories," she exclaimed to reporter Aline Mosby. "Now I'm talking about casting and percentages. I'm learning a lot about this business. I have a whole new set of muscles working." During the interview, the reporter asked her to reflect on her status as a Hollywood sex symbol. "I can't remember the last time I wore a sweater in a movie. Those days are over; I hope I've grown out of that. I can't compete with Jayne Mansfield and others any more."

During another interview with Hollywood columnist Bob Thomas, Lana said that she felt relieved to be freed from her studio contract, although she still owed MGM five movies over the next five years. "At least I can read scripts from other studios," she told him. "And I can talk about my own deals instead of what the studio tells me to do."

She seemed unnaturally confident for someone who craved stability over most everything else. Before walking off the studio lot after her last movie, *The Prodigal*, she wanted to visit the sound stages that had propelled her career over the past seventeen years, but she believed that would be a sign of weakness. Instead, she traced her finger across her neck as if her throat had been slit, got into her car, and left.

As Lana drove home, she came to the realization that she was aging out. She tried to blame MGM's decision to release her on the studio's excitement over a relatively new form of entertainment. MGM just could not afford to make multimillion-dollar motion pictures in the age of television.

But in reality, the studios were simply adhering to the age-old tradition of replenishing the supply. As Joan Crawford had once been forced from her throne to make way for Lana, she would now have to step down as reigning queen of Hollywood and hand that title over to a younger Marilyn Monroe. It made all the sense in the world, but Lana was devastated—and ripe for the taking.

When she began work on a new movie for Universal Studios called *The Lady Takes a Flyer* in April 1957, she received a mysterious phone call from a man identifying himself as Mr. John Steele. It was the same name that Stompanato had used when he had attempted to date and then extort actress Janet Leigh a couple years prior. Lana had never heard the name John Steele before and told operators at the Universal switchboard that she would not accept his calls.

But one day, while she was seated in the makeup chair, Stompanato somehow managed to get past the switchboard screeners. Lana still refused to take the call, but she asked her makeup artist and close friend Del Armstrong to phone back and find out exactly who John Steele was and what he wanted from her. Armstrong did her the favor and spoke to Mr. John Steele.

"All he wants is to send you some flowers," he told Lana. "I told him there wouldn't be anything wrong with that."

Stompanato followed through on his promise and sent several bouquets to her dressing room the following day.

"There were so many of them that they wouldn't fit into my dressing room," she wrote later. "There was a card, of course, with just the name John Steele and a telephone number."

Lana loved the intrigue and the attention. Stompanato and Cohen had baited the hook. Now they just had to wait for Lana to bite.

She sat with the card for a few days as the scent of the floral arrangement remained strong in her dressing room. Finally, she picked up the card and dialed the telephone number on the back. He answered the phone in a deep-throated voice, one that Lana found "pleasantly masculine."

"The flowers are overwhelming," she began. "But do I know you, Mr. Steele? Have we met?"

He admitted that he did not know her but that he had been admiring her from afar for some time.

"I know your good friend Ava Gardner," he told her.

Gardner was living in England now, so Lana could not reach her quickly to confirm. Mr. Steele continued the conversation and asked her to have dinner with him. Lana made it a rule never to talk to strangers, but there was something so interesting and sexy about him that she did not hang up the phone. She told him she did not date men during film production.

"But on weekends?"

"Weekends, I spend with my family," she told him. "My mother and my daughter."

Stompanato refused to give up. At Cohen's urging, he asked her to lunch and then simply for a cocktail.

It was time for Lana to add a little mystery of her own to the mix. She was enjoying the pursuit. "I have your telephone number and I might call you again if I have some free time." She smiled and hung up the phone.

Stompanato was smiling too. Contact had been made. It was now time to launch into phase two of the operation. He and Cohen believed in the use of overwhelming force, just like sending wave after wave of Marines onto the beaches of the Pacific islands. Stompanato would be relentless in his pursuit of victory.

When Lana showed up to the movie set the next day, she was met with more flowers as well as record albums by her favorite artists. How Mr. Steele had known about her musical tastes, she had not a clue. In all likelihood, he and Cohen had paid people close to her for such useful information. For several more days, Lana put up a brave front and resisted the seduction. Finally, she picked up the phone to let him know he had made his point.

"I'll be working late here [at the studio]," she told him. "But if you'd like to stop by for a drink after I get home, I might be able to see you for a little while. But call first."

Lana gave her mystery man her home telephone number. After the disturbing breakup with Lex Barker, she had moved out of her home in Holmby Hills and was now renting a luxury apartment in Hollywood.

When filming had wrapped for the day, she climbed into her big gray Cadillac, the car she dubbed the Baby Whale, and drove back to her place. She parked in her usual spot outside the building and fetched her script from the back seat. As she turned around, Lana noticed a car parked under a streetlamp across from the apartment house. There was a man sitting inside. With the script in hand, Lana turned back toward the building. She could hear a car door opening and closing behind her. She peered over her shoulder and saw that the man was now following her.

Lana clutched her car keys, holding the jagged edge of one key out to use as a weapon if she had to, raced into the building, and found the elevator. She punched the number to her floor and breathed a sigh of relief as the lift began moving. She was safe—for now. Lana entered her apartment and asked her maid Arminda if anyone had called. The servant said no, and Lana then proceeded into her bedroom. At that moment, there was a loud knock on the front door. Arminda answered while Lana quickly changed her clothes. A short time later, Arminda entered the bedroom.

"Mr. Steele is here," she told Lana.

"But he was supposed to telephone," Lana explained, still unnerved by her frightening retreat in the parking lot. She then paused for a moment. The whole thing was silly. There was nothing for her to be afraid of. It had been a simple case of miscommunication. "What does he look like?"

"A nice-looking man," Arminda said with a grin.

"Well, show him into the living room."

Lana left her mystery man waiting for a few minutes more. When she entered the living room, he stood up off the couch. She looked him over and liked what she saw. He was tall, dark, and muscular. She hid her immediate attraction under a veil of annoyance while asking him if he had been following her.

"Do you drive a black Lincoln Continental?"

"I do."

"You should have telephoned beforehand."

"I didn't mean to start off on the wrong foot."

"Well, you have."

It was no mistake that Stompanato did not follow Lana's order to call her ahead of time. He liked to keep women guessing and on edge, especially those who he wanted to exploit for his own ends.

"Would you like me to leave?" he shrugged.

He stared at her with puppy-dog eyes, and she felt empathy toward him.

"Oh well, you're here now. Just don't do it again," Lana replied, trying to regain the upper hand.

She offered him a drink while Arminda cooked Lana's dinner. They made small talk about their mutual friend Ava Gardner, and he told her they had only dated a few times but it never escalated to a full romance. After the drink, Stompanato, a.k.a. John Steele, asked if he could see her again.

"It's possible," she told him. "But only if you call in advance."

When she returned to her dressing room at Universal Studios the following day, it was packed once again with flowers. He telephoned her, and this time, the switchboard operators allowed the call to get through without hassle.

"Why don't we meet for lunch at my apartment?" she offered.

Stompanato smiled. This had been too easy. A few bouquets of flowers, a brief meeting, and now she wanted sex. But Lana was not interested in an intimate encounter, at least not yet. She asked for a clandestine lunch at her place because she did not want to be seen in public and photographed with a man she didn't really know.

When Lana returned to her apartment for their lunch date, Arminda handed her a tiny package that had been delivered to her door. Lana opened it to find a gold watch and a bracelet inset with diamonds with her initials on the back.

John Steele showed up a few minutes later carrying a silver tray full of vermicelli smothered in white clam sauce. It was her favorite dish. How could he have possibly known?

By now, Stompanato and Cohen had compiled a full dossier on Lana. They knew what she liked and didn't like, both at the lunch table and in bed.

Lana told her suitor that she could not accept such a lavish gift. When she asked him what he did for a living to afford such an expensive watch and bracelet, he muttered something about being in the record business. Lana didn't press further. By now, she was smitten by his dark good looks and his fawning attention toward her. "Whatever his profession was, he clearly knew how to court a woman," she remembered.

After lunch, she invited him into her bedroom to make love. He undressed and presented her with his massive penis, which came with its own nickname, Oscar, because it was the size and shape of an Academy Award.

She had never experienced such passion before, certainly not with Artie Shaw, Steve Crane, and especially Bob Topping.

"He has the stamina of a bull," Lana later told a friend. "He can't seem to get enough. A little rest and he's on fire again."

Completely breathless afterward and lying in bed under moist sheets, she teased him about his finances.

"Do you have a money tree?" Lana cooed while rubbing his hairy chest.

"No," he laughed. "Just the leaves."

In reality, Stompanato was funding the operation through Cohen and with money he received from another con job. While dating Lana, he was also seeing the wife of a wealthy Hollywood doctor. Her name was Rosemary Trimble. She would later deny any affair with Stompanato, but he kept a gold ring with the inscription "From Here to Eternity—Rosemary and John." He also shared three secret bank accounts with Trimble. One of the accounts had a balance of $25,000, which was completely wiped out by a personal check that Stompanato paid to himself for the full amount.

A portion of Trimble's money was used to pay for a full-length portrait of Lana that he had commissioned from a local artist. The painting, of Lana lying on a recliner in her negligee, would later hang on a wall in her apartment.

CHAPTER TWENTY-ONE

THE DREAM

Lana and Stompanato quickly became a hot item as the couple danced and dined all over Hollywood, at nightspots such as Tail o' the Cock on La Cienega Boulevard and most frequently at the Formosa Cafe, where they had their own designated booth. She introduced him to her friends as John Steele. Most of their dinner companions were oblivious to his real identity, but if Stompanato noticed a hint of recognition, he would stare the man or woman down, giving them the signal to stay quiet.

Cafe Formosa and the booth dedicated to Lana and Stompanato as they look today
(photo by Casey Sherman)

One day, Lana's friend and former costar Mickey Rooney made a surprise visit to her apartment. He burst through the front door waving an old copy of *Confidential* magazine.

"Lana, you can tell me to go to hell," Rooney began. "But for your own good, there's something you should know. It's about your friend."

"Well, what is it?" she asked nervously.

"You're seeing a man whose real name is Johnny Stompanato!"

Lana was floored. "But that's impossible. He wouldn't lie to me. We care for each other!"

Rooney handed her the magazine, which contained an article about Stompanato and his criminal ties to Mickey Cohen.

"Lana, I assure you. His name is Johnny Stompanato," Rooney continued. "He has a record. And not only that, he is associated with Mickey Cohen. You've heard of *him*?" Her head began to spin as Rooney continued to quiz her. "Those flowers he's been sending you. Do you know where they came from?"

Lana grabbed a card from the flower shop and showed it to Rooney.

"That shop is owned by Mickey Cohen," he pointed out. "I doubt very much that your friend Johnny had to pay for the flowers."

Hours later, Lana shared the revelation with her friend, makeup artist Del Armstrong.

"Dear God, Lana. I've heard that name," he said and shuddered.

"I can break it off," she told him.

Lana hoped that she would have the strength to follow through, especially when she confronted Stompanato himself. But he continued his chain of lies.

"I've always told you the truth," he told her.

She looked for some small sign of deceit in his tone and demeanor but found none. Stompanato was one cool customer.

"Then why are you using the name John Steele?"

"It's my name, I've been using it for years," he replied nonchalantly.

At that point, how could she argue? This was Hollywood, after all, and Lana had been using a stage name since she was fifteen years old. But Stompanato was not an actor. Or was he? She needed answers.

"John, just give me the truth. Why did you lie to me?"

He paused for a moment, trying to come up with something plausible to say.

"All right, I'll be honest with you," he began. "I felt that if I used my name, you might have read something about me in the papers and made the connection with Mickey Cohen. So my name is Johnny Stompanato, so what?"

"So, I think we'd better cool this whole thing," Lana told him. "I think we'd better not see each other anymore."

Stompanato smiled and let out an awkwardly loud laugh. "Just try getting rid of me."

His response set her on edge. Was it a desperate plea from a lover? Or was it a warning from a very dangerous man?

Lana tried to distance herself from Stompanato. She began dating other men, but Stompanato was relentless. He and Cohen could not afford to let her wriggle off their hook.

He called so often that she had to place her telephone off its hook. She began locking the door to her apartment and her bedroom door in case he managed to break in. Lana's fears were realized one evening when Stompanato climbed up the fire escape outside her building and forced his way into her apartment through a locked back door. Lana awoke to the creaking sound of her bedroom door as it opened. She stared at the entryway and noticed a large figure in the darkness. Before she could let out a scream, Stompanato ran toward her bed and pounced on her. Lana passed out from the terror and awoke to find his hulking body over hers, with a pillow covering her face. He then pushed the pillow away, spread her legs, and attempted to kiss her.

"Get the hell out of here," she yelled. "Or I'm calling the police!"

Stompanato laughed at her again. He knew Lana had just signed on for another movie and could not afford the bad publicity that a police call would bring. Fred Otash and his boss at *Confidential* would have a field day with this. Otash would make sure the police response would be heavy and ultimately embarrassing for Lana.

She did not report the break-in or the sexual assault that followed. Instead, the whole affair made her aroused.

"His consuming passion was strangely exciting," she wrote in her memoir. "Call it forbidden fruit, or whatever. But his attraction was very deep—maybe something sick within me—and my dangerous captivation [with him] went far beyond lovemaking."

Lana hated to admit it to herself, but she was lured to the dark side by the same gravitational pull that had cost her own father his life. Now, instead of pushing Stompanato away, Lana dragged him closer.

He too had a change of heart. Initially, he and Cohen had plotted to extort the movie star, but Stompanato was falling madly in love with her. Still, this did not mean he would not use her for his own personal gain. But the game itself had changed. He was no longer interested in blackmail or dirty sex movies. Instead, Stompanato saw Lana as his ticket to legitimacy in Hollywood. Much like his idol Bugsy Siegel had attempted with the Flamingo, Stompanato was hoping to leave the mob behind and pursue his dream of becoming a successful businessman. For Stompanato, that meant producing big-budget movies in Hollywood. He would use Lana as the key to unlocking his future. In an effort to achieve his goal, Stompanato would have to keep his girlfriend on a short leash. Whenever she got tired of him and threatened to leave, he refused to let her go.

"I'd rather see you dead first," he warned her.

Stompanato forced Lana to keep up with appearances, despite the ongoing tension in their relationship. The more times that he could be seen with her on his arm, the better the chances that he would be welcomed into polite society. Reporters like Florabel Muir followed the couple to public and private events, including a going-away party for Ricardo Montalbán at the Imperial Gardens, a Japanese restaurant in LA, where Lana was photographed wearing the outfit of a "lovely Nipponese maiden." Stompanato was no longer referred to as an associate of gangster Mickey Cohen. Instead, Muir wrote that he was simply "a proprietor of a gift shop."

Mickey Cohen was also making an effort to go legitimate, at least in the eyes of the public. He befriended the Reverend Billy Graham, and the two met in New York City to pray together. Just as Stompanato was now referred to as a gift shop owner, a newspaper account of the bizarre meeting between one of America's most trusted religious figures and one of the nation's most notorious mobsters described Cohen as an "ex-gangster turned nurseryman."

"I'm sincerely interested in anything that's the correct thing in life," Cohen told reporters after reading the Bible with Billy Graham. The reverend, for his part, said he believed Cohen was leading a new life and that he was "sincerely interested in spiritual things." The newspaper reporter went on to write that "Cohen was raised in the Jewish faith, but said that he was never a very religious person."

As he had done before with *Life* magazine, Cohen also offered himself up for another major interview, this time on live television for ABC News in New York with a young reporter named Mike Wallace, long before his iconic tenure on the television news program *60 Minutes*. It was Billy Graham's idea to have Cohen sit down in a television studio with Wallace and answer his questions. It would be a great promotion for Graham's crusade. If he could convert a Jewish killer like Cohen to Christianity, he could convert anybody. Instead, the interview was a disaster for Cohen. He flew to New York City, where he was put up in the Hampshire House across from Central Park. He was paid $2,000 for travel and expenses. When asked during a preinterview what he thought of Los Angeles police chief William H. Parker, Cohen called him a "sadistic cocksucker."

For a young television host like Mike Wallace, Cohen was a gold mine and would help to propel his talk show and elevate his career nationwide. When cameras rolled the next day, Wallace began the interview by asking Cohen if he had ever killed anyone.

"I have killed no man in the first place that didn't deserve killing by the standards of our way of life," Cohen replied. "In all of these, what you would call *killings*, I had no alternative. It was either my life or their life. You couldn't call these cold-blooded killings." When asked again to describe LAPD chief Parker, Cohen sanitized his answer for live television. "This man has no decency, [he is] a known degenerate, in other words, a sadistic degenerate of the worst type…an alcoholic and other adjectives, including 'disgusting.'" Cohen also denied that he had converted from Judaism to Christianity but admitted that Graham had a tremendous influence on him.

After the interview aired, Parker sued both Cohen and ABC for $2 million and demanded a retraction. The case would eventually be settled out of court with Parker being awarded nearly $46,000. Cohen was not happy. He sent a telegram to the newspapers in Los Angeles stating in typical Mickey-speak, "Any retractions made by those spineless persons in regard to the television show I appeared on with Mike Wallace on ABC network(s) does not go for me."

CHAPTER TWENTY-TWO

ANOTHER TIME, ANOTHER PLACE

Mickey Cohen's television interview had kicked up the dust on his long and murderous criminal career and his relationship with Johnny Stompanato. Lana now felt that Stompanato's past was closing in on her, and she was aching to break free. But she remained under his control both physically and mentally. Stompanato had even begun spending time with Cheryl.

He met the girl at a Culver City horse stable, where he had purchased a red Arabian mare named Rowena for her to ride. Cohen had actually paid for the horse. Cheryl was now fourteen years old and stood five feet eight inches tall. She towered over her mother and was a bit gangly, having yet to fully grow into her own body. Cheryl also carried deep scars that no one else could see.

After the molestation at the hands of Lex Barker, she had attempted to run away from Catholic school in April 1957. She recounted the incident years later in her heart-wrenching memoir, *Detour*. "Mother obviously didn't give a damn about me... I had never seen downtown Los Angeles, but I knew it was seedy and that no one would look for me there."

Her disappearance from the Sacred Heart Academy in nearby Flintridge had sparked a citywide police search. While briefly on her own, she met a man at a coffee shop and asked him for a ride to a hotel. The story and her life could have ended there, but the man turned out to be more noble than her movie-Tarzan stepfather. He brought her straight to a police station in East Los Angeles, and Lana was then called to pick her up. The incident was not kept quiet, as someone at the precinct tipped off the press. Cheryl's escapade was front-page news across the country with a headline that screamed "School-Hating Daughter and Lana Turner Reunited." The story also carried a photograph of Cheryl being escorted from the police station by a somber-faced Lana and her father, Steve Crane. Gossip columnist Louella Parsons scolded Cheryl in print for allegedly proving "that the problems of youth are not confined to the poor or underprivileged."

Cheryl soon transferred from parochial school to Emerson Junior High School in West Los Angeles, where Lana could keep a closer eye on her. The teenager learned that her mother was dating Johnny Stompanato during a casual conversation at her mother's apartment.

"Darling, Mother has met a very nice gentleman," Lana told her daughter. "His name is Johnny Stompanato and he has a horse."

Eager to ride the horse, Lana scheduled a visit to the stable a short time later. When Cheryl laid eyes on Stompanato, she was bemused to see "a thick-shouldered man with a suntan and slicked down wavy hair. His boots and Levi's seemed incongruous with a diamond pinky ring."

"Call me John," he told her flatly. He grabbed Lana by her slim waist and headed for the stalls. "She's yours to ride," he told Cheryl while pointing at Rowena. "She spooks easy as hell."

Cheryl was surprised to learn that Stompanato was an expert horseman. He trained Cheryl to ride Rowena over the next few months while she promised to brush the horse and clean out the stall.

A friend of Cheryl's father, Steve Crane, now a successful nightclub owner, kept his horse at the same stable. The friend watched Stompanato's riding lessons with Cheryl and telephoned Steve Crane. "He's putting his hands all over your daughter!" the man exclaimed.

Crane then called Lana's apartment and demanded to speak to her new boyfriend. "My daughter is the most important thing in the world to me," he said in a stern voice. "And I do care what happens to her."

Lana should have seen the warning signs, but once again, she failed herself and Cheryl. While Lana was jumping from film project to film project, she felt no worry that Stompanato was spending more time with Cheryl than she was. He would take the teenager for ice cream and fill her head with the idea of becoming a family.

"I want you to know that I really care for your mother," Stompanato told Cheryl. "Wouldn't it be nice if she and I got married. Then I'd always be your friend like this."

During her summer vacation, he put her to work in his Westwood gift shop where he sold pieces of pottery and wood carvings to tourists. Stompanato barely paid attention to the few customers he had and spent most of his time in a back office talking on the phone.

That July, Lana sent Cheryl and Mildred to a ranch in Colorado where her daughter would have the opportunity to improve her horse-riding skills. While staying in Estes Park, in the heart of the Rocky Mountains, Cheryl was thrown from a horse while riding bareback and suffered broken ribs and a concussion. She was taken by ambulance to a local hospital and then transferred to a medical facility in Denver and fitted for a body cast. Cheryl was injured, embarrassed, and once again front-page news. "Fall Injures Daughter of Lana Turner," the United Press reported. Most reports about the horse-riding accident included Cheryl's previous attempt to run away from school. Lana flew from LA to her bedside in Colorado. She then asked Cheryl why she was prone to such emergencies, especially while her mother was away. It was an odd observation. Cheryl brushed it off and was released from the hospital a week later and sent back to Los Angeles to recover at her grandmother's house in Beverly Hills.

Despite his promise of becoming a family, Cheryl Crane did not fit into Stompanato's lifestyle. Her erratic and even accident-prone behavior was taking Lana's attention away from helping him build his new career. At one point, he even tried to convince the teenager to move to Woodstock, Illinois, and live with his stepmother.

"Mom has a big house," he told Cheryl. "And there are lots of kids like you at Woodstock High School. You could change your name and make a lot of friends. Lana thinks this is a great idea."

There is no proof that Stompanato ever floated this notion to Lana. But with Cheryl out of the way, Stompanato could get Lana to focus on two new movie projects that he had been developing on his own. He told his friends that he was a movie producer now, although he had zero experience financing or making films. Stompanato felt that he did not need to understand the business, as he figured that was what he had Lana for. Hungry screenwriters sent him their scripts with the hope that he would pass them on to Lana, who had just formed her own independent production company called Lanturn Productions. Stompanato found two scripts that he liked, but he did not have the money to option the materials from the screenwriters. When he brought up the scripts to Lana, she brushed him off. She had already found her next movie project. Lana was excited about her new venture and the power she had in owning her own production company, which was very rare for an actor, especially for a woman in the 1950s.

After nearly two decades at MGM and a round-robin of films for other studios, Lana embraced the responsibility of shepherding projects for her own company. She leaned on her columnist friends to spread the word that she was fast becoming the film industry's new power player.

"Hollywood has a new Lana Turner. Claiming her days as a sweater girl and wife are over, the glamor queen has turned producer and sharp business lady," industry columnist Aline Mosby wrote.

During a sit-down interview at her apartment, Lana told Mosby that she could not compete with actresses like Jayne Mansfield and Marilyn Monroe anymore.

Lana also revealed that she had acquired six new projects for Lanturn Productions. "Now I'm talking about casting and percentages," she said with excitement in her voice. "I don't know which way is up. I'm learning a lot about this business. I have a whole new set of muscles working… One day I hope to stay in the movie business, but let somebody else be in the movies. I would just act now and then when the right story came along."

She also confided to the reporter that she had no intention of ever marrying again. Her divorce from Lex Barker was still not final.

"I just try to live my life day by day."

When Stompanato read the article, he wanted to cut her face. Lana had not told him that she already had six movies planned, and none of them were based on his scripts. The fact that she had openly shared her feelings about never marrying again also came as a gut punch. Nothing was going according to his plan. She had not responded to his threats, so Stompanato would have to try a softer tactic now.

"He was gentle, more like the person I'd known at first," she recalled. "He said I must not judge him on his past—he was a changed man, even his threats meant nothing. I would see—the old Johnny Stompanato was long gone."

Lana wanted to believe him. But she had to set aside her feelings about their relationship and instead focused all her attention on making her company successful. She had a great deal invested in her first film, called *Another Time, Another Place*. The script was based on a 1956 novel called *Weep No More* written by novelist Lenore Coffee, who had been cranking out screenplays in Hollywood since 1919. By the time she met Lana, the writer had become jaded by the so-called Hollywood machine and had decided to write books instead. "They pick your brains, break your heart, ruin your digestion," she remarked about the studio system. "And what do you get for it? Nothing but a lousy fortune."

Coffee's story centered on an American reporter working in London during the final months of World War II. The character, named Sara Scott, falls in love with a British reporter, Mark Trevor, who is a married man. After he's killed in a plane crash while covering an RAF mission in France, Sara decides to move in with Trevor's wife and young son while she compiles his war reporting for a new book. Sara grows close to the wife and son and is torn about her affair with Trevor before finally revealing the truth at the end of the film.

Lana loved the complexity of the story and its lead character, whom she would play on the big screen. She was not fond of the title *Weep No More*, and in her new role as producer, she had it changed to *Another Time, Another Place*. She also hired a young Canadian screenwriter named Stanley Mann to adapt the novel. Lana had heard great things about Mann, who had just adapted Arthur Miller's *Death of a Salesman* for Canadian television.

Lana decided to shoot the film not on some Hollywood soundstage but in England, where the story was set. The production would be expensive, but she hoped it would be worth it, both professionally and personally. She needed time and space away from Stompanato, and filming for months in London and Cornwall would allow her that. Stompanato had presumed that he would be accompanying her overseas, but she adamantly refused. "But, I'll write," she promised.

Instead of taking her boyfriend, Lana traveled with her makeup artist Del Armstrong, whom she also made an associate producer on the project. After arriving in Great Britain, Lana met with her director, Lewis Allen, a British native who had once directed propaganda films for Prime Minister Winston Churchill during WWII. Allen was on loan to Lana's company from Paramount Pictures, the studio that would distribute the film. Producer and director huddled over the key role of Mark Trevor, Lana's love interest in the movie. Twenty well-established British actors would be considered, but Allen and Lana decided to offer the role to a complete unknown.

The actor's name was Sean Connery. The twenty-seven-year-old Scottish truck driver, lifeguard, and model had done some minor work in theater, television, and film. Despite his inexperience, Lana believed there was something uniquely special about him. Connery was tall, muscular, and darkly handsome. His sex appeal was off the charts, but could he act? As producer and costar, Lana would have to teach him the ropes.

"He often missed his marks or forgot his key lines, to the annoyance of the director," she remembered. "Because I was co-producer, I had to work to smooth things out to ensure that the schedule went ahead as planned."

Although Lana was safely thousands of miles away from Stompanato, she struggled during her time in England, where the climate was cold and damp and the food was bland. She had initially booked a suite at London's luxurious Dorchester Hotel, but the drive to the movie set was too long, so she rented a large home in Hampstead Heath, which was closer to Elstree Studios, where the interior scenes would be filmed.

In an effort to cheer up his boss and costar, the young Connery rode Lana on the back of his motorcycle across the English countryside, and the two began a friendship that observers believed had turned intimate. Rumors of the budding romance reached Stompanato back in Los Angeles. He had been writing to Lana since production began, and she diligently wrote him back out of fear that he would hop on a plane to England, wanting to hurt her.

"Sweetheart, please keep well because I need you so," she penned in a love letter. "And so you will always be strong and caress me, hold me tenderly at first, and crush me into your very own being."

He wrote her back with equally flowery prose. "My dearest Lana, I am so filled with love for you at this moment, I wish I could write in a hundred languages. I can tell you right now, if I ever get you in my arms again, it will take a team of wild horses to break it up!"

Lana knew she was playing with fire. Her letters of comfort had the opposite of their intended effect. Instead of soothing Stompanato's heart and ego, the letters sent him into a heated, jealous rage. He would kill Connery if he had to in order to have Lana all to himself.

Short on cash, he went to Mickey Cohen and asked him to loan the money for a plane ticket to London. Cohen had given Stompanato $900 to buy the horse for Cheryl, but he was now going through a divorce with LaVonne, and money was tight for the so-called reformed gangster.

"Hey, listen to me, for Christ Almighty" he told Stompanato. "Tell Lana you ain't got that kind of money to live to that standard in life. If she wants you to be in Paris for two weeks, you ain't making that kind of money, and I can't be giving it to you. She ought to understand that. Tell her to send the tickets and you'll go."

Stompanato made a long-distance phone call to Lana in England and begged her for a reunion. She was exhausted after long shooting days and homesick for Hollywood, and in a vulnerable moment, she agreed to his request. She called her travel agent and booked a one-way ticket for him to meet her in London. Stompanato used a fake passport and flew under his alias John Steele.

After a ten-hour flight from LA, he arrived in England and was met at the airport by Lana's driver. He loaded his bags in the limousine and sat in the back like a VIP during the ride out to Hampstead Heath.

At first, the reunion was everything Lana had hoped for. He was loving, kind, and funny. For two weeks, Stompanato acted like the changed man he had promised her he was. But Stompanato wasn't there just to provide companionship; he was trying to muscle in on her production company. He kept telling her about a book that he wished to option. He even suggested starring in the movie himself. Stompanato looked at the handsome but inexperienced Sean Connery as an example of what he could become—a producer and Hollywood heartthrob.

Lana kept resisting his pressure, and that did not sit well with Stompanato. He then brought up the two scripts that he wanted to produce. The first was called *Love Betrayed*, written by Philip Cogburn, about two beautiful women who fall in love with a famous aviator. Stompanato suggested that Lana and

Ava Gardner could play the female leads while he would be cast in the role as the handsome pilot. The second screenplay was titled *The Bartered Bride*, which he thought could be a starring vehicle for Lana and Frank Sinatra. She shot both ideas down. Lana had also refused to let him visit her on the set of *Another Time, Another Place*. In an effort to make Stompanato feel he was not a prisoner in Hampstead Heath, she ordered her driver to take him for lunch and shopping in London.

Stompanato felt emasculated by her treatment of him. He didn't want to be a kept man like the gigolo he once was. He wanted power and prestige. He wanted what Lana had, and he was going to try to take it. His gentle demeanor was not working, and he would have to revert to his true nature as a violent thug. Angry that she was keeping longer hours at the studio while keeping him away from the production, Stompanato accused her of having an affair with Connery. Finally, Lana had had enough.

"Get the hell out of this room," she hollered. "I want you to pack your bags and go home!"

He stormed out of their bedroom for a few seconds and then stormed back in.

"I've had it with your orders," he shouted. "You get this straight. I'm not leaving here and you can't force me out!"

Lana threatened to call the police. Stompanato knocked the telephone out of her hand and grabbed her throat. As he began choking her, she somehow managed to let out a scream.

Lana's thickly built British maid Annie rushed up the stairs and pulled Stompanato off her. He clenched his fists and lunged at Lana once more, but the servant blocked his body with her own.

"Don't come near me," the maid warned him. "I'm not afraid of you. Miss Turner is, but I'm not. So help me God, you come any closer and I'll kill you!"

Stompanato glared down at the fearless, hefty Cockney maid and knew she was deadly serious. He fled to London while Lana tried her best to recover from the attack. Stompanato had choked her so badly that she suffered strained vocal cords. She stayed away from the set for two weeks, telling her director and crew that she had a bad case of laryngitis. The production was forced to shut down in her absence, which cost her thousands of dollars. When Lana finally returned to the set, the director had to settle for filming walking shots and scenes without dialogue until her voice had healed.

Stompanato returned a few days later to check on Lana's recovery. He tried to explain his violent temper to her. "It's because I love you so much," he said.

Lana waved off the hollow apology and ordered him out of the house.

"I'm not gonna leave," he told her. Lana tried blocking out his words, so Stompanato offered her a frightening ultimatum. "I'm serious. I can take care of Cheryl and your mother too. Don't think I won't do it."

He let his threat sink in while Lana choked back tears.

"I can have it done; no one will ever know where it came from."

The following day, while Lana was working, Stompanato bribed her driver to take him to the movie studio. He stuck a revolver in his waistband and hopped in the back of the limo. He arrived a short time later, just as Lana was filming a love scene with Sean Connery. As the actors kissed before the cameras, Stompanato overheard a production assistant telling another member of the crew, "It looks like those two have had plenty of practice."

Stompanato grabbed the gun and moved it to his breast pocket. The director yelled, "Cut!" and the two actors walked off the set, smiling and laughing with each other. Connery had his arm draped over Lana's shoulder. At that moment, Stompanato appeared out of the shadows.

"You keep away from her!" he shouted to Connery.

Stompanato pulled the revolver out of his pocket and aimed it at the actor's chest. Lana let out a bloodcurdling scream. Connery did not cower. Instead he reacted swiftly, grabbing Stompanato's wrist and twisting it behind his back. Feeling intense pain, Stompanato let out a squeal as he dropped the weapon. The future James Bond then spun Stompanato around and delivered a piercing blow to his nose, knocking him bleeding to the floor. Connery kicked away the pistol while Stompanato pulled out a handkerchief and applied it to his gushing nose. "You'll get yours, you motherfucker," Stompanato told him.

Before Connery could punch him again, security guards separated the two men and escorted Stompanato out of the studio.

Chapter Twenty-Three

The Mexican Standoff

Stompanato had been barred from the set of *Another Time, Another Place*, but he was still somewhere in England. Lana was terrified for her own safety, and she could not afford another violent incident on set, as Paramount Pictures could tear up the contract with Lanturn Productions and decide against distributing her film. She had to find a way to get him out of the United Kingdom, so she consulted with her friend and associate producer Del Armstrong.

"Why don't we get him deported?" he suggested.

"That wouldn't be possible, would it?" Lana asked.

Armstrong reminded her that Stompanato had traveled on a fake passport. He was also carrying a firearm, which was against the law in Britain.

"I've already checked," Armstrong explained. "I went to Scotland Yard."

Lana immediately grew nervous. "You did? You told them about me?"

Armstrong shook his head no. "I didn't mention any names. But they would have the cause to do it. Not only is it possible, Lana, it's the only way."

Lana finally agreed to the plan and spoke to a detective at Scotland Yard, explaining the situation with Stompanato. She handed the phone to Armstrong to go over the details.

While this conversation was happening, Stompanato was attempting to call Lana's phone line. The operator tried placing him on hold but instead patched him into the call between Armstrong and the Scotland Yard detective. Stompanato listened silently without saying a word while the two men went over their plan to deport him. When the call was finished, he took a taxi to the movie studio and threatened to kill Lana. Two British police officers appeared and ordered him off the lot and back to his room to pack. Reluctantly, Stompanato obliged and was soon escorted to the airport and ordered onto the next plane back to Los Angeles.

After filming was completed, Lana stayed in England to wrap up dubbing and all other postproduction work. She was glad Stompanato was gone but was growing more nervous that he was now back in Hollywood, where he could harm Cheryl and Mildred. She wrote him a few letters in an attempt to make peace and had her attorney Greg Bautzer keep a close eye on her daughter and her mother. When *Another Time, Another Place* was officially wrapped, Lana decided she would reward herself with a vacation to Acapulco, Mexico. She had just accomplished something she had never dreamed possible: producing her own Hollywood movie. Despite all the turmoil, she had grown as a creative force, and her British crew had even voted her "the nicest glamor girl to work with."

During her most recent correspondence with Stompanato, she mentioned that she would be headed to Mexico after the shoot, but she never gave him or her partners at Paramount Pictures her itinerary. Lana's goal was to recharge her batteries in a quiet, tropical place with no stress. Since there was no direct flight from London to Mexico, she first had to fly to Copenhagen and change planes there for the marathon journey to Acapulco. When Lana landed in Denmark, she was met on board the plane by a man carrying a single yellow rose.

"Who is this from?" she asked.

"A gentleman," he replied. "Would you please step this way?"

Confused, Lana followed the man off the aircraft. It was a late afternoon in January, and winter had cast its bleak shadow over the runway. Lana could not see through the darkness and drizzle as she maneuvered gingerly down the airplane steps to the tarmac. She struggled with the handrail while also holding her purse and jewel case. Lana saw an outstretched hand at the bottom of the steps, and she took it. She mouthed the words "Thank you" and looked up. She was startled to see the face of Johnny Stompanato illuminated by a floodlight on the runway.

Lana froze. *How could he have known I would be here?* she thought.

She turned and took a step back toward the plane. Stompanato grabbed her wrist and squeezed tightly. He guided her away from the plane in silence. Lana was too shocked, too terrified to say a word. He escorted her to the terminal, where a slew of reporters awaited them. Stompanato had set up the whole scene. He had shown that he was a producer after all. Light bulbs flashed in her dazed eyes. Someone handed her flowers. Lana was then asked to sit down and answer questions for her adoring fans from across Scandinavia. She was given a hot cup of coffee and nearly finished it in one gulp. Stompanato sat at a small table nearby, watching Lana like some KGB spy.

Lana fielded the questions as best she could, giving short and robotic answers. After the gaggle of reporters got their quotes from the Hollywood star, they departed quickly, and Stompanato grabbed Lana by the elbow and took her outside to a stretch limousine that was idling on the curb. She continued to smile for photographers until she got into the vehicle.

"What the hell are you doing here?" she asked him with spittle dripping over her carefully colored lips.

"I wanted to surprise you," he said with a sly grin.

"Well, you certainly did!" she shot back angrily.

Stompanato then informed her that he would be flying to Mexico with her. Lana protested mightily and attempted to get out of the limo. He pulled her back down onto the plush seat cushion.

"I'm already booked on the same flight," he said. "Lana, you know in your blood I'm never gonna let you go."

Stompanato then brought up his deportation from England, calling it "some stunt."

"It was the only way that I could convince you we were finished."

"But we're not finished."

Stompanato had been in Copenhagen for several days waiting for her to arrive. During this time, he spent $840 on a champagne party with several women at a luxury hotel and rented a car for $506. When approached with the bills, he told the hotel clerk and car rental salesman, "Send them to Lana Turner." Again, fearing scandal and concerned about her movie and her production company, she paid his debts without protest. He had also racked up similar bills in Paris and Brussels.

Lana felt like she was a hostage who had been kidnapped by a gangland killer. She was right, but there was nothing else she could do now but allow him to travel with her to Acapulco. She was afraid of calling the police again. By traveling with Stompanato, she could keep a close eye on him while keeping him far away from Cheryl and Mildred.

Before touching down in Mexico, Stompanato had already foamed the runway with the press, portraying himself to gossip columnists as Lana's knight in shining armor. "Lana Turner's boyfriend Johnny Stompanato made a hurried trip to Acapulco to be near her," Sidney Skolsky wrote in his column. "And at this writing, their romance is like wow!"

Lana had booked a one-room suite at a luxury resort called Villa Vera. The hotel room had a spectacular view of Acapulco Bay, and there was a glistening swimming pool right outside her door. "You're not staying here," she told Stompanato. "Get yourself a hotel."

Stompanato threw up his hands. "It's January, the big season. You know I can't find any place now."

He asked her to call the concierge and book a separate room for him, one that she would undoubtedly be paying for. The desk clerk told her the place was booked solid. Frustrated, she asked if she could stay at another hotel while Stompanato used her suite. The clerk scrambled and found another room for Stompanato. But it wasn't a room at all. The concierge had placed a cot in a utility closet. Outraged, Stompanato refused to budge. "This has gone far enough," he told Lana. "I'm staying with you!"

She ordered dinner in her suite and shared her meal with him, hoping to calm him down, but he continued to yell at her with a mouthful of food. Lana ordered him to his room, and he left, slamming the door behind him. "I hope I don't see you here in the morning!" she shouted as he stepped outside.

"Oh, you'll see me!"

Early the next morning, Lana heard a loud knock on her door.

"It's John."

She rolled over in bed and tried to hide under the covers while he kept pounding.

"I'm exhausted," she sighed. "Just let me sleep."

"Open the door!"

Lana did not move. Seconds later, she watched in horror as the wooden doorframe began to split apart. Then Stompanato crashed his shoulder through the door.

"God damn you!" he huffed. "You know better than to lock doors on me!"

Lana felt her throat constricting. She could imagine that terrifying scene in England replayed here. Once again, she tried to calm him down. "I wasn't trying to lock you out," she lied. "I was just tired."

Her explanation seemed to placate him. Stompanato told her he had taken a taxi into town the night before and walked the streets for hours, thinking about ways that he could improve their volatile relationship. Lana acted like she cared. She nodded her head, knowing her feigned interest was the only thing stopping him from strangling her in her bed.

"Don't worry, I'll take care of everything," he pledged. "This is going to work. It'll be okay."

Lana didn't believe him, not anymore. But she kept her true feelings to herself. She knew he was a conniving, evil bastard. As he had done in Copenhagen, Stompanato used the Mexico trip as a public relations tool, constantly feeding items to reporters in Hollywood. Occasionally, a columnist would bite. "Lana Turner's boyfriend, Johnny Stompanato (of Italian descent and Beverly Hills), has all the wolfesses gasping in Acapulco, because of how manly he looks in his bathing trunks" wrote Hollywood reporter Earl Wilson. "But they stay away because the word is out—He belongs to Lana."

A few nights after he apologized to Lana, Stompanato proved once again that he was full of nothing but lies and empty promises. He showed up at the foot of her bed while she was sleeping. This time, he had a gun in his hands. He had purchased the weapon from a local gun dealer to fend off iguanas, as he was terrified of them. Now he had the pistol, a snub-nosed revolver, pointed at her head. He stared at her with wild eyes.

"If you aren't going to be with me, you're not gonna be with anyone else," he whispered. "I'm not kidding with this gun. Take your choice."

He slapped her hard across the face. She tried slapping him back, but he punched her in the stomach. Lana doubled over in pain.

She had no choice at the moment. All she knew was that she could not live in fear for the rest of the trip. Instead, she wanted a truce with Stompanato. She wanted to lower his defenses. The only way to do that was to throw herself at him sexually. Lana would offer him her body night after night in the hope that he would not try to kill her again. Her ruse was a success. Even the concierge of the hotel thought they were madly in love. She sat on Stompanato's lap while he sunbathed and fondled him in the pool. Lana made him feel like the man he wanted to be and not the man he truly was. But in reality, she had no love for him, no desire. She put her body on autopilot while her brain worked out some way to get rid of him forever.

CHAPTER TWENTY-FOUR

AND THE OSCAR GOES TO...

While Lana was trapped in Mexico with Stompanato, she received a call from her new agent, Paul Kohner.

"Lana, Lana, you've been nominated for Best Actress for *Peyton Place*!"

"What, nominated?"

"By the Academy," Kohner explained.

Lana was confused. She had filmed *Peyton Place* the year before. The movie was based on a hugely popular and steamy bestselling novel written by New Hampshire–based author Grace Metalious. Instead of playing the role of a stereotypical sex siren, the thirty-seven-year-old Lana was cast in the matronly role of Constance "Connie" Mackenzie, the mother of eighteen-year-old Allison, a beautiful ingenue played by Diane Varsi. Although she was the most recognizable star among the ensemble cast, Lana's screen time was limited.

"I didn't do all that much in *Peyton Place*," she insisted.

"Well, others think it was a wonderful performance," the agent gushed. "Aren't you happy about that?"

The news was so overwhelming that Lana did not know how to feel or react. She had worked and struggled for years to be taken seriously as an actor. There were times when she never dreamed she would be discussed in the same breath as Elizabeth Taylor, Joanne Woodward, and Deborah Kerr, but here she was named alongside each of them in consideration for Hollywood's top prize. Lana was universally lauded for her performance. *New York Times* critic Bosley Crowther called her work "remarkable."

She could not celebrate her nomination in Acapulco thanks to Stompanato's constant barrage of menacing threats. Lana had satiated him with sex, but her Oscar nomination made him feel inferior once again. He showed her his pistol as a symbol of his power over her.

"Just to remind you I have it and that it's still aimed at you."

"And if you killed me, what would you get?" she asked.

"I'd throw myself on top of you and shoot myself," Stompanato replied with desperation in his voice. "If I don't have you, I have nothing to live for."

After spending three months in the hot Mexican sun, Lana returned to Los Angeles, where once again, Stompanato had gathered a welcoming party for her arrival. Photographers captured pictures of Lana faking a smile with Stompanato by her side, along with Cheryl, who greeted them both on the tarmac. Stompanato made sure his silk shirt was unbuttoned to his navel so that his bare, hairy chest was prominent in the photos. The story of their return was splashed on the front page of the *Los Angeles Times* along with a photo. But Stompanato's attempt to generate publicity for himself blew up in his face as the accompanying headline read "Lana Turner Returns with Cohen Figure." In the body of the article, he was described not as a pet shop owner or ceramics manufacturer. Instead, the reporter identified Stompanato as "a former Mickey Cohen associate." To make matters even worse, Lana went out of her way to clarify the situation for the press.

"There is definitely no romantic interest between us," she said, pointing to the deeply tanned gangster.

She knew her words might trigger another beating, but she no longer cared. Her goal now was to distance herself publicly and privately from Stompanato.

Lana stayed at the Bel-Air Hotel while she searched for a house to rent. She felt that her luxury apartment was too small for her now and it sent the wrong message. She wanted to live in the heart of Beverly Hills with all the other movie moguls. Lana found a beautiful two-story colonial mansion with black shutters and a curved brick walkway and tennis court on North Bedford Drive. It smelled of wealth and respectability, and she put a deposit down with a move-in date of April 1, 1958.

In the meantime, for the month of March, she would prepare for the Academy Awards, where not only was she in the running for Best Actress, but she had been tapped by the Academy to present the Oscar for Best Supporting Actor. This meant she would have to choose a bombshell outfit to wear to the gala while also bracing herself to deliver a bombshell of her own.

For weeks, Stompanato believed he would be escorting Lana down the long red carpet on Oscar night. He smiled at the thought of his boyhood chums and his mob buddies reading the newspapers and watching the newsreel accounts that would place him front and center on Hollywood's biggest night. He had come a long way thanks to Lana, and the Academy Awards would provide him with the opportunity to join the elite of the film industry. But his battered and bruised meal ticket had other plans.

Lana told Stompanato he would not be her date for the Oscars and that she planned to take her daughter and her mother instead. She steeled herself for the blow to come. But instead, Stompanato sulked and whined.

"I'm good enough to fuck you, to make love to you and hold you in my arms all night, but I'm not good enough to be photographed with you walking the red carpet?"

The reality was no, he was not good enough for her. But she quickly had to think up another explanation. She decided to blame Mickey Cohen for her decision. Lana cited the recent publicity surrounding the couple and the numerous mentions of Stompanato's ties to the notorious gang boss. She was now running a production company, and she was concerned that investors and film distributors would not do business with her if they believed Lanturn Productions was a front for the mob.

"It's your own fault," she told Stompanato. "If you hadn't been linked to Mickey Cohen, it would be different."

Stompanato agreed it was a bad look. "But you're not going to the ball afterward," he told her.

"If I win, which is unlikely, I have to go," she replied.

Stompanato attended each of her dress fittings. Lana had drawn sketches of a strapless gown with scales and handed it off to her designer, who then created the dress to her specifications, complete with a white lace trim that hugged her lean figure. Lana looked like a mermaid from a Hans Christian Andersen fairy tale.

On the night of the Oscars, Lana added a huge diamond bracelet to her ensemble, jewelry she had won in her divorce from Bob Topping. She poured herself a vodka and soda and toasted her outfit in front of Mildred and Cheryl.

"If they don't like the dress, to hell with them!" she exclaimed before downing her cocktail.

The limousine finally arrived, and Lana, her daughter, and her mother all got in. Johnny Stompanato was nowhere in sight.

The long, black car rolled toward Pantages Theater on Hollywood Boulevard where the ceremony was being held. Lana was visibly nervous; she stared at her trembling hands and recited the names of the Best Supporting Actor nominees under her breath. She was less worried about winning or losing an Oscar than about speaking before a large crowd of her industry peers. She feared she would stumble over the names of two foreign actors among the nominees: Vittorio De Sica, who was nominated for the big-screen adaptation of Ernest Hemingway's *A Farewell to Arms*, and Sessue Hayakawa, who played the cruel Colonel Saito in *The Bridge on the River Kwai*. After navigating heavy traffic, the limousine finally arrived at the red carpet.

"Well, my dear, win or lose tonight, you can definitely be proud of yourself," Mildred told her before the trio stepped out in front of a virtual sea of camera bulbs. Lana and her mother remembered the moment when they had first arrived in Hollywood with their battered suitcases after the murder of Virgil Turner so many years before. Their dream had become their reality. Lana posed radiantly for the photographers with Cheryl, wearing a green chiffon party dress, and the matronly attired Mildred by her side before walking down the ramp into the theater. Standing across the street on bleachers, adoring fans called her name. "Lana, Lana!"

She lost a shoe on her way in and limped to her seat while a publicist was sent back to retrieve her slipper. Lana sat briefly before being ushered backstage. She gazed over the crowd, looking for any sign of Stompanato. It would be just like him to muscle or bribe his way into the event. He was not there. While backstage, Lana exhaled and was given her instructions and told to wait for her cue. She could hear the familiar voice of her friend and Oscar cohost Jimmy Stewart on stage bantering with Janet Leigh and actor Don Murray. Moments later, Lana heard Stewart call her name, and she proceeded swiftly onto the stage in her fishtail dress while the orchestra serenaded her. She smiled when she reached the podium and thanked him for the warm introduction. As the tuxedo-wearing Stewart turned away, Lana grabbed for his arm.

"Jimmy, don't leave please," she said.

"Oh, why? Ya nervous?" he asked.

"No… It's just that I like you!"

Her comment drew laughter and an "aw shucks" comical smirk from Stewart.

"Now I'm nervous," he told the audience as guests erupted with laughter.

Lana then announced the nominees slowly, as to not mispronounce their names. She then tore open the envelope and declared Red Buttons the Oscar winner for his performance in *Sayonara*.

An hour or so later, John Wayne, dressed in tails and white tie, entered center stage to announce the Best Actress recipient. Joanne Woodward's name was called to pick up her first Academy Award, while Lana clapped graciously in the crowd. She had a strong feeling that Woodward would take home the Oscar, so she was not completely disappointed. At least Lana was free from the ordeal of omitting Stompanato's name from her acceptance speech. She could only imagine the headache that slight would have caused her.

After the ceremony, Lana's limo driver failed to show up at the theater. She thought, at least for a moment, that Stompanato had paid the driver to stiff the movie star on her big night. She piled Cheryl and Mildred into a cab, and they drove to the lavish after-party at the Beverly Hilton Hotel, where Lana smoked cigarettes and drank a few more vodka and sodas while chatting with Cary Grant, William Holden, and Clark Gable. Sean Connery was seated at their table. Lana felt secure in the presence of the Scotsman, as he would surely punch out Stompanato again if he tried to crash the party. Connery gazed fawningly at his costar and nudged Cheryl.

"Cheryl, love, look over there at your mom," he said. "That's what I call a star!"

Cheryl watched as her mother held court with Sophia Loren, Kim Novak, and Joan Collins. "I've never seen her this happy," the fourteen-year-old gushed.

Connery danced with Cheryl before Lana cut in and spent the next hour twirling around the dance floor, smiling and laughing with her daughter.

At the end of the evening, another limousine was called to take them all home. Cheryl spent the night with Lana at her bungalow at the Bel-Air Hotel. Both walked barefoot through the garden paths to Lana's two-bedroom suite. Lana fished out the room key from her purse and stepped inside. Music was playing softly in her bedroom.

That's odd, she thought to herself. *I don't remember leaving the radio on.*

Lana escorted Cheryl into the guest bedroom to help her undress. They made small talk about Cheryl's teenage crushes on some of the boys in her class. Lana warned her against getting on the back of any boy's motorcycle, especially after her horse-riding accident in Colorado.

"Oh, I forgot to tell you, I've rented a house, a nice big one on North Bedford Drive."

Lana told Cheryl that her bedroom had its own fireplace and that she would have her own telephone in her room, a must-have for any teenage girl.

"When do we move in?" Cheryl asked.

"April first, one week away."

Cheryl crawled into bed and felt the peck of her mother's lips on her cheek. It had been a great night for both of them, perhaps the greatest night of their lives.

Lana closed the door and headed for her bedroom, where the music still played. The room was dark, but she could see the figure of a man sitting on a chair by her bed. Lana's heart sank. She flicked on the light switch, and there he was, Johnny Stompanato, and he was smiling.

"You didn't expect me, but here I am," he whispered. "You've had your evening of fun, but now I'm here. You can't get rid of me that easily."

Lana did not respond. She walked over to the mini bar and made herself a vodka and tonic to steady her nerves. She downed the glass and faced him.

"John, I don't know why you're here," she said in a low voice. "But you can't stay. Cheryl is sleeping in the next room and the door is open."

"Close it!"

Lana did not want to engage in another fight and begged him to leave. Stompanato refused to move. She poured herself another glass of vodka and drank it.

"Don't have another drink," he said. "You're always boozing."

He then ordered her to sit down and tell him about her night.

"John, I'm very tired, please go home."

"You spent enough time yakking about it with Cheryl, but now you have no time for me? Is that it?"

Once again, she pleaded with him to go. Stompanato sprang from the chair, grabbed Lana's shoulders, and squeezed them hard.

"You no-good bitch!" he yelled loud enough for Cheryl to hear in the next room. "How dare you tell me to leave."

"Please, John, don't do anything," Lana begged with tears streaming down her face, smudging her makeup. "For God's sake, Cheryl is here!"

Stompanato raised his hand and slapped her hard across the face. She felt a burning sensation as one of her earrings pushed into her cheek.

"Don't you dare touch me!" she cried.

"I'm not gonna touch you, I'm gonna give you the beating of your life!"

He then slammed Lana against the closet door. Her head hit the wooden frame, and she thought she was going to pass out. Stompanato grabbed her again and punched her with his closed fist. She fell to the floor. He picked her up and threw her on the bed.

Cheryl was reciting her nightly prayers when she heard the violent commotion coming from her mother's room. She reached for the telephone in the room and thought about calling for help. Would it only make it worse? Would Stompanato kill her mother if Cheryl called the police? She placed the telephone receiver back on the handle and prayed for the violent storm to cease. But Stompanato wasn't finished.

He leapt on Lana and pinned her arms back on the bed.

"No, no, please don't," she whimpered. "Don't hit me anymore."

"Now do you understand?" he hissed. "You will never pull anything like that on me again."

She closed her eyes, hoping he would let her go.

"You will never leave me out of anything," he continued. "If you go anywhere, I'll always go there too. I let you get away with it this time, but never, ever again as long as you live!"

"Anything you say. But get off me. Leave me alone."

Stompanato let out another sinister laugh. He let her off the bed, and she stumbled toward the bathroom. Lana looked into the mirror. Her chin was swollen and her teeth were bloody. She ran the faucet and cupped cold water into her mouth, swishing blood and spitting it back into the sink while Stompanato stood in the doorway admiring his work. He ordered her to bed and sat back down on the chair, watching her closely for the rest of the night. Lana closed her swollen eyes but could not sleep. She pulled the bedspread over her head and pretended he was not sitting only a few feet away glaring at her. When dawn broke, Stompanato reached over and kissed her bruised cheek. Lana kept her eyes closed until he finally left the bungalow.

Cheryl tiptoed into the room to check on her mother. The bedroom looked like it had been hit by a tornado. The closet door was ripped from its hinges, and a broken lamp was left on the floor.

"Good morning, Mama. How are you?"

"A little tired, darling. I didn't sleep well," Lana lied. "How about you? Did you sleep well?"

"Oh, yes," Cheryl lied right back to her. "Just fine."

Chapter Twenty-Five

GOOD FRIDAY

Lana's Beverly Hills mansion as it looks today (photo by Casey Sherman)

Lana moved into her new home on North Bedford Drive in Beverly Hills one week after the Academy Awards. She still wore dark glasses and a kerchief to cover her face, as her makeup did little to hide the purple bruises on her cheeks and chin. Stompanato maintained a terrifying presence, covering her like a glove as she packed her furniture and wardrobe to bring over to the new house. Lana realized she had no silverware to bring, so she headed over to Pioneer Hardware in Beverly Hills, where she bumped into celebrated hair stylist Sydney Guilaroff. They discussed the recent tragedy involving Elizabeth Taylor's husband, Mike Todd, who had perished in a plane crash in New Mexico.

"It's horrible, isn't it?" Lana said of the crash. "Do you think Elizabeth would like me to come out and visit her?"

Guilaroff, a close friend of Taylor's, was staying at her home to aid her in her grief. He agreed that a call and a visit from Lana would be appropriate.

"Call her anytime," the hairdresser said. "And when I tell her it's you on the phone, I'm sure she'll be glad to talk to you." He followed Lana as she continued to browse through the store. "What are you doing at Pioneer Hardware?" he asked.

"We need a new kitchen knife," she answered nonchalantly.

Lana bought a set of knives and then drove to pick Cheryl up from the dentist. The teenager had had a wisdom tooth pulled, and the dentist had given her prescription medication to dull the pain. Lana put her daughter to bed and went about packing the rest of her belongings in her rented apartment. Cheryl drifted off to sleep but was woken up by a loud bang. At first, she thought she was hallucinating. The fourteen-year-old thought she was reliving the nightmare that had occurred back at the bungalow on Oscar night. She quickly realized that her bad dream was all too real. Stompanato was shouting at her mother once again.

"Motherfucker," he told her. "You'll do what I say or I'll cut up your face." Instinctively, Lana touched her bruised cheek while Stompanato smiled. He knew his threat was getting through to her. She was a wreck.

"Maybe I'll have it done for me," he said while working through his plan. "No one will ever want to look at that pretty face again!"

Stompanato did not beat her this time. Instead he marched out the door, leaving Lana trembling inside. Lana went to check on Cheryl.

"Please tell me what it's all about," her daughter pleaded.

"Baby, things aren't good between Johnny and me," Lana confessed. "I don't know what to do."

"Leave him, Mother," Cheryl told her. "Make him vanish."

Lana scoffed at the idea at first. She admitted to Cheryl that she was afraid of Stompanato and that he would cut her face or kill her if she ever left him.

"Baby, he held a razor to my face."

Lana also feared the bad publicity if police were called to remove him from her residence. She was desperate and trapped, but she tried to hide her true feelings from her daughter. She told Cheryl not to worry, and the girl drifted back to sleep. Lana returned to the kitchen and continued to pack. She placed the new set of knives in a cardboard box and taped it shut.

Cheryl spent the evening at Mildred's while Lana finished packing. The next morning, Cheryl woke up to the incessant honking of a car horn outside. Stompanato was in the driveway in a new white Ford Thunderbird convertible. He saw the teenager peek her head out from the curtains, and he waved at her. Stompanato looked like the carefree, harmless boyfriend who she had come to know—before he had brutalized her mother in the bungalow at the Bel-Air Hotel. Maybe she had imagined it after all?

She ran gleefully outside. "Hi, Johnny, have you seen it?" she asked about Lana's new house. "Is it wonderful? Have you seen my room and everything?"

"See for yourself," he replied. "We can be there in three minute. Where's your stuff?"

Cheryl stuffed her bags in the back of the Thunderbird, and Stompanato sped out of Mildred's driveway headed toward North Bedford Drive. Cheryl liked the speed and the roar of the T-bird's engine.

"Faster, Johnny, faster!" she squealed.

He smiled and pressed his lizard-skin shoe down on the accelerator. He gripped the steering wheel as his ID bracelet danced on his wrist. Cheryl could make out the inscription when it flashed in the sun. It read *Lanita*.

They rolled up to the curved driveway at 730 North Bedford Drive and were met by Lana at the front door. Stompanato unloaded Cheryl's suitcases while her mother gave her a tour of their new home. Lana and Stompanato did not speak to each other, but there appeared to be a silent truce between them. Stompanato put some of his clothes in her closet, a sign that he wasn't going anywhere.

"You okay?" Cheryl asked her mother.

"Fine," she muttered.

Lana was suffering alone and needed to confide in someone about her physical and mental abuse. Later in the day, she sat down with Mildred and told her everything—the beatings, the constant threats, and the rapes. Lana was repelled by Stompanato now, but that did not stop him from taking what he believed was his. Mildred telephoned Beverly Hills police chief Clinton Anderson. The police chief was well aware of the menace that Stompanato presented, but his hands were tied. Chief Anderson told Mildred that any complaint against Stompanato needed to be filed by Lana herself.

"Mildred, please have Lana call me about this, will you?" he asked.

Lana never made the telephone call.

A couple days later, on April 4, 1958, Lana went shopping for some pots, pans, and dishware. Stompanato went with her, hovering over her as she picked out more items for her kitchen. Lana admitted that she was not a good cook, but now she was at least willing to try.

Most of the stores were open, even during the Good Friday holiday. They returned to North Bedford Drive in the late afternoon. Lana had scheduled a cocktail hour with her friend Del Armstrong, as she was excited to show off her new home. She opened the front door to find Armstrong already there, making himself comfortable in the living room. Stompanato glared at Armstrong but did not say a word. He knew Armstrong had coordinated his deportation from England a few months before. Armstrong had brought a friend with him, whom Stompanato paid no attention to as he carried Lana's shopping bags into the kitchen. The friend, Bill Brooks, had worked with Lana on the production of *The Sea Chase* costarring John Wayne. While Stompanato was bouncing around the kitchen, Brooks leaned forward on the couch and whispered to Lana.

"Who did you say that fellow was?"

"Johnny Stompanato," she replied.

"I believe I used to know him," Brooks told her. "If it's the same one, we were at military academy together. Kemper, in Missouri. Class of '43."

Lana was startled. Stompanato had never told her that he had attended military school. But what really jumped out at her was Brooks's claim that they had both graduated in 1943. She did the math quickly in her head, and it did not compute. If Brooks was right, it meant that Stompanato was much younger than he claimed to be.

Stompanato entered the room, and Brooks reached out his hand.

"Remember me?" he asked.

"Sure, I do," Stompanato replied nervously before quickly leaving the room again.

With Stompanato out of earshot, Brooks asked Lana what he was like now. She shared a knowing glance with Del Armstrong, and both looked at the floor. Brooks picked up on the message.

"When we went to school together, he was bad news."

"What do you mean?" Lana asked.

Brooks leaned in closer. "He caused a lot of trouble there. He was a thief. I'd be careful of him."

Stompanato's old military school chum had no idea that Stompanato had been battering her mercilessly for months, but he could see the weariness in her eyes. The atmosphere was growing more uncomfortable for everyone, so Armstrong suggested that he and Brooks leave. Armstrong suggested that they all meet for dinner, but Lana told him she had too much unpacking to do. After the men left, Lana marched upstairs to confront Stompanato over lying about his age.

"I heard you say that you never wanted to be seen going out with a younger man like a lot of dames in Hollywood," he said, trying to defend himself. "You once told me that you didn't want to be Norma Desmond supporting a gigolo."

He was referring to the classic Billy Wilder film *Sunset Boulevard*, in which an aging actress, Norma Desmond, played by Gloria Swanson, gets involved with a young screenwriter played by William Holden. Hollywood looked the other way when actors dated younger women. Humphrey Bogart was forty-five years old when he fell in love with and married twenty-year-old Lauren Bacall. There was only a four-year age difference between Lana and Stompanato, but it presented a bad look as far as she was concerned.

He switched topics and asked her to loan him $4,000. He had used her as his personal bank vault since they began dating. This time, however, she flatly refused his request. There was no such thing as a loan to Stompanato, as he never paid off his debts. Stompanato yelled at her and then fled the house. She climbed the stairs to Cheryl's room and found her daughter working on a physiology term paper that was due after the holiday weekend.

"It's too much," she told Cheryl. "I just learned that Johnny has been lying to me about something else, his age. He's not forty-three, he's only thirty-three. That makes me close to five years older than he is. Oh, shit. I'm such a fool!"

Lana began to cry. Cheryl hugged her mother in an attempt to console her. They rocked back and forth for a few seconds until Lana pushed away and braced herself.

"I'm going to get rid of him," she said defiantly. "Tonight. I don't know how. Baby, this isn't going to be easy."

Lana hoped Stompanato would stay gone for the rest of the night and that she could end their relationship coldly with a phone call, but he returned to her North Bedford Drive mansion at 8:30 p.m. He said he wanted to take her to a movie. She agreed at first but then bowed out, telling him she was too tired. Lana did mention that she planned to have dinner with Del Armstrong and Bill Brooks the next night—without him. Stompanato barked at her again, reminding her that he would cut up her face and destroy her movie star looks.

Lana retreated upstairs to her bedroom, hoping he would stay in the kitchen. Instead, he pounded up the steps behind her, breathing down her neck. "You damn bitch! You're not getting rid of me that easy."

Cheryl heard Stompanato's booming voice, which was now drowning out the volume of the television set in her bedroom where she was watching an episode of *The Phil Silvers Show*.

"Now, look. I told you that I don't want to argue in front of the baby," Lana said, referring to her fourteen-year-old daughter.

"Why the hell not?" he countered. "She should hear the truth about you—everything!"

Lana turned around and ran downstairs toward her wet bar off the kitchen while Stompanato followed. She poured herself a drink with trembling hands.

"You break promises!" he shouted. "You said you would go to a movie and now you've changed your mind. And now you're gonna get drunk. You drink too much!"

Lana drained her glass and lit a cigarette to calm her nerves. Her whole body was shaking now.

"Just leave me alone," she screamed.

"You'll do as I say!"

Before he could strike her, Lana rushed back upstairs and locked her bedroom door behind her.

Stompanato failed to notice that a large carving knife that Lana had recently purchased was now gone from its sheath in the kitchen. He raced after Lana and reached for her bedroom doorknob. He jiggled it but could not get in.

"Open this motherfucker or I'll break it down!"

Fearing that he would shatter the doorframe, just as he had done in Acapulco, Lana unlocked the door. Stompanato stomped into the room like a mad bull.

"Don't fuck with me, or you'll live to regret it. That is, maybe you'll live," he warned. "Maybe not. Cunt, you're dead. After I've taken care of you, I'll go after Cheryl and Mildred. I'll mutilate all three of you bitches!"

Lana went black for a moment. All the rage growing inside her had made her blind. Suddenly, there was a frenzy of motion in the bedroom. A sharp eight-inch knife was flashed and pointed at Stompanato. With one thrust, the blade penetrated his abdomen, slicing into one of his kidneys, striking a vertebra, and puncturing his aorta. He stepped away from the knife, a plume of blood now expanding from where the weapon had entered his body. He clutched the gaping wound and groaned. Seconds later, Johnny Stompanato, gangster, conman, and abuser, was dead.

CHAPTER TWENTY-SIX

GET ME GIESLER!

With Johnny Stompanato lying dead in her bedroom, Lana made four frantic telephone calls. The first call was to her mother, Mildred; the second to a doctor; and the third to her ex-husband and Cheryl's father, Steve Crane. Her final call was to attorney Jerry Giesler.

Giesler was on a hot streak. Over the past few years, he had defended Errol Flynn against statutory rape charges, he had represented Charlie Chaplin for allegedly violating the Mann Act (which prohibited anyone from transporting women across state lines for sex), and he fought to free Robert Mitchum after the actor got busted with a marijuana joint at a party in Laurel Canyon.

Giesler sped over to North Bedford Drive in a chauffeured car and was ushered quietly inside Lana's home by Steve Crane and Mildred Turner. He was shown Stompanato's body and immediately called his clean-up man, private investigator Fred Otash, to join him at the scene.

Lana's personal physician, Dr. John MacDonald, had already declared Stompanato dead.

Otash despised Stompanato and was happy to see his lifeless body sprawled out on the carpet of Lana's pink bedroom. Otash looked around the bedroom and got to work. It took the private investigator two full hours to stage the crime scene to Giesler's satisfaction. The attorney gathered Lana and Cheryl in the bedroom. Otash overheard Lana weeping. "My career, what's going to happen to my career?" she sighed between heavy sobs.

Her immediate threat had finally been eliminated. Stompanato was dead and no longer capable of murdering her or harming Cheryl and Mildred. While Lana was distraught with worry about her film career, Giesler had to address his most serious concern—keeping her out of the electric chair. If Lana was to be charged with murder, a prosecutor could have easily proven premeditation given all the fights the couple had engaged in over the past year. Witnesses like Del Armstrong and even Sean Connery would be forced to testify about their volatile relationship.

Giesler huddled with Lana and her fourteen-year-old daughter and painstakingly walked them through his plan. Content with the narrative he was about to weave for police and the public, Giesler finally dialed the authorities.

When police officers were summoned to North Bedford Drive more than 120 minutes after Stompanato was stabbed to death, there was something peculiar about the setup in Lana's bedroom. Investigators were surprised to see that there was little or no blood on the rug, and the bedroom walls were damp and appeared to have been recently scrubbed. Stompanato's body looked like it had been moved from its original location. Also, the cover had been taken off Lana's bed and was nowhere to be found. "It looked like a hog had been butchered on it," Giesler reportedly told friends later on. The murder weapon, the kitchen knife, was located on the sink in the en suite bathroom. The fingerprints on the handle were wiped clean. It also looked like all the bathroom towels were missing from their racks, possibly used to soak up all the blood in the room. Were the bloody linens now stuffed in the trunk of Otash's car to be burned later?

Despite the obvious questions, detectives allowed Jerry Giesler to tell them what they saw. The attorney presented the scenario this way. He said that Cheryl had overheard a violent argument between Lana and Stompanato in the master bedroom and that he had threatened to cut Lana "good." At that moment, according to Giesler, Cheryl ran down the stairs and grabbed a butcher knife from the kitchen. The purpose was only to scare Stompanato, the attorney claimed.

The teenager then rushed back up the stairs to break up the fight between the two quarreling lovers. Cheryl placed the knife on the floor outside her mother's bedroom. She pounded on the door, begging for Stompanato to leave Lana alone. At that moment, she heard Stompanato yell, "Cunt, you're dead!"

Giesler looked at the detectives and then nodded over to Cheryl. "She picked up the knife from the floor and forced her way into the room. She witnessed Stompanato behind her mother with his arm raised, ready to attack," he told police. "She took a step forward and Johnny ran into the blade."

When asked whether Stompanato had any last words, the teenager spoke up. "He said, 'My God, Cheryl, what have you done?'"

Uniformed police officers traced Stompanato's body with chalk, took photographs, and searched every room for evidence. Giesler told Cheryl to change out of her evening robe and into some clothes, as they would need to give a formal statement at police headquarters. They left the crime scene on North Bedford Drive in Giesler's car, while Cheryl's father, Steve Crane, followed closely behind in a police car. Mildred was completely distraught and was driven home by another officer.

The neighborhood was now crawling with police, paparazzi, and curious onlookers. Author Dominick Dunne lived around the corner from Lana in a mansion on Walden Drive. He rushed over to the scene with his wife. "I stood outside Lana Turner's house and watched the comings and goings," he later wrote. "I wanted to be right in there with Jerry Giesler and Lana, listening to them getting their story straight."

Giesler's car pulled up to police headquarters where officers quickly whisked him, Lana, and Cheryl into Chief Anderson's office. The police chief asked Cheryl to explain what happened for the official record.

"Don't ask her, ask me," Lana blurted out nervously.

"Lana, please be quiet," Chief Anderson ordered. "I want to hear it from her."

Giesler nodded to Cheryl. The teenager repeated what her attorney had told investigators at the scene. Both Lana and Giesler were impressed with Cheryl's soliloquy.

"I thought he was going to get her," the girl told Chief Anderson. "I ran downstairs to the kitchen and grabbed the first big knife I could find and raced back upstairs." Cheryl went on to say that as Stompanato turned to attack Lana, "I plunged the knife into his stomach with all my might."

Lana jumped in. "I didn't know what was happening," she claimed. "I thought she was poking Johnny with her finger." She then told the police chief that she had been trying to break off the relationship with Stompanato since Christmas and that she was afraid of him.

Jerry Giesler butted in and declared that the killing was a case of justifiable homicide. The lawyer knew that even if Cheryl was put on trial, the state of California prohibited the death penalty for minors. That would not be the case if Lana herself was charged with the crime.

A police matron was called to Anderson's office to retrieve the teenager.

"Cheryl, go with her," Chief Anderson said quietly. "You'll be spending the night here."

"No!" Lana screamed. "Let me go with her!"

This was not how it was supposed to go, Lana thought. Giesler had not prepared her for the possibility that Cheryl would go to jail.

The fourteen-year-old was taken out of the office and placed in a cell. Lana was allowed to see her a short time later. Her heart sank when she saw Cheryl behind bars.

"Will you open the door, please?" Lana asked the police matron, who stared back with a blank expression on her face. "Open that door!" Lana screamed.

The female guard obliged, and Lana rushed into the small cell, grabbing hold of Cheryl and squeezing hard. The two collapsed on a jail cot, and Lana wept.

"You'll be all right," Lana whispered, her guilt over the entire affair punching a hole in her stomach. "You're the most important one in the world, to all of us. Don't be afraid."

She promised her daughter that she would return in the morning to take her home. Lana kissed Cheryl before stepping out of the jail cell with the metal bars closing loudly behind her.

"I wish I were like Mother," Cheryl told the jail guard. "At least she is able to cry. I can't."

"Then you must sleep," the guard replied.

"I can't," Cheryl said in frustration. "I just can't."

Reporters were gathered now outside Beverly Hills police headquarters. News photographers snapped pictures while reporters shouted a flurry of questions at Lana and Giesler.

"Why won't they let me bring my baby home?" she cried.

"There will be no trial," Giesler said adamantly to reporters. "After all, the girl is only fourteen. There is no justification for a trial."

Gielser escorted Lana into the back seat of his car, where she crouched down and hid away from the circling newsmen and women. Giesler suggested that he take her to a secure and secret location, but Lana just wanted to go home. When they arrived back at the mansion on North Bedford Drive, they saw ambulance attendants carrying Stompanato's body out of the front entrance of the house. He was brought out on a stretcher and covered in a white sheet. Lana could not stifle her scream, which echoed outside Giesler's car. He told her to be quiet.

"Stop it, Lana, stop it!" he said before shoving her down to the floor of the back seat. The attorney ordered her to stay still. He then stepped out of the vehicle and approached the swarm of reporters. "Lana has gone away for the night," he told them. The media had been held far back enough not to have heard Lana's gut-wrenching cry.

Stompanato's body was placed in an ambulance and taken away. The assembled throng of reporters all jumped in their cars and followed the sirens away from North Bedford Drive to the local morgue.

At the same time, Mickey Cohen had pulled up to one of his favorite night spots called the Carousel. He noticed the fountain boy inside with a telephone receiver held to his ear. The kid got excited when he saw Cohen walk in. The fountain boy handed the phone to Cohen. "It's a news guy from the *Journal-American* in New York," the kid said.

Cohen listened.

"Mickey," the reporter began. "Is Johnny dead or is he still alive?"

Cohen's face crinkled. "What the hell are you talking about?"

"What do you mean?" the reporter asked. "Don't you know what happened? Johnny got stabbed!"

"Where, in New York?"

Stompanato had told Cohen that he was planning a trip to New York City with Lana for the Easter holiday.

"No, at Lana Turner's place out there in Los Angeles," the reporter clarified. "In Beverly Hills."

At that moment, Cohen was confused, sad, and angry.

"Well look, let me get off the phone will ya? And I'll find out what it's all about!"

"Will you call me back?" the newsman asked eagerly.

"I'm not gonna promise that I'll call you back," Cohen replied with a frown. "I'm going to run over to Lana's and see what this is all about."

The gangster left the Carousel, hopped back in his car, and drove with abandon over to North Bedford Drive. He pulled into the circular driveway as Jerry Giesler was walking out the front door. Seeing Mickey Cohen, the attorney immediately grew fearful for Lana's safety.

Giesler approached the gangster. "Mickey, do me a favor. If Lana sees you, she's gonna fall out altogether."

Cohen tried to brush past Giesler, but the lawyer begged him to stop.

"John's dead," Giesler confirmed. "The body's at the morgue. Don't blow your top about it. I want to talk with you. I'd go over to the morgue with you, but I don't want to leave her right now. You want to wait out here for me?"

"No, I wanna run over to the morgue," Cohen said anxiously. "I'll see you later. Don't worry about me." He backed away, got into his car, and drove over to the city morgue.

When Cohen arrived, he overheard the medical examiner on the telephone with Stompanato's stepmother, Verena, back in Woodstock, Illinois. "Can you speak to her?" the medical examiner asked Cohen, pushing the phone his way.

"Mickey, are you sure it's really John?" she asked frantically.

"Well, I haven't seen him yet, Mrs. Stompanato," he replied, stifling his own tears. "Because they didn't clear me to see the body or whatever the bullshit."

Verena gave Cohen authorization to identify Stompanato's body, and he was then led down a corridor and into an examination room. Once there, he stood over the body while an attendant lifted the sheet. It looked like Stompanato was sleeping. His eyes were closed, but his body was now cold. Cohen wept for his friend and the man he had originally plotted with to compromise and squeeze Lana Turner for all she was worth. He felt a wave of guilt as he clutched his beefy hands into tight fists.

Cohen then returned to the medical examiner's office and called the stepmother back.

"Yeah, it's John," he confirmed. "He's dead, gone."

She then asked Cohen if he would take charge of the body.

"If you want me to, I'll do it," he told her. "Naturally, I'm not gonna say no. But you know there's gonna be a lot of publicity this way. It's gonna blow the thing out of proportion."

"There's nobody else out there, you're the only one," she pleaded. "I want you to make arrangements to send John back here to Woodstock."

Cohen told Verena that he would fulfill her request.

Jerry Giesler arrived at the morgue a short time later. The attorney told Cohen that Lana's teenage daughter, Cheryl, had killed Stompanato in self-defense while trying to stop him from attacking her mother. The story did not make sense to Cohen.

"Johnny was an athlete... If somebody came to challenge him, he could stand up for himself pretty well," Cohen later wrote in his memoir.

Stompanato was also a combat veteran from WWII. If he could survive attacks from Japanese soldiers and kill in return, how could he have fallen victim to a teenage girl with a knife?

Mickey Cohen promised himself that he would get to the bottom of what really happened between his friend and Lana and would make the guilty party pay for what they had done.

CHAPTER TWENTY-SEVEN

MICKEY'S REVENGE

In death, Johnny Stompanato had become as famous as his idol Bugsy Siegel.

Like the photos of Siegel's gangland murder, which were splashed across the front pages of newspapers and magazines around the world, the black-and-white image of Stompanato lying dead on Lana's carpet in his lizard-skin shoes was shared by news outlets far and wide. A police officer also posed with the eight-inch butcher knife used in the deadly stabbing.

Reporters were working overtime to get any new information about the crime and about Stompanato himself. They spoke to friends back in Woodstock, Illinois, who remembered him as a "likable" small-town boy who never got into any trouble but had glamorous ideals.

Police chief Anderson had gathered his own intelligence on Stompanato and told the press that he was no Boy Scout. Instead, Anderson described the dead man as a known gangster and gigolo.

"He acquainted himself with females of wealthy means," Anderson said. "He courts them, and after he is deeply involved, borrows money and never repays the loan. When the victim's money is dissipated, he becomes interested in another woman. Usually he frequents expensive night spots to meet wealthy-type females."

Stompanato's older brother, Carmine, was asked to address those rumors. "I guess you could call Jack a gigolo," he replied, using his brother's childhood nickname. "But you couldn't call him a hoodlum. He was never convicted of anything."

Stompanato had a minor criminal record, with only two arrests for vagrancy, but he had developed a notorious reputation as a gangster in Hollywood, thanks to his friendship with and his work for Mickey Cohen.

Cohen looked disheveled and was near tears when he arrived at the Beverly Hills police department the following day to formally claim his friend's body. Officers refused to grant Cohen's request, demanding that a member of Stompanato's family show up and sign for the body and his personal effects. The normally nattily attired gangster was unshaven and wore a simple sport shirt that looked like he had slept in it the night before. "Who did it, who did it?" Cohen asked rhetorically to reporters. All reminded him that fourteen-year-old Cheryl Crane was responsible for Stompanato's death. The mobster scoffed at the notion and shook his head in disbelief. "I don't like the whole thing. He made no effort to dodge the knife. It just doesn't jell with me."

The gangster demanded to see Cheryl. He left the lobby and tried to get up to the second floor, where the teenager was sipping tea in her jail cell. She heard the commotion but had no idea that it involved LA's most notorious mob killer. Cohen was ultimately turned away before he could get anywhere near the girl.

This was the response that Jerry Giesler had feared the most. Cohen was too smart to buy the idea that a fourteen-year-old girl could knock off a muscular, tough ex-Marine like Stompanato. Cohen was determined to mete out his own style of justice. And that meant somebody was going to get hurt.

Giesler received a call from an unidentified man a short time later.

"We are sending people out from the east to take care of Lana," the caller threatened. "And they'll take care of you too!"

Giesler was used to such threats, having represented Bugsy Siegel for the murder of Harry Greenberg. Still, they made him nervous. Mickey Cohen was unpredictable, and he was emotionally wounded over the stabbing death of his friend. There was no telling what Cohen would do. Giesler believed his best defense was to go on the offense and throw cold water on the threats, at least for Lana's sake. He reported the call to the police and to the press.

"It's probably all baloney," Giesler told reporters. "But I had to tell [the] police for Lana's and my wife's sake."

Cohen was undoubtedly enraged. He sent his men out on patrol, searching for Lana in Hollywood. At least one of Cohen's henchmen carried a bottle of acid that he had planned to splash in the movie star's face. Gangsters back in New York were against Cohen's revenge plot. Stompanato was a small fish in their big pond, and Lana was a gigantic film star. They could only imagine the kind of heat that would be applied by the FBI if they targeted Lana Turner for maiming or death. But Cohen had never followed the rules laid out by the Mafia, and he would not start now.

An FBI memorandum was issued on April 7, 1958, stating that John Stompanato "was stabbed to death by Cheryl Crane, daughter of movie star, Lana Turner, on April 4, 1958, at Hollywood, California." The memo also noted that "the stabbing is a local crime and not within the Bureau's jurisdiction." The FBI may not have had a dog in the fight, but agents would continue to watch this case closely as it unfolded.

Lana remained secluded in her home on North Bedford Drive. Stompanato's white Thunderbird remained parked outside, along with several police cars. The house had become an impenetrable fortress. Lana ventured out only to drive back and forth to see Cheryl and did so under police escort.

The day after the stabbing, Cheryl was taken downtown to Juvenile Hall, which she later described as a "gray monolith" with heavy-meshed windows. She was ordered out of her blouse, wool skirt, and camel-hair coat. A guard handed her a bar of soap and told her to take a shower. Cheryl was given a prison-standard uniform, a loose cotton dress, and tie-string underpants to wear and escorted to her cell.

"The only sign of life was visible through a small window in the door," Cheryl remembered. "I could see the faces of girls through the chicken-wire glass as they jumped high to get a glimpse of me. I felt like an animal in a zoo."

Her parents visited her on the morning of Easter Sunday. Cheryl ran into her father's arms.

Lana sobbed through the thirty-minute visit, and Cheryl attempted to keep the conversation as light as possible. "I didn't tell them how awful the place was because that would have put a burden on them they couldn't lift."

Lana and Steve Crane told Cheryl they might be able to bring her home the following day. The teenager looked at her distraught mother and did not believe it. Although Cheryl was the one sitting in jail, facing a murder charge, she felt more protective of Lana at that moment. What would happen to her mother's life? What would happen to her career? Cheryl hugged her mother tightly once again.

That Monday, Cheryl was called out of her cell for a predetention hearing. Lana, Mildred, and Steve Crane filed into the Juvenile Hall court-room where Jerry Giesler was already seated at a table with a stack of files in front of him. The attorney told Judge Donald Odell that he would prove that the stabbing was a justifiable homicide, and he requested that Cheryl be released from jail and into the custody of her grandmother. William B. McKesson, the district attorney, argued against bail for the teenager. The judge agreed, telling Cheryl, Lana, and Giesler that she would be safer under guard at Juvenile Hall. Judge Odell was fearful that a crazed Mickey Cohen might kidnap or even kill the teenager.

After the hearing, Cheryl was taken to a day room at the facility where other juvenile offenders sat around playing cards and talking. The fourteen-year-old was an instant celebrity to the other girls in the room, who recognized her and asked her if she killed Stompanato. One female prisoner told Cheryl she did not believe she had committed the crime. "I bet your mother really did it," the girl said.

"I did it, I did it, I did it," Cheryl shouted back.

When Lana returned home to North Bedford Drive, she climbed up the stairs to her bedroom where her tormentor had taken his last breaths just two nights before. She took a powerful sedative and drifted off to sleep.

Images of Johnny Stompanato invaded her dreams. A long knife appeared in her subconscious, but who was wielding it? Was it her? Or was it Cheryl? It was all a blur to her now. Lana tossed and turned in her bed as she waited for morning to arrive.

But there would be no rest for Mickey Cohen. He was going to hurt Lana any way that he could. Since she was surrounded by a cone of police protection, Cohen would need to find another way to exact his revenge—at least for now.

The press had run with Giesler's narrative that Cheryl had killed Stompanato to end the months of verbal and physical abuse he had subjected her mother to. Cohen knew there was another side to the story, but he needed proof. That evening, he ordered burglars to break into Stompanato's apartment at the Del Capri Hotel in Westwood. Wearing masks, the men cut through the screen in the bathroom window and climbed inside. Cohen had told them what to look for. With flashlights in hand, they searched the apartment until they found a box containing undeveloped rolls of film featuring Stompanato having sex with various famous and semi-famous women (none of them were Lana) and a shaving kit that was filled with two passports and several letters written between Stompanato and the movie star. The burglars brought the items to Cohen, who buried the film for safekeeping but held on to the shaving kit. He then called columnist Walter Winchell and told him to meet at the Mocambo on the Sunset Strip. Cohen was going to offer Winchell what he thought was the biggest scoop in the whole Turner-Stompanato affair.

According to an FBI memo sent directly to Director J. Edgar Hoover in April 1958, Cohen turned the letters over to Winchell for both his column and national radio broadcast. Cohen also told Winchell that he had obtained two passports for Lana and Stompanato. This information seemed far-fetched, as Lana already had her own passport, which she had used to travel to Britain and then to Mexico. Cohen had most likely helped Stompanato get a passport under the pseudonym John Steele. In the report, Winchell called Cohen a "pathological liar."

Cohen also told Winchell that Stompanato's family was planning to bring a $1 million lawsuit against Lana. The columnist typed up the story and sent it to his editors. Winchell was then informed that the story was going to be "killed" because Stompanato's family members had refuted the claim. Winchell invited an FBI agent to meet him at the Beverly Hills Hotel to retrieve the letters, which were being kept in Winchell's safe deposit box at the hotel.

"Please review these letters and return them to me," Winchell told the federal agent.

The agent informed Winchell that the deadly stabbing was outside the Bureau's jurisdiction.

Winchell said he believed the letters violated federal extortion laws and demanded that they be reviewed immediately.

Mickey Cohen knew he could not trust Winchell, so he made carbon copies of the letters and went shopping for a friendly reporter who would print them in the newspaper.

The *Daily Reporter* published portions of twelve letters that Lana had written to Stompanato while she was filming *Another Time, Another Place* in England.

"My dearest darling love, all I want to write and say is that I love you," Lana wrote. "It was so wonderful to hear your voice again, Daddy!... Remember how much you mean to me. I have so many things whirling around in my brain to write to you—but bear with me—the next letter has to be better and longer. Until then, keep your arms around me so close and kiss me as I do you a thousand times." She signed the letter *Lanita*.

Cohen told his favorite reporter, Florabel Muir, that he had obtained the letters prior to Stompanato's death and that he knew nothing about the break-in at his apartment. He then tried to turn the focus back to the film star. Cohen said he was releasing the letters as proof that his friend was not an unwelcome guest at Lana's house, saying that he was "burned up over the way she acted after Johnny was knifed to death." He also accused Lana of being callous and cheap. "Lana and [Steve] Crane have shown no decency at all in this terrible accident," Cohen complained. "They wouldn't even tell Johnny's brother how he died. They didn't even offer to pay for the funeral, even if they did it as a grandstand play."

Cohen was also feeling the sting of a fresh conviction for battery and disturbing the peace. He had been put on trial for the brutal beating of a waiter for spilling coffee on his hands during a dinner to honor Sammy Davis Jr. at the Villa Capri, which was co-owned by Frank Sinatra. Cohen claimed that he was trying to protect the singer's elderly father from getting knocked over by the clumsy waiter. Despite the overwhelming evidence of his guilt, the gangster tried to blame Lana for the jury panel's decision to hold him accountable.

"A couple of hours before I'm due in court, she [Lana] says she's afraid of a reprisal by the mob," Cohen stated. "Then she asks for police protection, so naturally everybody thinks I'm guilty of punching a waiter. I used to think Lana was an okay gal, but now I know better. She's trying to ruin my reputation."

Jerry Giesler had not allowed Lana to read any of the news accounts following the Good Friday stabbing of Stompanato. She had been pilloried by the press as reporters dredged up her father's murder from long ago, all her disastrous marriages and subsequent divorces, and Cheryl's runaway attempt and horse-riding accident. But somehow, Lana received word that her letters to her dead beau had been leaked to the press by Mickey Cohen. She was sickened and depressed by the news and could only imagine what millions of people thought when reading them and cackling over all the affectionate words she had once used to describe her monster.

Giesler fretted over the letters too and wondered how they could impact the official inquest into the stabbing, which was scheduled for April 11, 1958, where Lana's career and her daughter's freedom would hang in the balance.

CHAPTER TWENTY-EIGHT

THE PERFORMANCE OF A LIFETIME

After the publication of Lana's love letters to Stompanato, his brother, Carmine, demanded that she and her daughter, Cheryl, both submit to polygraph tests. Like Cohen, he could not digest the idea

Lana Turner testifies at Stompanato Death Inquest on April 11, 1958 (Courtesy: Associated Press)

that Stompanato had been slain by a fourteen-year-old bobby-soxer. "My brother was six feet tall, he didn't drink. He stayed in good shape all the time. I just don't understand how a little girl like that would have taken him by surprise."

The elder Stompanato made these remarks to reporters as his younger brother was being laid to rest in his hometown of Woodstock, Illinois. Cohen had paid to ship Stompanato's body home and financed the funeral. Before guests were allowed into the funeral home, the crime boss paid a secret visit, standing over his dead underling's open casket, which was draped with an

American flag. Cohen placed his hand over Stompanato's heart. The deceased gangster wore evening wear and was dressed as if he were headed out for a night of dancing and not a cemetery. Cohen made sure Stompanato was outfitted in a lace-tufted tuxedo shirt with a black initialed handkerchief sticking out of the pocket of his slick suit coat. Cohen paid his respects and left a large purple wreath behind. It was unsigned.

After Cohen departed the funeral parlor, some six hundred mourners formed a long line as they each filed past the casket. A few hundred more onlookers stood across the street from the funeral home, soaking in the spectacle, as Stompanato's stabbing was the biggest news to hit Woodstock in years.

"I get a kick out of feeling a glamorous and wealthy movie queen was madly in love with him and no girl around here would have him," one woman said. "He was considered trash."

Another witness countered the claim, telling a reporter, "He was an operator with the girls. He was doing that in high school."

Inside the funeral home, Reverend Cecil Urch, pastor of the First Presbyterian Church, read the Twenty-Third Psalm. "The Lord is my shepherd, I shall not want," Urch preached. "He restores my soul; He leads me in the paths of righteousness, for His name's sake."

Stompanato's former high school principal sang the hymn "Abide with Me" before Stompanato's body was carried out of the funeral home and driven to Oakland Cemetery on the edge of town, where his casket was lowered into the ground beneath a tall elm tree. A seven-man rifle squad from the American Legion fired a three-round salute to the ex-Marine and WWII veteran, while his brother, sisters, and stepmother wept.

It was a glorious send-off for an ignominious man. When questioned by reporters after the service about Stompanato's criminal past, Reverend Urch replied, "I never praise the dead. If they deserve it, everyone knows what kind of life they led. So why gild the lily?" Urch said he was unfamiliar with the dead man. "I didn't know Johnny from Adam's off ox," he added, using a popular phrase of the time.

Stompanato's ex-wife Sara and their ten-year-old son, John Stompanato III, did not attend the service. Sara had remarried and was now living in Indiana. When she was asked about her ex-husband, she said, "He had a good heart, you know. But he never grew up."

An autopsy had been performed before the burial, and the medical examiner reported that Stompanato was suffering from congenital polycystic kidney disease and probably would not have lived a full life anyway. This was of no comfort to Carmine Stompanato, who pushed for a continuance of the official inquest into his brother's death so that a more thorough investigation could be mounted. His request was denied, and coroner Theodore J. Curphey scheduled the hearing for April 11, 1958.

Jerry Giesler was doing his best to shield Lana's daughter from more scrutiny. He called Curphey and urged that Cheryl not be called to testify.

"She has made a signed statement," he reminded the coroner. "I think the best interest of the girl would be served if she didn't testify."

Curphey agreed but ordered depositions from Lana, Steve Crane, and every police officer who had responded to 730 North Bedford Drive on the night of the stabbing.

Verena Stompanato hoped the inquest would reveal more information about Lana's involvement in her stepson's violent death. "I only feel that they should share the guilt," she said, referring to both Lana and Cheryl Crane. "I don't want that little girl to suffer all her life."

On the morning of the hearing, Mickey Cohen released another letter to the press; this one was penned by Cheryl to Stompanato. She had written the note during study hall at school, and it is filled with the typical musings of a giddy teenager. Cheryl wrote to Stompanato about her horse Rowena, her recent election to the student council, and her breakup with a jealous boy. She signed off with the words, "Love ya & miss ya loads, CHERIE."

Cohen told reporters the letter was proof that Cheryl adored Stompanato and would be the last person likely to murder him in cold blood.

The official inquest into the stabbing of Johnny Stompanato was held in a courtroom on the eighth floor of the towering Hall of Records building on Spring Street in downtown Los Angeles. Reporters and curious onlookers had been gathering outside there as early as 6:00 a.m. on the morning of April 11, 1958. Seats were set aside for the first forty spectators who arrived, while 120 seats were held for members of the media. ABC had set up a pool camera to film and share footage with other television networks.

Wearing a gray coat over a gray tweed dress and silver nail polish, a compliment to her perfectly coiffed platinum-blonde hairstyle, Lana pulled up to the building in a limousine twenty minutes before the hearing was set to begin at 9:00 a.m. She was flanked by a swarm of police officers, guarding her from any attack carried out by Cohen or his thugs. Cohen had already shown up for the hearing, which was presided over by coroner's deputy Charles C. Langhauser, and was the first witness scheduled to testify. He was ordered to take the witness stand so that the bailiff could swear him in. Cohen bullied his way to the bench and raised his right hand. Satisfied that everything he would testify to was now under oath, assistant district attorney William McGinley asked him to identify a photograph of Stompanato for the coroner's jury of ten men and two women. Cohen gazed at the panel and then addressed McGinley.

"I refuse to identify him because I may be accused of his murder."

Cohen's statement drew a loud roar from the gallery of onlookers. When asked to clarify his reasoning, the crime boss pointed a finger at Beverly Hills police chief Clinton Anderson.

"He said that Johnny and Lana were going together to finance my operations," Cohen replied, alluding to the honey trap that had set the wheels of their explosive romance into motion. "If he can say that, he can say anything and I'm not gonna testify about anything!"

Cohen was immediately excused from the courtroom. He smiled as he left the building. It was a triumph of sorts for the gangster, who still had jail time looming over his head for pummeling a waiter at the Villa Capri.

Spectators viewed the stubby Cohen just as they would a newsreel or cartoon short played in a movie house before the featured attraction. Before the main event, they patiently sat through the testimony of a few more witnesses, including a visibly shaken Mildred Turner; Steve Crane, who said under oath that Cheryl had called him and admitted that she stabbed Stompanato because he was about to hurt Lana; and the responding Beverly Hills police. Sitting nervously with her attorney Jerry Giesler, Lana was finally called to the witness stand.

"Please state your name," the assistant district attorney asked.

"Lana Turner," she replied.

"Where is your address?"

"730 North Bedford."

"Miss Turner, when did Mr. Stompanato arrive at your residence on April 4, 1958. Approximately what time?"

"A little past 8 o'clock," she replied.

"Would you please tell the jury the series of events from your first meeting with Stompanato [that day] until the conclusion of his death?"

Lana told the panel that Stompanato had picked her up at two o'clock in the afternoon to go shopping. She mentioned buying some light bulbs and even visiting a pet store, but she remained mum on the knife she had purchased at the hardware store that day. Lana went on to describe the cocktail hour with Del Armstrong and his friend but never mentioned that she got angry with Stompanato for lying about his age to her.

"Did you have an argument with Mr. Stompanato before he left your house the first time?" the prosecutor pressed.

"Well, not exactly an argument at that point," she claimed. "My friends had asked me if I would be able to perhaps have dinner with them and I said no…it was very late notice…and that if I was to go out, I would have to arrange for my mother so that she could either come to my house or my daughter could go to her as she was never to be left alone." Lana went on to explain that Stompanato got mad with her for even considering the idea that she would go out with friends without him.

So far, Lana had been forceful in her delivery to the jury, but now her voice was starting to crack. Assistant district attorney McGinley offered her a glass of water. The inquest was jam-packed with reporters, photographers, and scandal-hungry spectators, and the heat was rising in the courtroom. Lana was beginning to sweat in her tweed dress, and she dabbed her forehead with her handkerchief before continuing her testimony.

The atmosphere was surreal to her. It reminded her of a scene from *Peyton Place* in which her character was forced to testify in a murder trial. Her performance in that scene had garnered her the Academy Award nomination. Now, the lights were shining on her and the camera was rolling, but there was no director to yell, "Cut!"

She had prepared for her testimony with Jerry Giesler and treated it as if she were running lines for a movie, but this was now all too real. The prosecutor was going off script, and Lana was growing more nervous.

McGinley walked Lana through her recollection of the next couple of hours, landing on Stompanato's return to her mansion in midevening. Lana told the prosecutor that she had spoken with Cheryl, who was home from boarding school, earlier that day. "I told her that I'm going to end it with him tonight, baby, it's going to be a rough night. Are you prepared for it?"

"And when you told Stompanato it was over?" McGinley asked.

"He grabbed my arm and Mr. Stompanato started shaking me and cursing me badly, and saying as he told me before, no matter what I did or how I tried to get away, he wouldn't let me," she declared. "He said that if he said for me to jump, I would jump, and if he said for me to hop, I would have to hop."

Lana then paused, took another sip of water, and wiped away a tear from her cheek.

"He would even cut my face or cripple me," she continued. "And beyond that, he would kill me, my daughter, and my mother."

Everything Lana had told the prosecutor and the jury had been the truth up to that point. She then explained that she had tried in vain to shield her daughter from the violent storm that was now churning in Stompanato's warped mind.

"He was holding me and I turned around to face the door, and my daughter was standing there, and I said: 'Please, Cheryl, please don't listen to any of this. Please go back to your own room.'"

Lana testified that Stompanato then went into her closet and pulled out one of his jackets on a hanger and walked back to her with the hanger raised, "in a way like he was going to strike me with it. And I said, 'Don't ever touch me again. I am absolutely finished. This is the end. I want you to get out.'"

Lana looked over to her lawyer before continuing. Giesler nodded his head, giving her his approval to carry on. She was now going to offer the most pivotal testimony in the official inquest. It was make-or-break time for the Oscar-nominated actress.

"And after I said that, I was walking toward the bedroom door and he was right behind me. And I opened it. And my daughter came in, and I swear it was so fast."

Lana broke down sobbing, clutching the rail of the witness stand for support. The prosecutor gave her a moment to compose herself as the jurors hung on every word.

"I truthfully say I thought she had hit him in the stomach. As best I can remember, they came together. But I never saw the blade. Mr. Stompanato grabbed himself here," she said pointing to her midsection.

"For the record, the abdomen?" McGinley asked, clarifying Lana's testimony for the court stenographer.

"Yes, sir. And he started to move forward, and he made almost a half turn and he dropped on his back and when he dropped, his arm went out."

Lana had perfectly described the position that Stompanato's body was left in when police arrived. A photo of the crime scene had appeared in nearly every newspaper and was now seared in the minds of the jury.

"I still didn't see that there was blood or a wound until I ran over to him. And I saw his sweater was cut. And I lifted the sweater up and I saw this wound."

Lana added that she and Cheryl grabbed two wet washcloths and applied one to Stompanato's forehead and another to the wound.

"And she kept saying, 'Mommy, I didn't mean to do it. I didn't mean to do it.'"

Lana told the prosecutor that she tried to claim responsibility for the fatal stabbing when police arrived later. "And it is true. I did beg, 'Please—can't I say that I did it?' Because that's all I could think of at the time, that my daughter not be involved in anything like this."

Moments later, everyone's attention turned to the back of the room where a young man wearing dark sunglasses stood up and shook his fist.

"I want to testify," he demanded. "This whole thing is a pack of lies! The girl was in love with Stompanato. There was jealousy between the mother and the daughter over Johnny. He was a fine gentleman."

The mysterious man at the center of the outburst was named Stephen Trusso. He had been ordered by Cohen to raise the possibility that Stompanato had been the victim of a lover's triangle. Cohen had heard rumors that Cheryl had been molested by her stepfather Lex Barker, and he believed privately that Lana murdered Stompanato after catching him in bed with her daughter. It would explain why Stompanato was caught off guard and had no defensive wounds. It would also demonstrate why the bedspread had gone missing from Lana's mattress.

Trusso's demand was ignored by Charles Langhauser, and the man quickly fled the courtroom. When reporters caught up with him on the street, he told them, "Lana Turner wasn't trying to get rid of Johnny Stompanato, it was the other way around. He was trying to unload her and she wouldn't stop calling him, pestering him. That's what really happened!"

Lana stepped off the witness stand after giving two hours of graphic testimony and collapsed into the arms of Giesler and her mother, Mildred. She put on dark sunglasses and was rushed out of the courtroom and driven back to her home at 730 North Bedford Drive.

The coroner's deputy ordered the twelve-member jury into chambers for their deliberation. The panel of ten men and two women reviewed all the evidence presented in the sensational case for only twenty-three minutes before issuing their decision. They returned to the courtroom and handed Langhauser a note. The coroner's deputy ordered everyone in the room to remain silent while he read aloud the verdict.

"We [the jury] find the death was justifiable homicide committed by said Cheryl Crane in the belief that her mother's life was endangered."

The vote was ten to two.

A wave of applause spread across the courtroom. Jerry Giesler quietly thanked God that his legal strategy had paid off.

"After all I heard today, and unless some new facts are uncovered, it would not be my inclination to prosecute her [Cheryl Crane] on criminal charges," Los Angeles district attorney William B. McKesson said after the verdict. "In that event, she would be free and right back where she started."

Lana was notified of the decision after she had returned home. She too breathed a sigh of relief. She had placed her faith, her future, and her daughter's freedom in the capable hands of famed Hollywood attorney Jerry

Giesler. And after all the abuse and pain caused by nearly every man in her life, beginning with her father, Virgil, Lana Turner had finally come out victorious.

But the celebration was short-lived. When Giesler returned to his office after the verdict, his office telephone rang.

"You'll be killed for representing the people who took Johnny away from us," the caller told the defense lawyer. "We're gonna get you for getting Lana's daughter off. This is no kidding."

Before Giesler could respond, the phone went dead.

CHAPTER TWENTY-NINE

THE AFTERMATH

Johnny Stompanato was dead and buried, Lana was exonerated from any wrongdoing, and the coroner's inquest jury had ruled that Cheryl's act had been "justifiable," but the process of getting her released from police custody was still a complicated matter. Cheryl had lost four pounds while being locked up at Juvenile Hall. For exercise, she paced the length of her cell, walking heel to toe and then taking giant steps.

"All I wanted to know was, when am I getting out?" she remembered. "In this hardened environment, I had to go along to get along. I was also learning to talk street talk, to distrust authority and to doubt my worth."

A hearing was set in late April 1958 to review the evidence once again and determine where the girl would live if she was released from Juvenile Hall. Until then, juvenile court judge Donald Odell said it would be best for Cheryl to remain in police custody and to be "removed from all outside influences." Odell told Lana, Giesler, and Steve Crane that several possible outcomes would be considered if the teenager was to be let out of jail; Cheryl could be freed without reservations, she could be made a ward of the court and released to one of her parents, or she could be made a ward of the court and placed in a private or state institution.

Lana had not considered the third alternative and wept as she left

Juvenile Hall, where Cheryl was spending her days in her cell or out in the playroom discussing her situation with her caseworkers while doing her best to avoid the other young prisoners.

"She looks good, but has a slight cold," Steve Crane told reporters outside Juvenile Hall. "Sure, she's homesick. She's counting the days like anyone else."

Crane had hired his own lawyer, Arthur Crowley, to serve as Jerry Giesler's cocounsel.

"We will be fully prepared at the hearing to prove that there is no necessity to make Cheryl a ward of the juvenile court," Crowley promised. "We will prove through witnesses who will testify that Cheryl is a healthy and normal girl and that the death of Mr. Stompanato was merely an unfortunate accident in her life."

The fourteen-year-old was not allowed to read Crowley's quote in the newspaper or any other mention of her case while incarcerated, which was a good thing, since her tormentor and rapist, Lex Barker, had gone to the press with his own story about his former stepdaughter.

"Lana is far better than Cheryl, who appeared really earmarked," Barker told a reporter from the United Press. The actor had given the interview while in Rome, perhaps trying to create his own narrative about their relationship, should Cheryl tell authorities the disturbing details of his late-night trips to her bedroom. "That girl has always been a real disaster," Barker added. "She's the world's most spoiled girl… She's very strange, two-faced." The actor also alluded to Cheryl's allegations that he had repeatedly molested her while he was married to Lana. "My divorce depended on Cheryl… [the girl] told a story to her mother. I denied that it was true. But Lana always had one great fault, to believe her daughter first, though knowing that she was a girl full of complexes and accustomed to lie."

Jerry Giesler feared that a knock on Cheryl's credibility would not bode well for the teenager at the next court hearing. Judge Allen T. Lynch presided over the proceedings at the courthouse in Santa Monica, California. Unlike with the media circus that had surrounded the inquest, Lynch ordered the hearing closed to reporters and the public.

Lana arrived just before 9:00 a.m., with Jerry Giesler and Mildred at her side. Lana had recently moved out of the rented home at 730 North Bedford Drive and was now living in a small house on Canon Drive, as she could not stay in the same room where her onetime lover and abuser had been stabbed to death. Lana waited eagerly for Cheryl to arrive at the courthouse in a station wagon escorted by her two caseworkers. There was a heavy police presence outside, as authorities were still wary of Mickey Cohen and his gang. Cheryl was given a fresh, blue cotton dress to wear at the hearing. She had been allowed to take a sit-down bath, but she still felt dirty. Cheryl was also embarrassed to have three weeks of hair growth on her legs. The teenager saw her mother smoking nervously outside the hearing room and asked her for a puff.

"I don't know if I should," Lana said, gazing around the corridor for disapproving eyes.

"Oh, for God's sake, give the kid a cigarette," Mildred urged.

Cheryl took her mother's cigarette and inhaled the smoke deep into her lungs. She exhaled, watching the cloud of smoke drift to the ceiling before handing the cigarette back to her mother and entering the courtroom.

Eighteen witnesses were called to testify at the hearing. Although the district attorney had promised not to press criminal charges against Cheryl, Judge Lynch still held the discretion to order her to be tried as an adult for murder or manslaughter, since the results of the coroner's inquest were not binding in juvenile court. But Lynch had a teenager daughter of his own, and he treated Cheryl in a paternal manner as the hearing got underway.

The initial sparring in the courtroom was not between the judge and lawyers but between the attorneys themselves, as Giesler and Crowley battled over which parent, Lana or Steve Crane, would be the best choice to care for Cheryl if and when she was acquitted. The judge examined their qualifications for custody as well as their financial standings. Crane earned a nice living in the restaurant business, and Lana was a big movie star. Crane said he had paid all Cheryl's medical bills after her horse-riding accident in Colorado the previous summer and had received no money from Lana, who was now deeply in debt in her new production company Lanturn and was still repaying loans provided to her by her previous studio, MGM. Lana was also paying Jerry Giesler $1,000 per day and would see film profits only if the upcoming release of *Another Time, Another Place* was successful.

"A great part of me would like very much not to continue [in films]," Lana told the judge. "However, the fact is that it's the only work I know, and that I have been the sole support of my daughter and my mother. I wish I could say that I had enough put away that I wouldn't have to work. I don't. I must continue working."

Finally, it was Cheryl's turn to speak. Judge Lynch asked her which parent she would prefer living with if she were to be released.

"My grandmother," Cheryl replied.

The judge mulled her request. He then floated the idea that Cheryl could be placed in a boarding school under a different name in a different city to avoid any unwanted publicity.

"What would you think of that, Cheryl?" he asked.

"No," she replied flatly.

"You'd rather stay here and fight it out?"

"Yes."

"Now, that's courage," he told her.

Judge Lynch then heard arguments from the attorneys regarding the stabbing itself, along with more witness testimony. After ninety minutes, the judge handed down his decision. Cheryl would not be criminally charged, but she would remain a ward of the State of California until she was eighteen years old. Until that time, she would be released into the custody of her grandmother, Mildred Turner. The judge also decided that her parents could see her no more than once a week and were prohibited from taking her across state lines.

Dozens of reporters flocked around Lana as she left the courthouse in Santa Monica. Police officers formed a protective shield around the movie star as she was escorted to Giesler's limousine.

"I'm very happy," Lana told members of the press. "It was what I was praying for."

"It's a great relief for both parents to have their daughter out of Juvenile Hall," attorney Crowley added. "Both Steve and Lana are very happy."

Cheryl was escorted out of the courthouse by her caseworkers and her grandmother. While officers kept a watchful eye out for Cohen and his henchmen, they did not seem to notice two women in flowery hats slip their way through the police barricade. One of them reached Cheryl and stuffed two blue envelopes in her hand.

"Don't read them, don't read them," Mildred ordered.

The teenager did not listen. Once in the car, Cheryl tore open the envelopes and found legal letters inside. The girl had just been handed a subpoena to testify in a wrongful death suit filed by Johnny Stompanato's family.

It was yet another card for Mickey Cohen to play in this drama. He convinced Stompanato's brother, Carmine, to file a lawsuit against Lana for $1 million, just as he had promised Walter Winchell. Carmine, who worked as a barber in Woodstock, had no idea how to proceed with such matters and leaned on Cohen for guidance. The gangster told him he needed a local attorney in Woodstock to develop the legal paperwork. They found a small-town lawyer named Charles Parker to represent both Carmine and Verena Stompanato.

"We want to do all we can to clear Johnny's name," Parker told reporters. "It's just a question of how to go about it."

Cohen had airmailed Carmine Stompanato a transcript of the coroner's inquest.

After reading the transcript, Carmine lashed out at investigators. "No one told the whole story at the inquest," he complained. "There are a lot of loose ends in the investigation. A civil suit ought to clear them up."

Once the lawsuit was filed, Cohen's plan was to hire a lawyer in Los Angeles who was equal to the eminence of Jerry Giesler. When he announced the strategy to reporters, Carmine and his wife got upset. "We've given Mr. Cohen no instructions," Ruby Stompanato claimed. "If you ask me, Mr. Cohen talks too much!"

Mickey Cohen fervently believed that Lana had murdered Stompanato and had the chance to confront her with the allegation while both were dining at La Scala, a popular Italian restaurant in Beverly Hills. The gangster walked past Lana's table without noticing her. Lana's eyes followed Cohen through the restaurant before he sat down in a booth with members of his entourage. Fearing that Cohen would shoot her dead at her table, Lana rose quietly and slipped out the back door of the restaurant without touching her food.

Cohen remained angry and heartbroken over Stompanato's death, as he bore the responsibility of placing him in Lana's path. The honey trap he had set for Lana had become a bear trap for his friend and associate Johnny Stompanato.

Around this time, a Hollywood lawyer named Louis Blau turned up at Lana's home carrying a little box. Blau told her he had received the box from her former maid, Arminda. The maid claimed Stompanato had given her the box for safekeeping when he flew to London to confront Lana on the set of *Another Time, Another Place*. Stompanato had told Arminda the contents of the box were very valuable to him. Blau opened the box in front of Lana and pulled out a spool of exposed film.

"Now look at it," he said.

Lana took a strip of film and held it up against the light. Each frame showed Lana lying on a bed naked.

"Do you remember him taking these pictures?"

She shook her head no.

Another image showed a woman on the same bed with them performing fellatio on Stompanato. The photo was blurry, but Lana could see a woman with blonde hair inserting his cock in her mouth. Lana did not recognize the woman who gave John a blow job on film, nor did she remember engaging in a threesome. But then she recalled one weekend afternoon when John handed her a stiff drink. Lana fell into a deep sleep and did not wake up for several hours. She had blamed her blackout on overtiredness combined with the heavy alcohol content in her cocktail. But now, she suspected that Stompanato had drugged her.

Blau deduced that Stompanato did not take the pictures for his own personal porno stash but instead held on to them in an effort to blackmail her.

"Do you have any scissors?" Blau asked Lana.

She fetched a pair of sheers, cut the negatives into small pieces, and burned them in an ashtray.

Mickey Cohen's original plan to extort a truckload of money from Lana had gone up in smoke. But that did not mean the mobster still wasn't going to stick it to the movie star any way he could.

Cohen ordered Carmine Stompanato to hire another attorney, William J. Pollack, to handle depositions in the wrongful death case. Pollack was considered to be one of the best plaintiff lawyers in the United States. Instead of representing Stompanato's brother and stepmother in the case, Cohen thought the best strategy would be for his friend Pollack to represent Stompanato's ten-year-old son, John Stompanato III, who barely knew his father. The estimate for the $1 million lawsuit was lowered to a number that was more palatable to the judge—$750,000.

Cheryl was ordered to give her deposition behind closed doors at

Pollack's Hollywood office in June 1958. Pollack and Cheryl's attorneys Giesler and Crowley listened intently as the teenager tried to recount what had happened two months earlier. Because of the time restrictions the judge had placed on Cheryl as a condition of her release from Juvenile Hall, she had not had much opportunity to confer with her parents or her lawyers. During the deposition, Cheryl said Stompanato fell with his head against a dresser and his feet pointing toward the foot of the bed. Attorney Pollack claimed there was no way he could have fallen that way. "I think there are wide discrepancies between Lana's description of where the slaying happened, and where Cheryl said she saw the body lying," Pollack said after the hearing. "I am encouraged."

During the coroner's inquest, Lana had testified that Stompanato was fatally stabbed near the door of her bedroom, but Cheryl was now indicating that it happened on the other side of the room where the crime scene photographs were taken. Speaking to reporters, Pollack also claimed that Cheryl could not remember killing Stompanato. "She remembers going into the room and going toward John but not pushing in and pulling out the knife."

In early August 1958, the Los Angeles Superior Court reviewed Pollack's complaint and decided there was enough evidence to order a civil trial in the wrongful death case with Lana and Steve Crane both named as codefendants. In the complaint, the attorney accused Lana and Crane of negligence in summoning a local doctor instead of calling for an ambulance with the proper medical equipment that might have saved Stompanato's life. But more explosive was Pollack's assertion that strong doubt had been raised as to whether Lana or her daughter stabbed Stompanato or whether one assisted the other. Pollack was now linking Lana directly to the deadly incident as a coconspirator or as the killer herself.

The attorney also dropped another quarter of a million dollars from the lawsuit and was now seeking damages of $500,000 for the dead gangster's son. Without the legal case, Stompanato's estate was worth only $274, which included $50 in cash. When the story broke about his meager net worth, newspaper editors mocked him with headlines such as "Johnny No Millionaire; He Just Lived Like One" and "He Lived Big and Died Little."

A police search of Stompanato's apartment uncovered a .32-caliber revolver, two large photographs of Lana, and an inexpensive good luck charm from his ex-wife Helene Stanley. Detectives also found his little black book, which held the telephone numbers of June Allyson, Anita Ekberg, and Zsa Zsa Gabor, all reportedly honey-trap victims of Stompanato and Mickey Cohen.

While the case was pending, the juvenile court judge refused to allow Cheryl to return to her mother or her father. Instead, the girl, now fifteen years old, would stay with Mildred Turner. She enrolled as a student at Beverly Hills High School, where a school official praised Cheryl's work ethic and said that she was "very quiet and apparently happy here."

The school official did not mention that Cheryl was teased mercilessly by her classmates.

"Have you heard the assignment they gave Cheryl Crane?" one student asked a group of friends. "She works in the cafeteria in charge of knives."

Cheryl pretended not to hear the snide remark. "The knife joke was a horror for me," she remembered. "I'm told there were several Cheryl jokes going around the student body of 2,000… Before long I sort of melted into the crowd."

Cheryl dated a boy but felt no attraction for him. She was confused about her own sexuality until she read a lesbian pulp fiction novel written by Ann Bannon called *Odd Girl Out*. Cheryl recognized herself in the novel's main character, a shy college freshman named Laura Landon who falls in love with a sorority girl named Beth. Cheryl devoured more Bannon books and even asked her grandmother to read them. But Mildred was appalled by the material and later burned all the books.

As Cheryl continued to have relationship issues with Mildred while also navigating her return to teenage life, her mother was attempting to get her own life back on track. Lana signed with Universal Studios for a costarring role in the film *Imitation of Life*, where she would be paired with Sandra Dee and Robert Alda. Lana had initially believed the shocking scandal would be the end of her career. And while her movie with Sean Connery fell flat at the box office, her film *Peyton Place* received a 20 percent boost in ticket sales after the stabbing of Stompanato.

Lana may have lost out to Joanne Woodward for the Best Actress Oscar in 1958, but she ran away with the prize of "Biggest Hollywood Story of the Year." In December, national newspaper columnist Bob Thomas touted Lana and Johnny Stompanato for topping a year of scandal "when Hollywood's dirty linen was aired in public display." Thomas listed his top ten stories in Hollywood for 1958 in his year-end column. He placed the Stompanato stabbing first on his list, ahead of Mike Todd's deadly plane crash and the love triangle between Todd's widow, Elizabeth Taylor, Debbie Reynolds, and Eddie Fisher. "The death scene in Lana Turner's bedroom was more dramatic than any that could be concocted in a movie. Lana's daughter was cleared in the death, but the tragedy is not over."

Not by a long shot.

CHAPTER THIRTY

FADE OUT

Where was he getting all his money? That was what reporters and federal investigators wanted to know about Mickey Cohen, who in early 1959 still wore $250 custom-tailored suits and tipped waiters $100 at Mocambo while owing half a million dollars in back taxes. Cohen's only visible means of support was a silent partnership in a local ice cream business.

"He certainly isn't making it selling ice cream cones," one LA police official groused. "No ice cream man alive can pick up $200 tabs in nightclubs night after night."

Cohen referred to himself as an ex-mobster and was now living in a modest split-level apartment on Barrington Avenue in West Los Angeles and, in his words, "living off loans from friends." Yet he was still treated like the godfather of the Hollywood underworld, and once again, the IRS was after him. No one believed he had simply retired after a long life of crime, greed, and violence. Cohen proved he was still dangerous when he ordered a rival named Jack Whelan, known to reporters as an underworld muscleman and a lone-wolf bookie, murdered at a place called Rondelli's Restaurant in Sherman Oaks, California. Whelan had gone there for to meet with Cohen and to collect a $900 gambling debt, but he never reached his table. The bookie was shot and killed just six feet from where

Cohen was dining. Cohen was arrested on suspicion of murder, but the charges did not stick.

Three pistols were recovered from a trash can outside Rondelli's Restaurant. One of the guns had been registered to Johnny Stompanato. Detectives believed the firearm had been stolen from Stompanato's apartment along with his love letters to Lana shortly after he was stabbed to death.

While Los Angeles detectives grew more frustrated with their pursuit of the gangster, the IRS painstakingly and methodically built another strong case against him. Once again, Cohen could not outrun or outsmart government auditors and accountants. He was arrested and later convicted on charges that he had failed to pay $300,000 in taxes over a five-year period. Cohen was sentenced to serve fifteen years at Alcatraz, the island prison that had once held his hero Al Capone for the same offense.

When Alcatraz was closed for good, Cohen was transferred to a federal penitentiary in Atlanta. It was here that the devil went down to Georgia to finally collect his debt from the lying, murdering extortionist. After decades of close calls that included wild shootings and a destructive bomb blast at his home, Cohen was forced to feel the same pain that he had inflicted on others. One day, while the forty-nine-year-old gangster was working as a clerk in the radio and television shop of the prison, another inmate and former mental patient named Berl Estes McDonald crept up behind him and crushed his skull with a two-foot piece of lead pipe. Cohen dropped to the floor, bleeding profusely from an open wound in his head. He slipped into unconsciousness and remained in a coma for two weeks with a compound depressed fracture to his skull. Mickey Cohen would survive the attack, but he would never be the same again. The beating left him partially paralyzed.

Prior to the beating, the wrongful death lawsuit that had been engineered by Cohen against Lana was settled out of court for just $20,000, which was a huge drop from the previous demand of $500,000. Part of the reason for the deflated number was the judge's mistrust of Mickey Cohen, whom he called "a hoodlum" in court. He was also surprised that Lana's lawyer was willing to settle the case instead of going to trial.

"I don't want to tell you how to run your case," the judge told Lana's attorney Louis Blau. "But if it had been me, I would have been 1,000 percent sure that there is such a person as John Stompanato III before I parted with $20,000."

Lana felt great trepidation when she arrived on the set of her new film, *Imitation of Life*, in late 1958. The movie was a remake of another film that was based on a bestselling 1933 novel written by author and activist Fannie Hurst about race relations in America. Lana had read the script and believed *Imitation of Life* was life imitating art as far as her personal story was concerned. But Lana was desperate. She needed to work and quickly grabbed the offer from Universal, which paid her only $2,500 per week. To save face for his client, Lana's agent, Paul Kohner, also got her a cut of the movie's back end. It was a small perk, and neither thought it would generate any money.

Lana was excited to perform again, even though the role would be the most challenging, yet the most close to home of her long career. She was cast as Lora Meredith, an aging actress and single mother battling through a strained relationship with her teenage daughter, Susie, played by sixteen-year-old Sandra Dee. Lana's most pivotal scene came late in the film when she attended the funeral of her best friend. The set was dressed with a blanket of flowers covering a casket. Mahalia Jackson's haunting singing voice echoed through the Harlem church where the scene was being filmed.

"When I heard the first strains of that song in rehearsal, I simply broke down," Lana later recalled. "Images of my own life, my own dark fears flooded my mind and I dissolved into tears."

Lana ran from the set and locked herself in her trailer. Her hairdresser chased after her and found the distraught movie star curled up in a chair, weeping uncontrollably. The hairdresser attempted to comfort Lana and urged her to go back and finish the scene.

"I can't, I can't," she said amid breathless sobbing.

The hairdresser raised her hand and slapped Lana across the face. She had not been struck so hard since Stompanato had attacked her shortly before he was killed. At that moment, Lana wiped the tears from her reddened cheek and vowed that she would weep no more, unless the cameras were rolling. It was time to take her life back. With a new resolve, she returned to the church to finish the scene. She was in control now. Lana gave all the emotion that the scene had called for, not as a wounded woman who had nearly been destroyed by love for the past year but as the professional actor she had been and would become again.

"Cut, print!" the director yelled. "Brilliant, you gave it just what it needed!"

At the end of the shoot, Lana gifted Sandra Dee the sweater she had worn as a teenager herself in her first film, *They Won't Forget*. It was the garment that helped create a gigantic movie star.

Imitation of Life was a smashing success. One Hollywood writer called it a "superb movie of dramatic quality" and praised Lana's performance as "outstanding." Famed film critic Emanuel Levy would go on to tout *Imitation of Life* as "one of the four masterpieces directed in the 1950s." It was one of the studio's biggest hits in years. Lana's salary was boosted greatly because of her back-end deal, which paid out $2 million to her, the highest paying acting job of her career.

Universal backed the film with a strong promotional campaign, eventually sending Lana and her costars on a twelve-day publicity tour to Boston, Chicago, Cleveland, New York, and Washington, DC. During the promotional junket, Lana told one reporter that her entire view on life had changed since the Stompanato stabbing. "I have a feeling of being able to contain myself," she said. "I don't mean I'm aloof or pulling away from life. It's that I no longer jump without thinking."

Joining the cast of *Imitation of Life* had been a calculated risk for Lana. She could have waited for the notoriety surrounding her fatal breakup with Johnny Stompanato to cease, but she realized it would follow her for the rest of her life regardless. Would she rather hide in fear? Or did she have the strength to press on? Lana chose the latter, both for herself and for Cheryl.

Lana did not hide behind a pair of dark sunglasses, and her attorney Jerry Giesler was nowhere in sight as she readied herself to meet the media horde outside the Screen Actors Guild Theater in Hollywood for the world premiere of *Imitation of Life* in March 1959. Reporters and fans had been camped outside the theater for several hours, waiting for a glimpse of the now reclusive movie star. Spotlights danced across the night sky, and a red carpet was unfurled and set down under an awning outside the theater's entrance where celebrities like Natalie Wood and Robert Wagner smiled and waved for the cameras before heading inside to take their seats. About a half hour went by, and there was still no sign of Lana, the film's lead.

It had been less than a year since the stabbing of Stompanato, and virtually the only time she had appeared in public was to attend various court hearings about the fatal night in April 1957, which now included a custody battle with Steve Crane over her daughter, Cheryl, who was still under Mildred's care. There was murmuring in the crowd as to whether Lana would show up at all. Finally, a limousine pulled up to the curb outside the theater. Cameramen jostled for position while gleeful spectators craned their necks for a better view of the woman who had generated national and international headlines for the past eleven months.

The back door of the limousine was opened by the red carpet host, and out stepped not Lana but her beautiful teenage daughter into the bright lights of the red carpet. Wearing a fur stole over a sleeveless gown, Cheryl Crane, self-confessed killer, notorious problem child, and parental protector, offered a thin smile for the cameras. Hell was behind her, and it was now time for her coming-out party. Standing tall on the red carpet, Cheryl braced herself for a disparaging question or remark from a member of the press or the public. Instead, she was fawned over by the swelling crowd, which viewed her not as a murderous juvenile delinquent but as a Hollywood princess. The teenager's grin spread widely and confidently across her face.

Cheryl turned her attention back to the limousine where her mother was about to join her on the red carpet. Outfitted in white silk, white gloves, and ostrich feathers, Lana Turner looked a newer version of her older self. Radiant, glamorous, and in command of everyone's attention, she marched forward amid a sea of flashbulbs and applause with her right arm raised and her gloved hand waving triumphantly in the air as Cheryl walked beside her. The journey ahead for both mother and daughter would be full of peaks and valleys, but in that one moment, they owned the night.

AUTHOR'S NOTE

As was mentioned in this book, Lana Turner did settle the wrongful death lawsuit filed on behalf of Johnny Stompanato's son in 1961. It cost just $20,000, a mere drop in the bucket for her, but it saved her from the embarrassment of having to relive the horrible nightmare and perhaps even prevented evidence from being presented that would suggest that *she*, not Cheryl, had murdered Stompanato, as the Los Angeles district attorney had kept the door open for criminal prosecution in the sensational case. Since there is no federal statute of limitation in a capital murder case, Lana lived with this terrifying possibility hanging over her head for the rest of her life. She died from throat cancer in 1995 at the age of seventy-four. Her film and television career carried into the 1970s and 1980s when she appeared in her last role, a recurring guest spot on the TV soap opera *Falcon Crest*.

Lana outlasted and outshined her adversary Mickey Cohen. He would continue to experience lasting effects from his beating in prison. After his parole, the one time crime lord lived modestly in semi-seclusion in Los Angeles, occasionally speaking out about prisoner rights. Cohen had stomach cancer surgery in 1975 and died nearly a year later at UCLA Hospital. He was sixty-two years old.

Jerry Giesler wrote a book about his career titled *Hollywood Lawyer:*

The Jerry Giesler Story. In it, he discusses all his most famous cases except one—his defense of Lana Turner and Cheryl Crane. The omission is odd to say the least. Giesler suffered a fatal heart attack at his home in Beverly Hills in 1962. He was seventy-five years old.

Cheryl Crane's relationship with Lana remained complicated. There were more runaway attempts while she was a teenager, but Cheryl seemed to have gotten her life together as an adult. She wrote her own life story and her own version of the Stompanato stabbing in a 1987 book called *Detour: A Hollywood Story*. It's a well-told, heart-wrenching effort. Cheryl Crane sticks to the official version of events, despite the evidence that suggests she never touched the knife at 730 North Bedford Drive. Perhaps she too was concerned about the open-ended probe and wanted to spare her mother from the burden of a new investigation. Cheryl also wrote a mystery novel called *The Bad Always Die Twice*, the title a take on her mother's most famous film. At this writing, Cheryl is retired from a successful career in real estate and living in Palm Springs, California, with her longtime partner.

In preparation for this book, I spent time in Los Angeles researching Lana's life, visiting the house on North Bedford Drive in Beverly Hills, having lunch at the Formosa in the booth she had once shared with Johnny Stompanato, and even visiting the site of Mickey Cohen's bombed-out home in Brentwood. Most importantly to me, I took a walk to the TCL Chinese Theatre on Hollywood Boulevard, which was a short distance from my lodgings at the Hotel Roosevelt. I was familiar with the theater, as it hosted the world premiere of my film, *The Finest Hours*, in 2016. But I had never stopped to look at the handprints and footprints of all the Hollywood legends who are immortalized in cement there. I stood with the rest of the selfie-taking tourists, examining each slab of cement until I found Lana's, located just under the prints of actress Myrna Loy. I placed my hands in the indentations made by the actress on May 24, 1950. At that moment, I realized how important her legacy was and the great responsibility I had in telling her story the right way.

For decades, Lana had been described as a femme fatale, the real-life version of the character she had played in *The Postman Always Rings Twice*. But that's not the Lana Turner who I found writing this book. To me, Lana was a feminist hero and a pioneer.

Before there was Lady Gaga, Gwyneth Paltrow, Evan Rachel Wood, and Rosario Dawson, there was Lana Turner. Before there was Harvey Weinstein, Joss Whedon, William Hurt, and Mel Gibson, there was Johnny Stompanato. Masculine toxicity, sexual harassment, and violence against women are as indelible to the fabric of the entertainment industry as the fabled Hollywood sign. While many courageous women have stepped forward and buzz-sawed their way through the iron chains of their oppression through the global #MeToo movement, we all must offer thanks to a female star from the golden age of Hollywood who broke a vicious cycle of violence and took her life back. Lana Turner was the stuff that dreams are made of—Hollywood dreams. These dreams were shattered and rebuilt on a rain-soaked evening in the early spring of 1958 in an explosion of violence that screenwriters of the time would not dare imagine.

Casey Sherman, 2023

READING GROUP GUIDE

1. What was your impression of Lana Turner's "discovery" in Hollywood? What was the source of her fame, and how did that shape her career trajectory?

2. Errol Flynn has been quoted as saying that he could claim any girl he wanted as "star's perks." Do you think his behavior was as common as he claimed it was? Do you think anyone noticed or commented on his clear preference for underage performers?

3. What was the greatest motivator behind Lana's marriages? Why didn't any of them live up to her hopes and expectations?

4. Compare Lana's and Cheryl's childhoods. How did Lana's unexpected fame force both of them to grow up too soon?

5. How did Lana manage Cheryl's delinquency and rebellion? Do you think her parenting was colored at all by her previous failures to protect Cheryl?

6. What effect does the excuse "I love you too much" have on Lana when Stompanato tries to justify his violent behavior?

7. Despite her long history with violent men, Lana rarely called the police for assistance. What stopped her? Why is it so damaging to one's reputation to be a victim of violence?

8. Lana is devastated to learn that she is actually four years older than Stompanato. Why would an age difference like that be considered a bigger scandal than, for example, the twenty-five-year gap between Humphrey Bogart and Lauren Bacall?

9. Lana and Cheryl always stood by the story that Cheryl interrupted the fight and killed Stompanato herself, but the book suggests that story was an invention of Jerry Gieisler's. Do you buy the story that Lana killed Stompanato?

10. Grueling hours, sketchy prescriptions, and sexual abuse were all common in Lana Turner's Hollywood. How much do you think has changed for the movie business today following the #MeToo scandals and greater scrutiny on the industry?

ACKNOWLEDGMENTS

I would like to thank my literary agent, Peter Steinberg at Fletcher & Co., for suggesting this story to me. After the success of my previous book *Helltown*, Peter urged me to write something that felt as big as *Helltown*, which chronicles a serial murder case on Cape Cod involving Kurt Vonnegut and Norman Mailer. We kicked around some ideas, and he sent me a short *Life* magazine article about the enduring mystery surrounding Lana Turner and Johnny Stompanato. I was a huge fan of Raymond Chandler's classic LA crime noir novels and of *L.A. Confidential,* both the James Ellroy book and the Curtis Hanson film. I saw *A Murder in Hollywood* as my opportunity to add something valuable to the rich crime lore of Los Angeles.

I would also like to thank my editor, Anna Michels, and the incredibly supportive team at Sourcebooks. I am honored to be a part of the Sourcebooks family. I would like to thank film producers Jake Crane and Mark Robinson for encouraging me and for reading my pages. A special thanks goes to my management team at Gotham Group in LA, especially Ellen Goldsmith-Vein, Charlie Scully, and my attorney, Joel VanderKloot. Once again, another thank you to my longtime writing partner Dave Wedge for his continued support of my solo projects.

But this book could not have been completed without the love of my family. It starts with my beautiful wife, Kristin Sherman, whose unflappable patience with me is so admirable. It's just one of a million reasons that I love you. My daughters, Bella and Mia, are the wind beneath my wings all day, every day. I am so proud of you, and I hope you'll find Lana Turner as inspiring as I do. I'd like to thank my uncle Jim Sherman and my fearless mother, Diane Dodd. A special thanks also goes out to the Goldsmith-York family for your love and support. Finally, I would like to thank my beloved brother Todd Forrest Sherman. Todd had been a champion of all sixteen of my books and sadly passed away during the writing of *A Murder in Hollywood*. I miss my best friend every day. As I was writing Lana's story, my brother published his own novel, a gripping murder mystery set on Cape Cod called *Into the Realm*. Please check it out at any online retailer. You'll be glad you did.

BIBLIOGRAPHY

A daunting amount of research went into the writing of this book. I am grateful for all the work that reporters and writers have done over the years chronicling Lana Turner, Mickey Cohen, Johnny Stompanato, Cheryl Crane, etc. I am an old gumshoe who can remember sitting in cramped newsroom archives, police stations, and darkened libraries compiling notes from newspaper clippings or microfiche. While I still love to get my hands dirty, I was appreciative of all the resources that can now be found online. It makes my job a lot easier.

GOVERNMENT DOCUMENTS

Lana Turner FBI File 9–12601

Mickey Cohen FBI File 92-HQ-89947 Parts 1 and 2

Benjamin "Bugsy" Siegel FBI File 62–81518

Virgil Turner Death Certificate December 14, 1930, Office of San Francisco Medical Examiner

BOOKS, MAGAZINES, AND WEBSITES

Babcock, Richard. "American Gigolo." *Chicago Magazine*, March 28, 2008, https://www.chicagomag.com/chicago-magazine/april-2008/american-gigolo/.

Bair, Deirdre. *Al Capone: His Life, Legacy, and Legend*. New York: Doubleday, 2016.

"Brownsville." Brooklyn Jewish Historical Initiative. Accessed March 10, 2023, https://brooklynjewish.org/neighborhoods/brownsville-brooklyn/.

Buntin, John. *L.A. Noir: The Struggle for the Soul of America's Most Seductive City.* New York: Broadway Books, 2009.

Cohen, Mickey, and John Peer Nugent. *Mickey Cohen: In My Own Words.* New York: Prentice Hall, 1975.

Crane, Cheryl, with Cliff Jahr. *Detour: A Hollywood Story.* New York: Avon Books, 1988.

Davis, John H. *Mafia Kingfish: Carlos Marcello and the Assassination of John F. Kennedy.* New York: McGraw Hill, 1989.

Dunne, Dominick. *The Way We Lived Then: Recollections of a Well-Known Name Dropper.* New York: Crown, 1999.

Eschner, Kat. "The Columnist Who Shaped Hollywood's Most Destructive Witch Hunt." *Smithsonian Magazine,* July 28, 2017, https://www.smithsonianmag.com/smart-news/hollywood-columnist-who-shaped-its-most-destructive-witch-hunt-180964208/.

Eyman, Scott. *Lion of Hollywood: The Life and Legend of Louis B. Mayer.* New York: Simon and Schuster, 2008.

———. *20th Century-Fox: Darryl F. Zanuck and the Creation of the Modern Film Studio.* Philadelphia: Running Press, 2021.

Flynn, Errol. *My Wicked, Wicked Ways.* New York: G. P. Putnam's Sons, 1959.

Giesler, Jerry, and Pete Martin. *Hollywood Lawyer: The Jerry Giesler Story.* New York: Simon and Schuster, 1960.

Guerrero, Susana. "'Loathsome Dungeons': Remembering San Francisco's Disturbing Slaughterhouses." SFGATE, January 25, 2022, https://www.sfgate.com/food/history/article/Butchertown-was-San-Francisco-slaughterhouses-16749759.php.

Guilaroff, Sydney, with Cathy Griffin. *Crowning Glory: Reflections of Hollywood's Favorite Confidant.* Vancouver, BC: General Publishing, 1996.

Knight, Marcy. "Rose Marie, Who Performed at the Flamingo Opening in 1946,

Remembers It Well." *Memories of the Mob with Rose Marie* (blog), Mob Museum, November 3, 2017, https://themobmuseum.org/blog/rose-marie/.

Levy, Shawn. *The Castle on Sunset: Life, Death, Love, Art, and Scandal at Hollywood's Chateau Marmont.* New York: Doubleday, 2019.

Lewis, Brad. *Hollywood's Celebrity Gangster: The Incredible Life and Times of Mickey Cohen.* New York: BBL Books, 2009.

Lieberman, Paul. *Gangster Squad: Covert Cops, the Mob, and the Battle for Los Angeles.* New York: Thomas Dunne, 2012.

Matzen, Robert. *Fireball: Carole Lombard and the Mystery of Flight 3.* Pittsburgh: GoodKnight Books, 2017.

Morris, Edmund. *Dutch: A Memoir of Ronald Reagan.* New York: Random House, 2007.

Otash, Fred. *Investigation Hollywood!* Washington, DC: Regnery, 1976.

"Owney 'the Killer' Madden Owner of Harlem's Cotton Club 1925–1931." *Harlem World Magazine,* https://www.harlemworldmagazine.com/owney-the-killer -madden-owner-of-harlems-cotton-club-1925–1931/.

Porter, Darwin, and Danforth Prince. *Lana Turner: Hearts & Diamonds Take All.* New York: Blood Moon, 2017.

Roeburt, John. *Get Me Giesler.* New York: Belmont Books, 1962.

Root, Eric, with Dale Crawford and Raymond Strait. *The Private Diary of My Life with Lana.* Beverly Hills, CA: Dove Books, 1996.

Schwarz, Ted. *Hollywood Confidential: How the Studios Beat the Mob at Their Own Game.* Boulder, CO: Taylor Trade, 2007.

Server, Lee. *Handsome Johnny: The Life and Death of Johnny Rosselli: Gentleman Gangster, Hollywood Producer, CIA Assassin.* New York: Macmillan, 2018.

Shnayerson, Michael. *Bugsy Siegel: The Dark Side of The American Dream.* New Haven, CT: Yale University Press, 2021.

Turner, Lana. *Lana: The Lady, The Legend, The Truth.* New York: E. P. Dutton, 1982.

Wilkerson, W. R., III. *Hollywood Godfather: The Life and Crimes of Billy Wilkerson.* Chicago: Chicago Review Press, 2018.

NOTES

PROLOGUE

Mildred Turner was giving the man: Lana Turner, *Lana: The Lady, The Legend, The Truth* (New York: E. P. Dutton, 1982), 242.

"Call Jerry Giesler": Turner, *Lana*, 243.

CHAPTER ONE: A MURDER BY THE BAY

Under the name Ernie Johnson: "Murdered Man Believed to Be Robber Victim," *Oakland Tribune*, December 15, 1930.

Virgil Turner had returned home: Darwin Porter and Danforth Prince, *Lana Turner: Hearts and Diamonds Take All* (New York: Blood Moon, 2017), 4.

Mildred had suspected: Porter and Prince, *Lana Turner*, 9.

Added a diamond stickpin to the lapel: "Murdered Man."

The girl was now living: Turner, *Lana*, 19.

"I want a bike, Daddy!": Turner, *Lana*, 17.

in the slaughterhouse district: Susana Guerrero, "'Loathsome Dungeons': Remembering San Francisco's Disturbing Slaughterhouses," SFGate, January 25, 2022, https://www.sfgate.com/food/history/article/Butchertown-was-San-Francisco-slaughterhouses-16749759.php.

Turner was struck once: Virgil Turner autopsy report, Office of San Francisco Medical Examiner, December 14, 1930.

"There's a body": Virgil Turner autopsy report.

The next day's headline: "Murdered Man."

In the last paragraph: "Murdered Man."

"Put on your nice dress": Turner, *Lana*, 17.

Is my mother having a baby?: Turner, *Lana*, 17.

"You're the Cream in My Coffee": Porter and Prince, *Lana Turner*, 7.

Mildred had Judy wave: Turner, *Lana*, 12.

"huge medallion of shining gold": Turner, *Lana*, 18.

"Do you want to kiss your father goodbye?": Turner, *Lana*, 18.

Judy flinched: Turner, *Lana*, 18.

"The shock I suffered then: Lana Turner, "My Private Life," *Woman's Home Companion*, December 1951.

CHAPTER TWO: FROM BROOKLYN TO BOYLE HEIGHTS

"rawest, remotest, cheapest ghetto": "Brownsville," Brooklyn Jewish Historical Initiative, accessed March 10, 2023, https://brooklynjewish.org/neighborhoods/brownsville -brooklyn/.

Mickey Cohen's earliest memories: Mickey Cohen and John Peer Nugent, *Mickey Cohen: In My Own Words* (New York: Prentice Hall, 1975), 3.

"I was really looking to make a buck": Cohen and Nugent, *Mickey Cohen*, 3.

Mickey Cohen's official FBI file: Mickey Cohen FBI File 92-HQ-89947, Parts 1 and 2, https://archive.org/stream/MickeyCohen/Cohen%2C%20Meyer%20Harris%20 92-HQ-3156%20Part%201%20of%202_djvu.txt.

"I was making gin": Cohen and Nugent, *Mickey Cohen*, 5.

Instead, they were unforgiving and sadistic: Brad Lewis, *Hollywood's Celebrity Gangster: The Incredible Life and Times of Mickey Cohen* (New York: BBL Books, 2009), 7.

"I got a kick": Cohen and Nugent, *Mickey Cohen*, 7.

"It seems all us": Cohen and Nugent, *Mickey Cohen*, 7.

CHAPTER THREE: THE SODA FOUNTAIN

"We rattled our way": Turner, *Lana*, 25.

The sign had been erected: Mark McGroarty, ed., "The Saga of the Sign: The Rise, Ruin and Restoration of Hollywood's Biggest Name," Hollywood Sign Trust, 2018, https://assets .website-files.com/62311413466139dfed65b237/62d07604bddd685d1b9001a0 _The%20Saga%20of%20The%20Sign.pdf.

"Where will you live": McGroarty, "Saga of the Sign."

mother and daughter had survived: Turner, *Lana*, 16.

"All I noticed: Turner, *Lana*, 25.

"I'm afraid I'm a coward": McGroarty, "Saga of the Sign."

Mother and daughter bonded: Turner, *Lana*, 22.

"As I sipped the Coke": Turner, *Lana*, 26.

The man desperately wanted: W. R. Wilkerson III, "Writing the End to a True-to-Life Cinderella Story," *Los Angeles Times*, July 1, 1995, https://www.latimes.com/archives /la-xpm-1995-07-01-ca-19119-story.html.

"There's a gentleman": Turner, *Lana*, 26.

"Hello, young lady": Darwin Porter & Danforth Prince, *Lana Turner*, 14.

"He publishes the *Hollywood Reporter*": Turner, *Lana*, 26.

"Save your money": W. R. Wilkerson III, *Hollywood Godfather: The Life and Crimes of Billy Wilkerson* (Chicago: Chicago Review Press, 2018), 76.

Within the pages: Kat Eschner, "The Columnist Who Shaped Hollywood's Most Destructive Witch Hunt," Smithsonian Magazine, July 28, 2017.

He had a fascination: Porter and Prince, *Lana Turner*, 17.

"You're a very pretty girl": Turner, *Lana*, 27.

"This should get you into Zeppo's office": Turner, *Lana*, 27.

"Tell me Judy, how old are you?": Turner, *Lana*, 27.

"Men go home": Porter and Prince, *Lana Turner*, 17.

"Lift your skirt": Turner, *Lana*, 28.

"Well, you're very pretty": Turner, *Lana*, 28.

"You're in the picture": Turner, *Lana*, 28.

"**What about Lana?**": Turner, *Lana*, 30.

"**Just walk**": Turner, *Lana*, 31.

"**Lana's debut didn't require**": Porter and Prince, *Lana Turner*, 25.

"**Women walk the street**": United Press International, "Plunging Neckline, Falsies Get Blame for Rise in Sex Crimes," *Brooklyn Eagle*, December 16, 1949, https://bklyn. newspapers.com/image/52858517/.

"**Short on playing time**": Turner, *Lana*, 31.

CHAPTER FOUR: CHICAGO AND AL CAPONE

"**Never leave the joint**": Cohen and Nugent, *Mickey Cohen*, 19.

"**That Jew kid**": Cohen and Nugent, *Mickey Cohen*, 17.

"**sweet, but oh so vicious**": "Owney 'the Killer' Madden Owner of Harlem's Cotton Club 1925–1931," *Harlem World Magazine*, accessed March 11, 2023, https://www.harlemworldmagazine .com/owney-the-killer-madden-owner-of-harlems-cotton-club-1925–1931/.

"**Owney was really a guy to respect**": Cohen and Nugent, *Mickey Cohen*, 13.

"**We were stepping on the toes**": Cohen and Nugent, *Mickey Cohen*, 16.

"**Look, when I learned for sure**": Cohen and Nugent, *Mickey Cohen*, 18.

Capone had taken a ten-room suite: Deirdre Bair, *Al Capone: His Life, Legacy, and Legend* (New York: Doubleday, 2016), 211.

"**Only Capone kills like that**": Bair, *Al Capone*, 137.

"**I walked into his office**": Cohen and Nugent, *Mickey Cohen*, 21.

"**what a nice piece of work**": Cohen and Nugent, *Mickey Cohen*, 21.

"**People who never *knew* me**": Cohen and Nugent, *Mickey Cohen*, 22.

"**I respected his ways**": Cohen and Nugent, *Mickey Cohen*, 25.

"**What the fuck is the goof up**": Cohen and Nugent, *Mickey Cohen*, 29.

"**I got ribbed about this**": Cohen and Nugent, *Mickey Cohen*, 30.

"**Why did you break his head?**": Cohen and Nugent, *Mickey Cohen*, 32.

CHAPTER FIVE: TOO FAST, TOO SOON

Stitched into the flag's canvas: Frazer Pearce, "It's Not Every Day That Errol Flynn Sails into Your Life, but in 1930 He Spent a Month in Rockhampton," ABC Australia, August 14, 2021, https://www.abc.net.au/news/2021-08-15/errol-flynn-hellraiser-visit -to-queensland-towns/100373874.

Lana had recently been introduced: Porter and Prince, *Lana Turner*, 48.

"You saw a young lady you fancied": Errol Flynn, *My Wicked, Wicked Ways* (New York: G. P. Putnam's Sons, 1959), 60.

Then he invited her to join him: Porter and Prince, *Lana Turner*, 50.

"I just happened to look well": Flynn, *My Wicked, Wicked Ways*, 142.

Lana was ordered: Porter and Prince, *Lana Turner*, 44.

"He said that I was": Porter and Prince, *Lana Turner*, 45.

"Lana is just as oversexed": Porter and Prince, *Lana Turner*, 46.

"Dutch was not yet a one-girl guy": Edmund Morris, *Dutch: A Memoir of Ronald Reagan* (New York: Random House, 2007), 185.

"We had youth, we had beauty": Turner, *Lana*, 40.

"They'd give [me and Mickey Rooney] pills": Erin Blakemore, "The Golden Age of Hollywood Had a Dirty Little Secret: Drugs," History, updated November 6, 2019, https://www.history.com/news/judy-garland-barbiturates-hollywood-studio-drugs.

"I could have slept": Turner, *Lana*, 35.

"an all-American": Louis B. Mayer, "Judy Garland, Mickey Rooney, and Louis B. Mayer," tagcbs, January 5, 2013, YouTube video, 3:22, https://www.youtube.com/watch?v=th9gWYit-GQ.

"sing from the heart": Scott Eyman, *Lion of Hollywood: The Life and Legend of Louis B. Mayer* (New York: Simon and Schuster, 2008), 418.

"You're keeping late hours": Turner, *Lana*, 42.

CHAPTER SIX: THE RETURN OF THE KING

"I had the stick": Cohen and Nugent, *Mickey Cohen*, 44.

"Who was that gorgeous woman": Cohen and Nugent, *Mickey Cohen*, 44.

"He was young": Michael Shnayerson, *Bugsy Siegel: The Dark Side of the American Dream* (New Haven, CT: Yale University Press, 2021), 10.

"insane along certain lines": Shnayerson, *Bugsy Siegal*, 15.

"Jack [Dragna] wasn't pulling": Cohen and Nugent, *Mickey Cohen*, 41.

"You just move": Cohen and Nugent, *Mickey Cohen*, 36.

"I heard you were a fucking nut": Cohen and Nugent, *Mickey Cohen*, 38.

"It's his family heirloom": Cohen and Nugent, *Mickey Cohen*, 39.

CHAPTER SEVEN: HOLLYWARS

"The act itself hurt like hell": Turner, *Lana*, 44.

"Joan Crawford is doubtless": "Crawford and Fitzgerald," *New York Times*, February 25, 1979, https://www.nytimes.com/1979/02/25/archives/letters-crawford-and-fitzgerald-evil-humors-a-reckoning-dubois.html.

"If you want to see": Charlotte Chandler, *Not the Girl Next Door: Joan Crawford, a Personal Biography* (New York: Simon & Schuster, 2008), 5.

"I'd like to talk to you": Porter and Prince, *Lana Turner*, 63.

"Well, darling": Turner, *Lana*, 46.

"So, Lana dear": Turner, *Lana*, 47.

"blazes across the screen": Trailer for *These Glamour Girls*, directed by S. Sylvan Simon (MGM, 1939), https://www.imdb.com/video/vi3642016025/.

"If there was ever a point": Turner, *Lana*, 47.

"You're a gutty kid": Cohen and Nugent, *Mickey Cohen*, 51.

"I saw you talking": Shnayerson, *Bugsy Siegel*, 65.

"Permission granted": Lewis, *Hollywood's Celebrity Gangster*, 24.

"I talked him out of it": Lewis, *Hollywood's Celebrity Gangster*, 25.

"We got there in the evening": Shnayerson, *Bugsy Siegel*, 67.

"anti-Jew, rabble rousing": Lewis, *Hollywood's Celebrity Gangster*, 25.

"I started bouncing their heads together": Cohen and Nugent, *Mickey Cohen*, 69.

"Them two guys got in a fight": Cohen and Nugent, *Mickey Cohen*, 69.

"Why did you throw us": Cohen & Nugent, *Mickey Cohen*, 68.

CHAPTER EIGHT: THE NEEDLE

"Where am I?": Turner, *Lana*, 59.

"Mrs. Mildred Johnson": Turner, *Lana*, 59.

"Where's Artie?": Turner, *Lana*, 60.

"He never missed a chance": Turner, *Lana*, 48.

"If you go around with Ben Siegel": Shnayerson, *Bugsy Siegel*, 78.

"I'm determined to": Porter and Prince, *Lana Turner*, 97.

"How my life is going to change!": Turner, *Lana*, 50.

"I've lost her": Turner, *Lana*, 51.

"I'm sorry, I'm sorry": Turner, *Lana*, 51.

"He was clumsy and fumbling": Turner, *Lana*, 53.

"That son of a bitch!": Turner, *Lana*, 53.

"Well, you've really done it": Turner, *Lana*, 54.

"But Artie's in love with me!": Porter and Prince, *Lana Turner*, 103.

"Why did you do it?": Turner, *Lana*, 54.

"I admired Artie's talents": Turner, *Lana*, 55.

"What is this crap?": Turner, *Lana*, 59.

"Check her in as Mildred Taylor": Turner, *Lana*, 59.

"Get your things": Turner, *Lana*, 61.

"Well, I just found out": Turner, *Lana*, 63.

"What the hell do you mean": Turner, *Lana*, 64.

"MGM has strict taboos": Turner, *Lana*, 64.

"I went by myself": Turner, *Lana*, 64.

"I'm going to die": Turner, *Lana*, 65.

"You've threatened the life of my daughter": Turner, *Lana*, 66.

CHAPTER NINE: LANA MEETS BUGSY

"If you want me for Ivy": Turner, *Lana*, 71.

"Please don't blow anything into my eyes": Turner, *Lana*, 72.

"Stop it! You're hurting me": Turner, *Lana*, 73.

"I never heard of signing": Cohen and Nugent, *Mickey Cohen*, 60.

"Hey, look-it": Cohen and Nugent, *Mickey Cohen*, 60.

"All of you were stiff, sloppy drunks": Cohen and Nugent, *Mickey Cohen*, 60.

"have never seen entertainment": Trailer for *Dr. Jekyll and Mr. Hyde*, directed by Victor Fleming (MGM, 1941), https://www.imdb.com/video/vi4065312537/.

"Darling, I just heard that MGM": Porter and Prince, *Lana Turner*, 136.

"extraordinarily handsome": Porter and Prince, *Lana Turner*, 146.

"I was wrong about you": Porter and Prince, *Lana Turner*, 147.

"Mayer and Warner pay me off": Porter and Prince, *Lana Turner*, 148.

"He looks better": Porter and Prince, *Lana Turner*, 148.

"This Giesler's a great guy": Porter and Prince, *Lana Turner*, 149.

CHAPTER TEN: THE HOME FRONT

"Lana's name dominated": Porter and Prince, *Lana Turner*, 141.

"Get that Kraut": Porter and Prince, *Lana Turner*, 156.

"When I had time between pictures": Turner, *Lana*, 76.

"When there were men in the crowd": Turner, *Lana*, 76.

"that blonde whore": Porter and Prince, *Lana Turner*, 207.

"Now, Lana, here's where you come in": Turner, *Lana*, 80.

Lana attended Lombard's massive funeral: Robert Matzen, *Fireball: Carole Lombard and the Mystery of Flight 3* (Pittsburgh: GoodKnight Books, 2017), 302.

"For those whose pulses throbbed": Douglas Churchill, "'Honky Tonk' Opens Today," *New York Times*, October 2, 1941, https://www.nytimes.com/1941/10/02/archives /screen-news-here-and-in-hollywood-the-moon-and-sixpence-a-somerset.html.

"the modern Jean Harlow of celluloid": Review of *Somewhere I'll Find You*, directed by Wesley Ruggles, *Variety*, August 5, 1942, https://archive.org/details/variety147-1942-08/page /n7/mode/2up.

"likable enough but not especially stimulating": Turner, *Lana*, 77.

"Howard was brilliant": Turner, *Lana*, 78.

"god damnedest biggest hotel": Shnayerson, *Bugsy Siegel*, 86.

"She was strictly a lady": Cohen and Nugent, *Mickey Cohen*, 103.

"Look, the guy's probably gonna get": Cohen and Nugent, *Mickey Cohen*, 64.

"He's in the army!": Cohen and Nugent, *Mickey Cohen*, 65.

"We went over there": Cohen and Nugent, *Mickey Cohen*, 68.

"I'm gonna tell you": Cohen and Nugent, *Mickey Cohen*, 72.

"Are ya dead?": Cohen and Nugent, *Mickey Cohen*, 73.

"You'd come in there": Cohen and Nugent: *Mickey Cohen*, 74.

CHAPTER ELEVEN: ALONG COMES MR. CRANE

"heels over chin": Porter and Prince, *Lana Turner*, 215.

"I'm lonely unless": Porter and Prince, *Lana Turner*, 215.

"I got this paper": Turner, *Lana*, 83.

"I wasn't legally married": Turner, *Lana*, 84.

"He will not be free to marry": Turner, *Lana*, 84.

"Whatever we try": Turner, *Lana*, 85.

"Please, you're carrying my child": Turner, *Lana*, 85.

"My answer is no": Turner, *Lana*, 85.

"I demand that you remarry": Porter and Prince, *Lana Turner*, 222.

"It's a her, it's a her!": Turner, *Lana*, 87.

"I could hear the other babies": Turner, *Lana*, 88.

"Tell me, Mother": Turner, *Lana*, 88.

"I can't find the words": Turner, *Lana*, 89.

"It was only then that I realized": Turner, *Lana*, 92.

"Is Mr. Crane home?": Porter and Prince, *Lana Turner*, 215.

"I'm in love with another man": Turner, *Lana*, 96.

CHAPTER TWELVE: THE POSTMAN RINGS

Lana was now earning: Turner, *Lana*, 97.

"evil film": Eyman, *Lion of Hollywood*, 392.

"He Had to Have Her Love": Trailer for *The Postman Always Rings Twice*, directed by Tay Garnett (MGM, 1946), https://www.imdb.com/video/vi1520764185/.

"a tremendously tense and dramatic show": Bosley Crowther, "'The Postman Always Rings Twice,' with Lana Turner in a Star Role, Makes Its Appearance of the Capitol," *New York Times*, May 3, 1946, https://www.nytimes.com/1946/05/03/archives/the-screen-the-postman-always-rings-twice-with-lana-turner-in-a.html.

"Latins, I quickly learned": Turner, *Lana*, 105.

"Eva Perón wanted to be Lana Turner": Porter and Prince, *Lana Turner*, 312.

"It struck me that she had gone blonde": Turner, *Lana*, 106.

"Those eyes were like narrow slits": Turner, *Lana*, 107.

"It terrified and sickened me": Turner, *Lana*, 107.

"it is to be noted": Office Memorandum, March 12, 1945, Lana Turner FBI File 9–12601, https://archive.org/details/LanaTurnerFBI/Lana%20Turner%20FBI%20File%209-12601/page/n1/mode/2up.

"My God, if the dirty bitch": Office Memorandum, May 17, 1945, Lana Turner FBI File 9–12601, https://archive.org/details/LanaTurnerFBI/Lana%20Turner%20FBI%20File%209-12601/page/n1/mode/2up.

"Keep quiet if you know": Office Memorandum, May 17, 1945, Lana Turner FBI File 9–12601, https://archive.org/details/LanaTurnerFBI/Lana%20Turner%20FBI%20File%209-12601/page/n1/mode/2up.

"She kept this appointment": Office Memorandum, May 7, 1946, Lana Turner FBI File 9–12601, https://archive.org/details/LanaTurnerFBI/Lana%20Turner%20FBI%20File%209-12601/page/n25/mode/2up.

"Our LA Office advised": Office Memorandum, April 7, 1958, Lana Turner FBI File 9–12601, https://archive.org/details/LanaTurnerFBI/Lana%20Turner%20FBI%20File%209-12601/page/n33/mode/2up.

CHAPTER THIRTEEN: THE FLAMINGO

"What the hell?": Cohen and Nugent, *Mickey Cohen*, 77.

"You're outside three or four minutes": Cohen and Nugent, *Mickey Cohen*, 77.

"We have ascertained": Office Memorandum, July 18, 1946, Bugsy Siegel FBI File 62–81518, https://vault.fbi.gov/Bugsy%20Siegel%20/Bugsy%20Siegel%20Part%20 1%20of%2032/view.

"According to the FBI": Office Memorandum, July 21, 1946, Bugsy Siegel FBI File 62–81518, https://vault.fbi.gov/Bugsy%20Siegel%20/Bugsy%20Siegel%20Part%20 1%20of%2032/view.

"All my money and my friend's money": Office Memorandum, July 21, 1946, Bugsy Siegel FBI File 62–81518, https://vault.fbi.gov/Bugsy%20Siegel%20/Bugsy%20Siegel%20 Part%201%20of%2032/view.

"We'll make [Winchell] bring Hoover": Office Memorandum, July 21, 1946, Bugsy Siegel FBI File 62–81518, https://vault.fbi.gov/Bugsy%20Siegel%20/Bugsy%20Siegel%20 Part%201%20of%2032/view.

criticizing the construction of the Flamingo: Editorial, *Las Vegas Tribune*, August 8, 1946.

"I don't like to tell you": Shnayerson, *Bugsy Siegel*, 144.

"On the morning of [December] 25th": Marcy Knight, "Rose Marie, Who Performed at the Flamingo Opening in 1946, Remembers It Well," *Memories of the Mob with Rose Marie* (blog), Mob Museum, November 3, 2017, https://themobmuseum.org/blog /rose-marie/.

"like a set that MGM wanted to build": Shnayerson, *Bugsy Siegel*, 145.

"I know you love him": Shnayerson, *Bugsy Siegel*, 152.

"You don't own me, Ben Siegel!": Shnayerson, *Bugsy Siegel*, 164.

"You got armament?": Cohen and Nugent, *Mickey Cohen*, 79.

"I'm tired, Georgie": Shnayerson, *Bugsy Siegel*, 169.

"When someone smells flowers": Shnayerson, *Bugsy Siegel*, 170.

The hit man stood about fifteen feet away: Shnayerson, *Bugsy Siegel*, 171.

CHAPTER FOURTEEN: COHEN'S WORLD

Muir lifted the newspaper: Shnayerson, *Bugsy Siegel*, 172.

A photo of Siegel's foot: Shnayerson, *Bugsy Siegel*, 173.

"I wish I knew": Cohen and Nugent, *Mickey Cohen*, 80.

"Naturally, I missed Benny": Cohen and Nugent, *Mickey Cohen*, 81.

"Vaus, I understand": Will Vaus, "The Original Wiretapper," *Los Angeles Times*, April 4, 2008, https://www.latimes.com/archives/la-xpm-2008-apr-01-oe-vaus1-story.html.

"Be my guests": Lewis, *Hollywood's Celebrity Gangster*, 87.

"buried more bones": Allan May, "Frank Bompensiero San Diego Hit Man, Boss and FBI Informant," *Crime Magazine*, October 14, 2009, http://www.crimemagazine.com/frank-bompensiero-san-diego-hit-man-boss-and-fbi-informant.

The killers fled in a yellow convertible: "Gangland War! Cohen Held After Gunman Mows Down Aide," *Hollywood Citizen-News*, August 19, 1948.

"I have no idea": "Police Guard Cohen at Funeral," *New York Daily News*, August 23, 1948.

"You don't have to say nothing": Cohen and Nugent, *Mickey Cohen*, 121.

"Mickey's going to get his": "Gangland War!"

"I was following Mickey Cohen around": Florabel Muir, "Behind Hollywood's Silken Curtain," *New York Daily News*, August 4, 1957, https://www.newspapers.com/newspage/453991686/.

"What are you standing out here for?": Lewis, *Hollywood's Celebrity Gangster*, 111.

"I don't need protection": Lewis, *Hollywood's Celebrity Gangster*, 112.

"This is my jeweler friend": Lewis, *Hollywood's Celebrity Gangster*, 112.

"I'm hit": Lewis, *Hollywood's Celebrity Gangster*, 113.

Four bullets ripped: "Cohen Pal, State Agent, Near Death," *Los Angeles Mirror*, July 20, 1949.

The hit squad had tossed: "Mickey 'Gets His' Surrounded by Heavy Bodyguard," *Los Angeles Mirror*, July 20, 1949.

"Be on your guard": Lewis, *Hollywood's Celebrity Gangster*, 114.

CHAPTER FIFTEEN: ENTER STOMPANATO

"favorite Italian mother": Richard Babcock, "American Gigolo," *Chicago Magazine*, March 28, 2008, https://www.chicagomag.com/chicago-magazine/april-2008/american-gigolo/.

"I used to get confused": Babcock, "American Gigolo."

"He was my protector": Babcock, "American Gigolo."

"better than average intelligence": Babcock, "American Gigolo."

Stompanato stuffed a dynamite cap: Associated Press, "Slain Man Former Kemp Student," *The Sunday News and Tribune* (Jefferson City, MO), April 6, 1958.

"we have a wonderful bunch": Babcock, "American Gigolo."

Her name was Sara Utush: "Jack Stompanato Takes a Bride in China," *Daily Sentinel* (Woodstock, IL), May 19, 1946, https://www.newspapers.com/clip/38229505/johnny -stompanato-marriage-in-china/.

he met a rich, lonely man: "Too Much Cash, So Cohen Pal Goes to Jail," *Los Angeles Times*, May 12, 1952.

Stompanato later told the IRS: "Too Much Cash."

"Someone sent him to me": Cohen and Nugent, *Mickey Cohen*, 185.

Stompanato was fined $250: "High Court Rules Stompanato No Bum," *South Gate Daily Press*, April 22, 1950.

The blast, which occurred just fifty feet: "Homemade Bomb Explodes Near Home of Gambler Mickey Cohen," *Tulare Advance-Register*, August 2, 1949, https:// visaliatimesdelta.newspapers.com/image/513974502/.

"Now you've had it": Fred Otash, *Investigation Hollywood!* (Washington, DC: Regnery, 1976), 186.

"just the cutest thing I ever saw": Otash, *Investigation Hollywood!*, 96.

"entirely satisfactory": United Press International, "Gambling Czar in Seclusion as Cops Quiz Thug," *The Brooklyn Daily Eagle*, July 31, 1939.

"The Strip, a hunk of county": Aline Mosby, "Hollywood's Famed Strip Becoming Gasoline Alley," *Boston Daily Globe*, August 16, 1949.

"We've been writing the script": United Press International, "Film to Be Written from LA Headlines," *Knoxville Journal*, September 18, 1949.

"We don't want your scar tissue": "Mickey Cohen Heads for Ohio," *San Francisco Examiner*, August 6, 1950.

"He's gone and we're glad of it": "Mickey Cohen Heads for Ohio."

"Well, Mickey, I have never": "Editorial: The Governor Repeats," *Hollywood Citizen-News*, July 27, 1949.

"The situation is bad": "Editorial: The Governor Repeats."

"exhibitionist hoodlum": "Trouble in Los Angeles," *Life*, January 16, 1950.

Cohen was asleep: "Mobster Boss Escapes When Home Blasts," *Wichita Eagle*, February 6, 1950.

The heavy blast blew out every window: "Mobster Boss Escapes."

"It's a shame": "Mobster Boss Escapes."

"I just got back in bed": "Six Arrested in Probe of Cohen Home Bombing," *Fort Worth Star Telegram*, February 14, 1950.

"Guided as I was": Lewis, *Hollywood's Celebrity Gangster*, 140.

"He is heavy-set, heavy-browed": Estes Kefauver, "Mickey Cohen an 'Outlaw' After Split with Mafia," *Miami News*, July 31, 1951.

"I know he got his money someplace": "Pals Back Mickey, Cohen Speaks for Self Monday," *Hollywood Citizen-News*, June 16, 1951.

"I'm trying to find out": "Too Much Cash."

"I've always asked him [Cohen]": "Pals Back Mickey."

"People in my business": "Pals Back Mickey."

"I want to begin my sentence now": Cohen and Nugent, *Mickey Cohen*, 153.

"For the Whatever Became of Department": Dorothy Kilgallen, "For the Whatever Became of Department," *Times-Tribune* (Scranton, PA), March 17, 1952.

CHAPTER SIXTEEN: LANA IN TECHNICOLOR

"star's essentials": Turner, *Lana*, 125.

"What's that?": Turner, *Lana*, 127.

Built to resemble an English manor: Linda Stowell, "Helmsley Home Has Brought Bad Luck to Its Owners," *Associated News Press*, April 18, 1988, https://apnews.com/article/aea9e58509078a15e840d6574d6be50d.

"The master hall reminded me": Turner, *Lana*, 128.

"For God's sake, the guy's married": Porter and Prince, *Lana Turner*, 350.

"Sorry, I still won't": Turner, *Lana*, 130.

"Metro-Goldwyn-Mayer has just put Lana Turner": Margaret Bean, "After Comment on Late Picture and Lana Turner," *Spokesman-Review* (Spokane, WA), February 1, 1948.

"If you care for your movie career": Porter and Prince, *Lana Turner*, 353.

"splendiferous production": Bosley Crowther, "Lana Turner and Gene Kelly Top Cast of 'Three Musketeers,' Feature at Loew's State," *New York Times*, October 21, 1948, https://www.nytimes.com/1948/10/21/archives/lana-turner-and-gene-kelly-top-cast-of-three-musketeers-feature-at.html.

"She's one of the sweetest people": Aline Mosby, "Lana Turner Misunderstood Says Director George Sidney," *Times-Tribune* (Scranton, PA), May 21, 1948.

"He won't get a divorce": Porter and Prince, *Lana Turner*, 356.

"a blot on the character of America": "Many Deplore Bad Taste of Lana Turner Wedding," *Spokesman-Review* (Spokane, WA), May 16, 1948.

"Our grandfather made the money": Porter and Prince, *Lana Turner*, 358.

"At Round Hill": Turner, *Lana*, 141.

"Don't injure my face, you bastard!": Porter and Prince, *Lana Turner*, 365.

"I looked out of the window": Cheryl Crane with Cliff Jahr, *Detour: A Hollywood Story* (New York: Avon Books, 1988), 137.

"I'll show them": Turner, *Lana*, 159.

"This is the life that will be lost": Turner, *Lana*, 159.

CHAPTER SEVENTEEN: THE BEAUTIFUL AND THE BAD

"jagged laceration across the lower quarter": Porter and Prince, *Lana Turner*, 385.

"It hurts, it hurts": Turner, *Lana*, 159.

"That's utterly ridiculous": Turner, *Lana*, 160.

Her injury was declared "accidental": "Turner Hospitalized with Wrist Slash," *Times-Tribune* (Scranton, PA), September 13, 1951.

Cheryl had also been told: Crane, *Detour: A Hollywood Story*, 148.

"Your signature will be immortalized": Eric Root with Dale Crawford and Raymond Strait, *The Private Diary of My Life with Lana* (Beverly Hills, CA: Dove Books, 1996), 154.

"We're already grooming other blondes": Porter and Prince, *Lana Turner*, 377.

"First, your makeup is all wrong": Root, *My Life with Lana*, 154.

"They all copy me": Root, *My Life with Lana*, 157.

"adequate": Bosley Crowther, "'The Merry Widow,' With Lana Turner and Fernando Lamas, Opens at Loew's State," *New York Times*, September 25, 1952, https://www .nytimes.com/1952/09/25/archives/the-merry-widow-with-lana-turner-and-fernando -lamas-opens-at-loews.html.

"I don't suppose you've ever seen": Crane, *Detour: A Hollywood Story*, 157.

"Why don't you just take her": Turner, *Lana*, 164.

"And I hope you'll keep": Turner, *Lana*, 164.

"that Miss Turner had no part": Thomas M. Pryor, "Lana Turner Gets New Leading Man," *New York Times*, October 23, 1952, https://www.nytimes.com/1952/10/23 /archives/lana-turner-gets-new-leading-man-montalban-replaces-lamas-in-latin .html.

"short on originality": "The Screen in Review: 'Latin Lovers' Has Lana Turner Struggling with Problem of $37,000,000 at the State," *New York Times*, August 13, 1953, https://www.nytimes.com/1953/08/13/archives/the-screen-in-review-latin-lovers -has-lana-turner-struggling-with.html.

"the private lives of the famous and notorious": Trailer for *The Bad and the Beautiful*, directed by Vincente Minelli (MGM, 1952), https://www.imdb.com/video/vi2170356761/.

CHAPTER EIGHTEEN: TARZAN THE TERRIBLE

"I doubt that in today's moral climate": Turner, *Lana*, 180.

"If the photographers don't get out of here.": Crane, *Detour: A Hollywood Story*, 165.

"Lana Turner, Lex Barker wed": "Lana Turner, Lex Barker Wed in Italy Ceremony," *Los Angeles Times*, September 8, 1953.

"Cheryl, I'm your father now": Crane, *Detour: A Hollywood Story*, 166.

Topping lied to Cheryl: Crane, *Detour: A Hollywood Story*, 144.

"I want to show you something": Crane, *Detour: A Hollywood Story*, 171.

"This is a man's rabbit": Crane, *Detour: A Hollywood Story*, 172.

"Of course, not everyone would understand": Crane, *Detour: A Hollywood Story*, 172.

"Time for another lesson": Crane, *Detour: A Hollywood Story*, 179.

"You know what they do to girls": Crane, *Detour: A Hollywood Story*, 180.

"I'm not going to do this anymore": Crane, *Detour: A Hollywood Story*, 204.

"Lana, I want you to come": Crane, *Detour: A Hollywood Story*, 205.

"He's been coming into my room": Crane, *Detour: A Hollywood Story*, 206.

"Why didn't you come to bed?": Crane, *Detour: A Hollywood Story*, 207.

CHAPTER NINETEEN: JOHN STEELE

"Why are you behind the camera": Paul Harrison, "Harrison Turns Hollywood Spotlight on Three New Faces," *Ogden (UT) Standard-Examiner*, May 22, 1939, https://www.newspapers.com/clip/6973207/the-ogden-standard-examiner/.

Gilbert's marriage to Stompanato: International News Service, "Actress Weds," *Long Beach Independent*, February 12, 1949, https://www.newspapers.com/clip/38232410/stompanato-marries-helen-gilbert/.

"During our short marriage": Babcock, "American Gigolo."

"his pockets had too much jingle": "Too Much Cash."

"Yesterday, heedless of the possible peril": Paul V. Coates, "Well, Medium and RARE," *Los Angeles Mirror*, July 8, 1952.

Stompanato's impending nuptials: Erskine Johnson, "Helene Stanley and Johnny Stompanato Have Set a Wedding Date," *La Crosse Tribune*, January 24, 1953.

"I thought Johnny really loved you?": Babcock, "American Gigolo."

"one time bodyguard for Mickey Cohen": "Actress Awarded Divorce from Mate," *Progress Bulletin* (Pomona, CA), February 10, 1955.

"I gotta see you on something important": Cohen and Nugent, *Mickey Cohen*, 85.

"I'm all washed up with gambling": "Don't Roust Mickey, Lawyer Warns Police," *Hollywood Citizen-News*, October 11, 1955.

"Mickey's going to be a good little boy": "Don't Roust Mickey."

"The Stompanato-Mickey Cohen blackmail angles": Lana Turner FBI File 62–81080, https://archive.org/details/LanaTurnerFBI/Lana%20Turner%20FBI%20File%20Extracts%20-%20Cross%20References/page/n27/mode/2up.

CHAPTER TWENTY: THE PLAN

the two gangsters reverse engineered: John H. Davis, *Mafia Kingfish: Carlos Marcello and the Assassination of John F. Kennedy* (New York: McGraw Hill, 1989), 392.

"And does it feel wonderful": Aline Mosby, "Lana Turner Shuns Glamour Roles," *Alva Review-Courier*, June 16, 1957.

"At least I can read": Bob Thomas, "Actress Lana Turner Freed from Studio Contract," *Springfield News*, April 18, 1956.

Before walking off the studio lot: Turner, *Lana*, 189.

"All he wants is to send you some flowers": Turner, *Lana*, 196.

"There were so many of them": Turner, *Lana*, 197.

"The flowers are overwhelming": Turner, *Lana*, 197.

"Weekends, I spend with my family": Turner, *Lana*, 197.

"I'll be working late here": Turner, *Lana*, 198.

"But he was supposed to telephone": Turner, *Lana*, 199.

"Whatever his profession was": Turner, *Lana*, 200.

"He has the stamina of a bull": Porter and Prince, *Lana Turner*, 506.

"Do you have a money tree?": Turner, *Lana*, 200.

"From Here to Eternity—Rosemary and John": "New Stompanato Secrets Found," *Stockton Daily Record*, April 15, 1958.

CHAPTER TWENTY-ONE: THE DREAM

"Lana, you can tell me to go to hell": Turner, *Lana*, 202.

"Dear God, Lana": Turner, *Lana*, 202.

"It's my name": Turner, *Lana*, 203.

"Get the hell out of here": Turner, *Lana*, 205.

"His consuming passion was strangely exciting": Turner, *Lana*, 205.

"I'd rather see you dead first": Turner, *Lana*, 214.

"lovely Nipponese maiden": Muir, "Behind Hollywood's Silken Curtain."

"I'm sincerely interested in anything": Associated Press, "Mickey Cohen and Billy Graham Pray Together," *Modesto Bee*, April 2, 1957.

"sadistic cocksucker": Cohen and Nugent, *Mickey Cohen*, 171.

"I have killed no man": Cohen and Nugent, *Mickey Cohen*, 172.

The case would eventually be settled: Lee Mortimer, "New York Confidential," *Post-Star* (Glens Falls, NY), October 23, 1957.

"Any retractions made by those": Lewis, *Hollywood's Celebrity Gangster*, 206.

CHAPTER TWENTY-TWO: ANOTHER TIME, ANOTHER PLACE

"Mother obviously didn't give a damn": Crane, *Detour: A Hollywood Story*, 214.

While briefly on her own: "Lana Turner's Daughter Found Safe," *Buffalo Evening News*, April 1, 1957.

"School-hating": "School-hating daughter and Lana Turner Reunited," *Philadelphia Enquirer*, April 2, 1957.

"that the problems of youth": Louella Parsons, "Louella's Movie-Go-'Round," *Albuquerque Journal*, April 14, 1957.

"Darling, Mother has met a very nice gentleman": Crane, *Detour: A Hollywood Story*, 221.

"a thick-shouldered man with a suntan": Crane, *Detour: A Hollywood Story*, 222.

"She spooks easy as hell": Crane, *Detour: A Hollywood Story*, 222.

"He's putting his hands": Crane, *Detour: A Hollywood Story*, 223.

"I want you to know": Crane, *Detour: A Hollywood Story*, 223.

Cheryl was thrown from a horse: United Press International, "Fall Injures Daughter of Lana Turner," *Indianapolis Star*, July 25, 1957.

She then asked Cheryl: Crane, *Detour: A Hollywood Story*, 230.

"Mom has a big house": Crane, *Detour: A Hollywood Story*, 231.

"Hollywood has a new Lana Turner": Aline Mosby, "Lana Turner Shuns Glamour Roles," *Memphis Press-Scimitar*, June 13, 1957.

"He was gentle, more like the person": Turner, *Lana*, 206.

"They pick your brains": Lynda Obst, "Oscars for Doorstops," *New York Times*, May 18, 1997.

"But, I'll write": Turner, *Lana*, 206.

"He often missed his marks": Turner, *Lana*, 206.

"**Sweetheart, please keep well**": United Press International, "Some of Lana Turner's Love Letters to Stompanato Bared," *Daily Advertiser*, April 9, 1958.

"**My dearest Lana**": "Lana Turner's Love Letters."

"**Hey, listen to me**": Cohen and Nugent, *Mickey Cohen*, 187.

"**Get the hell out of this room**": Turner, *Lana*, 208.

"**Don't come near me**": Turner, *Lana*, 209.

"**It's because I love you so much**": Turner, *Lana*, 209.

"**I'm serious**": Turner, *Lana*, 210.

"**You keep away from her!**": Porter and Prince, *Lana Turner*, 517.

"**You'll get yours**": Porter and Prince, *Lana Turner*, 518.

CHAPTER TWENTY-THREE: THE MEXICAN STANDOFF

"**Why don't we get him deported?**": Turner, *Lana*, 210.

"**the nicest glamor girl to work with**": Dorothy Manners, "The English Crew and Grips Voting on Lana," *Orlando Sentinel*, October 27, 1957.

"**Who is this from?**": Turner, *Lana*, 213.

"**What the hell are you doing here?**": Turner, *Lana*, 214.

"**Send them to Lana Turner**": "[Stompanato] Meets Lana in London," *Windsor Star*, October 18, 1957.

"**Lana Turner's boyfriend**": Sidney Skolsky, "Lana's Boyfriend Made Hurried Trip to Acapulco," *Hollywood Citizen-News*, February 4, 1958.

"**You're not staying here**": Turner, *Lana*, 215.

"**This has gone far enough**": Turner, *Lana*, 215.

"**I hope I don't see you here**": Turner, *Lana*, 217.

"**I'm exhausted**": Turner, *Lana*, 217.

"**Lana Turner's boyfriend, Johnny Stompanato**": Earl Wilson, "It Happened Last Night," *Durham Morning Herald*, February 5, 1958.

"**If you aren't going to be with me**": Turner, *Lana*, 219.

CHAPTER TWENTY-FOUR: AND THE OSCAR GOES TO...

"Lana, Lana, you've been nominated": Turner, *Lana*, 220.

"I didn't do all that much": Turner, *Lana*, 220.

"remarkable": Bosley Crowther, "The Screen: Drama in 'Peyton Place,'" *New York Times*, December 13, 1957, https://www.nytimes.com/1957/12/13/archives/the-screen-drama -in-peyton-place-american-town-star-of-film-at-roxy.html.

"Just to remind you": Turner, *Lana*, 222.

Stompanato's attempt to generate publicity: "Lana Turner Returns with Cohen Figure," *Los Angeles Times*, March 20, 1958.

"I'm good enough to fuck you": Porter and Prince, *Lana Turner*, 525.

"It's your own fault": Porter and Prince, *Lana Turner*, 525.

"If I win, which is unlikely": Turner, *Lana*, 223.

"If they don't like the dress": Crane, *Detour: A Hollywood Story*, 243.

"Well, my dear": Crane, *Detour: A Hollywood Story*, 7.

"Jimmy, don't leave please": *30th Academy Awards*, directed by Alan Handley, aired March 26, 1958, on NBC.

"Cheryl, love, look over there": Crane, *Detour: A Hollywood Story*, 10.

"I've never seen her this happy": Crane, *Detour: A Hollywood Story*, 11.

"Oh, I forgot to tell you": Crane, *Detour: A Hollywood Story*, 14.

"You didn't expect me": Turner, *Lana*, 226.

"You spent enough time yakking": Turner, *Lana*, 227.

"I'm gonna give you the beating": Turner, *Lana*, 228.

"Good morning, Mama": Turner, *Lana*, 232.

CHAPTER TWENTY-FIVE: GOOD FRIDAY

"It's horrible, isn't it?": Sydney Guilaroff with Cathy Griffin, *Crowning Glory: Reflections of Hollywood's Favorite Confidant* (Vancouver, BC: General Publishing, 1996), 195.

"You'll do what I say": Crane, *Detour: A Hollywood Story*, 18.

"Please tell me what it's all about": Crane, *Detour: A Hollywood Story*, 19.

"Hi, Johnny, have you seen it?": Crane, *Detour: A Hollywood Story*, 23.

"Mildred, please have Lana call me": Crane, *Detour: A Hollywood Story*, 23.

"Who did you say that fellow was?": Turner, *Lana*, 237.

"You once told me": Porter and Prince, *Lana Turner*, 528.

"I just learned that Johnny has been lying": Crane, *Detour: A Hollywood Story*, 28.

"Now, look. I told you": Turner, *Lana*, 238.

"You break promises!": Turner, *Lana*, 239.

Lana rushed back upstairs: "Slaying in Lana Turner's Bedroom," *Morristown Gazette*, April 6, 1958.

"Open this motherfucker": Crane, *Detour: A Hollywood Story*, 31.

"That is, maybe you'll live": Porter and Prince, *Lana Turner*, 529.

A sharp eight-inch knife: "Slaying in Lana Turner's Bedroom."

slicing into one of his kidneys: Associated Press, "Daughter, 14, Fatally Stabs Lana's Gigolo," *Orlando Sentinel*, April 6, 1958.

CHAPTER TWENTY-SIX: GET ME GIESLER!

"My career, what's going to happen to my career?": Porter and Prince, *Lana Turner*, 533.

"It looked like a hog": Porter and Prince, *Lana Turner*, 535.

"She picked up the knife": Crane, *Detour: A Hollywood Story*, 33.

"He said, 'My God, Cheryl'": Turner, *Lana*, 240.

"I stood outside Lana Turner's house": Dominick Dunne, *The Way We Lived Then: Recollections of a Well-Known Name Dropper* (New York: Crown, 1999), 32.

"Don't ask her, ask me": Turner, *Lana*, 244.

"I thought he was going to get her": "Slaying in Lana Turner's Bedroom."

"I thought she was poking Johnny": "Daughter, 14, Fatally Stabs Lana's Gigolo."

"You'll be spending the night here": Turner, *Lana*, 245.

"Will you open the door, please?": Turner, *Lana*, 245.

"I wish I were like Mother": Crane, *Detour: A Hollywood Story*, 256.

"Why won't they let me": "Daughter, 14, Fatally Stabs Lana's Gigolo."

"There will be no trial": "Daughter, 14, Fatally Stabs Lana's Gigolo."

"Stop it, Lana, stop it!": Turner, *Lana*, 246.

"It's a news guy": Cohen and Nugent, *Mickey Cohen*, 188.

"Mickey, do me a favor": Cohen and Nugent, *Mickey Cohen*, 189.

"Well, I haven't seen him yet": Cohen and Nugent, *Mickey Cohen*, 189.

"There's nobody else out there": Cohen and Nugent, *Mickey Cohen*, 189.

"**Johnny was an athlete":** Cohen and Nugent, *Mickey Cohen*, 189.

CHAPTER TWENTY-SEVEN: MICKEY'S REVENGE

a "likable" small town boy: "Homefolk Called Him Likable," *Knoxville News Sentinel*, April 6, 1958.

"He acquainted himself with females": "Homefolk Called Him Likable."

"I guess you could call Jack": "Homefolk Called Him Likable."

"Who did it, who did it?": Crane, *Detour: A Hollywood Story*, 254.

"I don't like the whole thing": "Lana Turner's Love Letters."

"We are sending people": Associated Press, "Lana's Lawyer Says He's Had Death Threats," *Salisbury Times*, April 26, 1958.

"It's probably all baloney": "Giesler Airs Threats in Turner Case."

"was stabbed to death": FBI Memorandum, April 7, 1958, Lana Turner FBI File 9–12601, https://archive.org/details/LanaTurnerFBI/Lana%20Turner%20FBI%20File%20 9–12601/page/n29/mode/2up.

"The only sign of life": Crane, *Detour: A Hollywood Story*, 258.

"I didn't tell them": Crane, *Detour: A Hollywood Story*, 259.

"I bet your mother really did it": Crane, *Detour: A Hollywood Story*, 261.

Cohen turned the letters over to Winchell: FBI Memorandum, April 18, 1958, Lana Turner FBI File 9–12601, https://archive.org/details/LanaTurnerFBI/Lana%20Turner %20FBI%20File%209–12601/page/n35/mode/2up.

"Please review these letters": FBI Memorandum, April 18, 1958, Lana Turner FBI File 9 –12601, https://archive.org/details/LanaTurnerFBI/Lana%20Turner%20FBI%20File %209–12601/page/n35/mode/2up.

"My dearest darling love": Associated Press, "Lana Turner Letters Imply Romance Cooling Off," *Daily Reporter* (Dover, OH), April 10, 1958.

"burned up over the way she acted": United Press International, "Stompanato Buried, Lana Omits Wreath," *Arizona Republic*, April 10, 1958.

"A couple of hours before I'm due": United Press International, "Mickey Cohen Convicted of Slugging Waiter," *The State* (Columbia, SC), April 8, 1958.

CHAPTER TWENTY-EIGHT: THE PERFORMANCE OF A LIFETIME

"My brother was six feet tall": United Press International, "Slain Man's Brother Seeks Lie Test for Lana Turner," *Vancouver Sun,* April 9, 1958.

"I get a kick out of feeling": "Stompanato Buried, Lana Omits Wreath."

"He was an operator with the girls": "Stompanato Buried, Lana Omits Wreath."

"I never praise the dead": "Stompanato Buried, Lana Omits Wreath."

"He had a good heart": Associated Press, "Military Rites at Woodstock for Victim," *The Times* (Munster, Indiana), April 9, 1958.

"She has made a signed statement": "Court Decision Holds Cheryl Until Hearing," *Austin American-Statesman*, April 8, 1958.

"I only feel that they should share": "Slain Man's Brother."

"Love ya and miss ya loads": United Press International, "Cheryl Wrote Chatty Letter to Stompanato," *Fort Worth Star-Telegram*, April 11, 1958.

"I refuse to identify him": United Press International, "Hoodlum Threatened to Kill Three of Us, Lana Testifies," *Press Democrat* (Santa Rosa, CA), April 12, 1958.

"Miss Turner, when did Mr. Stompanato": United Press International, "Testimony of Lana Turner at Inquest in Stompanato Killing," *Philadelphia Inquirer*, April 12, 1958, https://www.newspapers.com/clip/27420352/the-philadelphia-inquirer/.

"Did you have an argument": "Testimony of Lana Turner."

"I told her": "Testimony of Lana Turner."

"He would even cut my face": "Testimony of Lana Turner."

"He was holding me": "Testimony of Lana Turner."

"And after I said that": "Testimony of Lana Turner."

"I truthfully say I thought": "Testimony of Lana Turner."

"I still didn't see": "Testimony of Lana Turner."

"And it is true": "Testimony of Lana Turner."

"This whole thing is a pack of lies!": United Press International, "Victim's Friend Creates
    Stir at Knife Slaying Inquest," *Salt Lake Tribune,* April 12, 1958.

"Lana Turner wasn't trying": "Victim's Friend Creates Stir."

"We [the jury] find the death": "Testimony of Lana Turner."

"After all I heard today": "Testimony of Lana Turner."

"You'll be killed for representing": "Police Step Up Guard," *Arizona Republic,* April 26,
    1958.

CHAPTER TWENTY-NINE: THE AFTERMATH

Cheryl's act had been "justifiable": "Coroner Backs Cheryl in Death of Lana's Lover," *Tulsa*
    Daily World, April 12, 1958.

"All I wanted to know was": Crane, *Detour: A Hollywood Story,* 272.

"removed from all outside influences": United Press International, "Cheryl Crane Has
    Hearing Today," *Rhinelander Daily News,* April 24, 1958.

"She looks good": "Cheryl Crane Has Hearing Today."

"We will be fully prepared": "Cheryl Crane Has Hearing Today."

"Lana is far better than Cheryl": United Press International, "Cheryl Real Disaster, Barker
    Quoted," *Nashville Tennessean,* April 10, 1958.

"I don't know if I should": Crane, *Detour: A Hollywood Story,* 279.

"A great part of me would like": United Press International, "Lana Turner Still in Movies to
    Earn a Living," *Fort Worth Star-Telegram,* July 1, 1958.

"My grandmother": Crane, *Detour: A Hollywood Story,* 280.

"You'd rather stay here": Crane, *Detour: A Hollywood Story,* 281.

"It was what I was praying for": Associated Press, "Judge Places Cheryl Crane in Custody
    of Grandmother," *Fort Worth Star-Telegram,* April 25, 1958.

"Both Steve and Lana are very happy": "Judge Places Cheryl Crane."

"Don't read them": Crane, *Detour: A Hollywood Story*, 282.

"We want to do all we can": "Kin of Slain Johnny to Sue Lana," *Quad-City Times*, April 15, 1958.

"No one told the whole story": "Kin of Slain Johnny."

"We've given Mr. Cohen": "Kin of Slain Johnny."

"Mickey Cohen fervently,": Cohen and Nugent, *Mickey Cohen*, 192.

"Now look at it": Turner, *Lana*, 253.

"I think there are wide discrepancies": United Press International, "Cheryl Telling New Story, Attorney Says," *Knoxville News-Sentinel*, June 24, 1958.

newspaper editors mocked him: United Press International, "He Lived Big and Died Little," *Press Democrat* (Santa Rosa, CA), November 30, 1958.

"very quiet and apparently happy here": Associated Press, "Cheryl is in School," *Commercial Appeal* (Memphis TN), October 26, 1958.

"Have you heard the assignment": Crane, *Detour: A Hollywood Story*, 298.

but she ran away with the prize: Bob Thomas, "Stompanato Death Called Biggest Hollywood Story," *State Journal* (Lansing, MI), December 18, 1958.

CHAPTER THIRTY: FADE OUT

"He certainly isn't making it": James Bacon, "He's Noisy for the Quiet Life," *Battle Creek Enquirer and News*, January 4, 1959.

Cohen was arrested on suspicion: United Press International, "3 Pistols at Site of Slaying," *Indianapolis Star*, December 8, 1959.

Berl Estes McDonald crept up behind him: Associated Press, "Mickey Cohen is Beaten with Pipe in U.S. Prison," *Tuscon Daily Democrat*, August 14, 1963.

"I don't want to tell you": Associated Press, "Lana Turner Must Pay $20,000 to Stompanato Boy," *Terre Haute Tribune*, October 10, 1961.

"When I heard the first strains": Turner, *Lana*, 253.

"I can't, I can't": Turner, *Lana*, 254.

"Brilliant, you gave it just what it needed!": Turner, *Lana*, 254.

Lana gifted Sandra Dee: "Charmed Sweater," *Chattanooga Daily Times*, March 1, 1959.

"superb movie of dramatic": "Life: Superb Movie of Dramatic Quality," *Valley Times* (North Hollywood, CA), March 21, 1959.

"one of the four masterpieces": Emanuel Levy, "Imitation of Life (1959): Sirk's Glorious, Oscar Nominated Melodrama Starring Lana Turner, Sandra Dee, and Juanita Moore," Emanuel Levy Cinema 24/7, August 15, 2009, https://emanuellevy.com/review /imitation-of-life-1959–6/.

"I have a feeling": Rick Du Brow, "Lana Tells About Changes in Personal Life," *Evening Herald* (Shenandoah, PA), March 17, 1959.

Don't miss *Helltown*, another thrilling true crime narrative from Casey Sherman!

PROLOGUE

MAY 12, 1974

The prisoner closed his dark eyes and inhaled, taking the warm air of midspring deep into his lungs. He blocked out all the noises around him and, for a brief moment, imagined himself back in Provincetown, sitting at the far edge of MacMillan Pier, staring out at the seemingly endless horizon of Cape Cod Bay where the Pilgrims had first set foot in the New World in 1620. He could almost hear the squawk of seagulls dive-bombing for squid and the echo of waves slapping against the old wooden pylons while his bare feet dangled carefree over the side. For the past four years, he had held on to the belief that he would return there one day.

Along with that belief had come a promise, a wager he had made with himself. He would try desperately to swallow any sudden urges to kill again.

Tony Costa opened his eyes and rubbed his spectacles with his denim shirtsleeve. Before him stood not the shifting sands and rolling dunes of Race Point. Instead, he gazed wearily at the twenty-foot-high walls of concrete that surrounded him and the prison guards with cocked, loaded rifles perched atop eight observation towers that offered them a clear view of the crowded yard below.

The bell sounded, and the prisoner soon fell into a long line with his fellow inmates. The new guys, those freshly convicted of serious offenses such as armed robbery, rape, and murder, stared at him and whispered among themselves. All were hardened criminals, but none were like him. They had not done what he had done.

Since the killing of self-professed Boston Strangler Albert DeSalvo, who was stabbed nineteen times in the prison infirmary six months earlier, the prisoner had become the most notorious resident at the Massachusetts state penitentiary at Walpole. Much had been written about all the gruesome crimes that had been attributed to him, but in his mind, no one had told the story the right way—from his point of view, from the killer's perspective.

Costa dawdled for a moment, allowing himself to get pushed to the back of the line. One by one, the inmates escaped the light of late afternoon and disappeared into the catacombs inside the prison that eventually led them back to their narrow, steel-encrusted cells. Costa craned his neck to allow the sun to touch his nose one last time before the natural light was replaced by the flickering fluorescent bulbs inside the jail that had plagued him with constant headaches since the moment he had arrived there four years earlier.

He returned to his cramped first-floor cell with its double bunk, exposed metal toilet, and small writing desk and sat himself in front of an old, borrowed typewriter, the machine he had used to write nearly four hundred pages over the past several months. Finally satisfied with the narrative structure of his uniquely twisted story, Costa landed on a title for his manuscript.

He struck the keys with his fingers, typing the word *Resurrection* in bold letters. On the next page, he wrote, "Truth demands courage, and rather than live a life of illusion, together we persistently sought the spiritual truth of life. And our search is only beginning."

He stared down at the thin piece of white writing paper with a grin of satisfaction. He was sure that the book would become a runaway bestseller. He wanted to be remembered not as a killer of young women but as a writer and a thinker who had helped to define the Age of Aquarius for a whole generation of readers. In his mind, this book would also cement his legacy as one of Cape Cod's great novelists, mentioned in the same breath as Kurt Vonnegut Jr. and Norman Mailer .Tony Costa then typed his name on the title page, yanked the leather belt from his prison-issued denims, and contemplated his next move.

CHAPTER ONE

1968

Edie Vonnegut was nervous about bringing the boy home to meet her father, who was holed up in his writer's shed off the back of their Cape Cod farmhouse on Scudder Lane. Seventeen-year-old Edie had learned to traipse lightly around her father, Kurt, especially when he was working.

"Wait here," Edie told her date, a handsome, young ice hockey player from nearby Hyannis. "He said that he wants to meet you. I'll be back in a sec."

Edie left the boy standing at the edge of Coggins' Pond at the back of the property as she tiptoed toward the wooden door and knocked.

"What?" an exasperated Vonnegut asked. "What now?"

Edie pushed open the door, paused for a moment to calm her nerves, and stepped inside. Standing at the threshold atop a wooden plank that held Thoreau's quote, *Beware of All Enterprises That Require New Clothes*, the daughter saw her father's lanky frame hunched over his Smith Corona typewriter with its space bar indented by his thumb from years of use and self-abuse. His head wore a halo of gray cigarette smoke, and underneath, Edie could see the grimace on his worn and wrinkled face. It was a look that terrified her siblings and on numerous occasions had sent their mother,

Jane, to the laundry room, where she would lock herself inside to cry alone for hours.

The boy heard a rumble of chatter coming from the studio, followed by the slamming of the door as Edie marched out with her arms flailing and her long, brown hair blowing in the Cape Cod breeze. She turned once to flip her father the middle finger and then stomped toward the main house, leaving the boy to fend for himself at the edge of Coggins' Pond.

The boy jogged up the hill just as Vonnegut exploded out of his study and intercepted him on the beaten path back to the house.

"I'm going to say one thing, so let me be perfectly clear," the writer barked. "Don't you fuck my daughter. Don't you dare fuck her!"

Vonnegut's words startled the boy. He had only come over to take Edie for ice cream and a movie, and now he was being subjected to a bizarre, sexual interrogation from the girl's domineering dad.

Scared and confused, the boy simply nodded and picked up his pace toward the main house.

Vonnegut watched him go and hoped that his words would sink in. The writer then retreated back to his studio and continued the daunting work of editing his latest novel, a book that he intended to call *Slaughterhouse-Five*.

Locked away in his study, Vonnegut reached for another Pall Mall and struck a match. After taking the smoke into his lungs, his mind returned to his daughter. She had been a real sweet kid, but now that she was older, she'd become a bitchy little flibbertigibbet.

He felt that he had a right to be overly protective of the teenager. She was beautiful after all. Edie was gifted with a svelte, athletic figure that had turned every boy's head at Barnstable High School. She wore her skirts short and her hair long, parted in the middle with brown curls cascading over her shoulders. Vonnegut knew he did not need to worry much about the boy he had just encountered in the backyard. The kid seemed polite enough. Instead, he fretted over a new crowd that Edie was hanging out with down the road in Provincetown. That group seemed aimless, uninspired, and hungry for only drugs and sex. Hippies were taking over the tip of Cape Cod, and Kurt Vonnegut Jr. feared that his precocious daughter could get washed away with the tide.

———————

Like Edie Vonnegut, Sydney Monzon was fascinated by Ptown, which was only a thirty-minute drive from the place where she grew up but a world away from her parents' stuffy home in the village of Eastham, which ran up the Cape's long, giraffe-like neck. Commercial Street, with its eclectic vibe, was the closest that Sydney could get to the counterculture eruption that was happening in places like Haight-Ashbury in San Francisco and Greenwich Village in New York, at least for now. She had recently told her sister Linda and her closest friends that she wanted a new life, one filled with adventure and exploration. Sydney was a year out of Nauset High School, where she had graduated in 1967. Blessed with a radiant smile and delicate features, Sydney made friends easily, but she was desperate to break away from the ordinary.

In her high school yearbook, she wrote that she was leaving with the belief that "the future holds more valuable hours than has the past." While her classmates waxed their surfboards to tackle the waves at nearby Coast Guard Beach, Sydney, or "Snyd" as she was called, could often be found curled up under a tree with her nose in a book. She loved to read the work of philosophers like Bertrand Russell and quoted them often. Sydney paraphrased Russell in her senior quote: "Some men would rather die than think; in fact, they do," she wrote. Sydney was drawn to intellectuals, which was why no one raised any concern about the friendship she had struck with Tony Costa, a handsome young man in Provincetown whom she called Sire. The pair was often seen riding their bicycles together down the narrow streets and alleyways in the center of town. Sydney had told her sister Linda that their relationship was casual and platonic. She was living with another man, a local fisherman named Roland Salvador, at the time. Still, Linda had her suspicions that her sister had fallen hard for her new friend and that Sydney's relationship with Roland had hit a dead end. On Friday, May 24, 1968, Linda Monzon left her two-room cottage at 25 Watson Court, in Provincetown's historic district, and began walking up the hill toward Commercial Street. At the top of the hill, she noticed a small figure standing next to a car. Linda recognized her sister immediately and smiled. Sydney was tiny: about four feet, eleven inches tall, she weighed less than one hundred pounds. Friends had playfully teased her that she had been the model for the Baby First Step doll, which was hugely popular among little girls at the time.

"Hey, Linda, can you come here?" Sydney shouted. "I need to talk to you."

"I can't, Sis," Linda said, looking at her watch. "I'm already late. I'll just see ya later."

Sydney gave her sister a troubled look. Linda waved it off as some minor boy trouble and made herself a mental note to dig in further when the sisters were alone. Linda kept walking while Sydney got into the passenger seat of Costa's car, a 1963 Oldsmobile, and drove away.

He took his eyes off the road briefly and let them rest on Sydney's body. She wore a pair of white Levi's bell bottoms with cuts above the knees and a sleeveless, pastel-orange blouse that was tucked into her small waistline. Her silky brown hair was parted in the middle and flowed over her shoulders. Sydney caught his gaze and then looked into the back seat where she spotted a pair of gloves, a laundry bag, and a small screwdriver.

"Where are we going, Sire?" she asked nervously.

Costa smiled. His eyelids were heavy.

"We need to get some pills," he told her. "And then I'll take you to a place where a thousand tiny Tinkerbells will descend upon you and carry you to fantasy's domain."

Sydney realized where they were headed: an ancient cemetery near Corn

Hill Beach in North Truro. They had gone there several times before to get stoned. But Costa was now out of drugs and low on cash. They would need to replenish the stash Bonnie-and-Clyde style. He rolled down his window to let in a gust of damp salt air. The breeze seemed to revive him. They drove past the doctor's office on Route 6A and saw that all the lights were out. The doctor had closed his shop early to enjoy the long Memorial Day weekend, the unofficial start to the busy summer tourist season on Cape Cod.

They waited for nightfall and switched seats. Sydney was now behind the steering wheel. She adjusted the cushion so that her bare feet could reach the pedal.

"All right, love. You can drop me off at the telephone booth over there by the hamburger stand," Costa told her. "When I'm done pillaging the doctor's office, I'll wait for you in the phone booth. I'll just pretend that I'm making a call if anyone shows up."

Sydney nodded. She could hardly imagine what her father, Bertram, a drywall contractor and U.S. Navy veteran, would think about the idea that his daughter was about to pull off a drug store robbery.

"I'll hide the dope over there," Costa said, pointing to a row of bushes. "We can pick the stuff up after we see that everything is all right. Then we'll head home, okay?"

"Yeah, I'll drive down the road a ways and will come back in about an hour. Is that cool with you, Sire?"

"That sounds groovy."

Sydney let the young man out and sped off. She drove back to Eastham, back toward her mundane past, where she had once fretted over simple things like decorating for the prom with its "Over the Rainbow" theme and working on the yearbook committee. Sydney had even supplied a baby picture for the Nauset Tides yearbook of her in a dress, balanced against the grill of her father's car. She had been the epitome of the all-American girl until the move up to Ptown. Sydney pulled the car over near the Eastham

290 · CASEY SHERMAN

Windmill and waited. The giant gristmill, with its large wooden sails, had towered over the town green since 1793. It was the oldest structure of its kind on Cape Cod and a source of great pride for local residents, but for Sydney, it was a symbol of a small town that was stuck too far in the past. She fiddled with the radio and landed on Hugo Montenegro's orchestral from the Clint Eastwood film *The Good, the Bad, and the Ugly*, which was nearing the top of the Billboard charts. She now felt a bit like a desperado herself as she sat in wait for her companion to make his score.

Tony Costa made his way ninja-like to the medical office just as a Truro police officer drove past on his nightly patrol. Stealthily, he crept toward the back of the building and tested a window to see if it was unlocked, but the office was totally secure. He then wedged a screwdriver into the muntins that separated the glass panes and tripped the lock.

Costa climbed into the office, drew the shades, and slid the gloves on both of his hands. He had put together his cat burglar kit in a hurry and realized now that he was wearing two left-handed gloves. The pill closet was located at the front of the building, so he navigated his way slowly through several small offices with locked doors. Costa had carpentry experience, so he easily managed to remove the doors by pulling out their hinges. He did not want to trash the office. His sole mission was to obtain the pills he needed and nothing more, at least not yet. He found the pill closet and examined it with a small penlight.

"Gold mine," he whispered to himself.

Suddenly, the penlight shut off. The battery was dead. He did not panic; instead, he pulled out a book of matches and a tiny glass of denatured alcohol from his laundry bag. Using a piece of clothesline rope for a wick, he lit the end to create a makeshift lantern. He had used the kit to cook up dope and had now transformed it into an alcohol lamp. He trembled with excitement as he gazed into the pill closet. He had never seen such an abundance of drugs before. Reading each label carefully, he stuffed sealed bottles of Nembutal, Seconal, Dexedrine, and so-called black beauties into his laundry bag, filling it to the brim.

Costa found his way back to the open window and slipped out as silently as he came.

He hid the drugs in the woods and strolled over to the phone booth to wait for Sydney. Two cars passed by before she pulled into the parking lot, hugging the steering wheel with her diminutive frame. He opened the passenger door and climbed in next to her.

"What happened, Sire? Where's the stuff?" she asked. "Did you get anything?"

"Did I get anything, love? There's more dope in there than a pharmaceutical warehouse," he replied. "The bag's over there in the pine grove. Let's go get it and get out of here."

Sydney drove over to the wooded area and watched as her companion retrieved the laundry bag.

"Are we headed back to Ptown?" she asked.

"I've got a stash in the woods," he told her. "You know the place. We can sort the stuff out there and put it all into the ammo cans. It'll be safer than riding all the way into town with it."

Costa had purchased several army surplus tank ammunition canisters that were airtight and water resistant. The cans were now buried in a thicket near Cemetery Road. Sydney stepped on the gas pedal, and soon the pair wound their way down the twisting country lane. She gripped the steering wheel tightly around each hairpin turn while her companion increased the volume of the car radio. The local station was now playing "Blue Turns to Grey" by the Rolling Stones, his favorite band.

He sang along with the tune, imitating Mick Jagger.

Sydney kept her focus on the road. The difficult drive was made worse by a heavy rain that began to pelt the windshield. She flipped on the wipers as he guided her off the main road to a dirt track, an old carriage trail, barely wide enough to fit his car. They could hear the bushes and long vines scraping against the sides of the Oldsmobile as they bounced over tiny moguls and deep puddles before coming to a small clearing about a mile into the woods.

"We're here," he told her, smiling.

Costa reached over and wrapped his long arms around her small shoulders. They kissed as droplets of rain rolled down the windshield like tears on a baby's cheek. Sydney moved closer, finally straddling him. He held her tightly, breathing heavy with excitement now, as he ran his hands over her compact body. Sydney met his soft touch with her own delicate caress.

This is perfect, he thought to himself. They were alone in the Oldsmobile, but they were not alone. The young man's split personality, an alter ego he had named Cory, had come along for the ride.

Don't do it, Cory, he urged the alter ego. *She doesn't deserve to die.*

Costa suddenly broke the embrace.

"Love, why don't we sort and stash this stuff now, before we get too involved in each other's bodies and minds and forget what we came here for."

Sydney nodded and adjusted her blouse. They got out of the car, and he grabbed the heavy laundry bag from the back seat. He reached for her hand as they ran through the rain toward a large pine tree at the edge of the clearing. Sydney giggled as the mud squished through her bare toes. She said something to her companion, but he didn't hear it. The young man's inner voice was now raging loudly in his skull.

He set the bag down at the base of the tree and dug through wet leaves until his fingers found one of the canisters. Sydney began rifling through the bag, handing him bottle after bottle. The drugs filled three full ammo cans.

"Are we done yet, Sire?" she asked him. "We're getting soaked to the bone out here."

"We are just about done, love," he responded. "Why don't you head back to the car?"

Tony Costa reached his hand inside a fourth ammo can and felt the thick wooden handle of a large knife.

"You fucked my head up bad tonight, Cory," he muttered to himself as he pulled out the weapon. "Let's leave her alone."

Suddenly, he felt the sharp edge of the blade against his neck.

You'll die too, motherfucker, Cory threatened. *Just like the rest of them.*

Costa looked over at Sydney, who was walking with her back turned toward the Oldsmobile. He jumped to his feet and gave chase, running toward her with the knife held high in his right hand. Sydney

The ancient cemetery in Truro, Massachusetts, where Tony Costa had lured his victims. © Casey Sherman

heard the rustling of leaves under his feet and then the splash of a puddle as he drew closer. She spun around quickly and could see her companion's crazed eyes, nearly illuminated in the darkness. Her own eyes followed his raised arm as it swung down upon her.

"Sire!" she screamed.

The blade cut into Sydney's shoulder, triggering a fountain of blood that sprayed across the young man's shirt. He lifted the knife and struck her again and again.

ABOUT THE AUTHOR

Casey Sherman is a *New York Times*, *Wall Street Journal*, *USA Today*, and *Boston Globe* bestselling author of seventeen books, including *The Finest Hours* (now a major Walt Disney Studios motion picture starring Chris Pine and Casey Affleck), and *Patriots Day* (now an acclaimed motion picture from CBS Films starring Mark Wahlberg and Kevin Bacon). Sherman's 2023 true crime bestseller, *Helltown*, is now in development as a limited television series for Amazon Studios. Sherman will serve as executive producer on the project, which is slated to star Oscar Isaac (*Dune*), with director Edward Berger (Netflix, *All is Quiet on the Western Front*), and produced by Team Downey (Robert Downey, Jr. and Susan Downey, HBO's *Perry Mason*). Sherman's other books include James Patterson's *The Last Days of John Lennon*, which spent more than twenty-three weeks on the *New York Times* bestseller list; *12: The Inside Story of Tom Brady's Fight for Redemption*; and *Hunting Whitey: The Inside Story of the Capture and Killing of America's Most Wanted Crime Boss*. Sherman has appeared on more than one hundred television and radio programs and is a contributing writer for *TIME* magazine, *Esquire*, *the Washington Post*, *the Daily Beast*, *Boston Magazine*, and the *Boston Herald*.